IAN ALLAN TRANSPORT LIBRARY

BRITISH
MOTORCYCLES
•Since 1900•

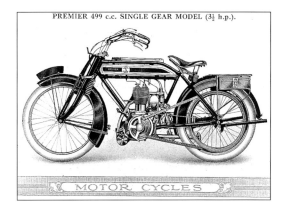

PREMIER 499 c.c. SINGLE GEAR MODEL (3½ h.p.).

MOTOR CYCLES

IAN ALLAN TRANSPORT
LIBRARY

BRITISH
MOTORCYCLES
•Since 1900•

PAUL COLLINS

IAN ALLAN
Publishing

Contents

Front cover:
The Vincent-HRD Rapide was promoted with the proud boast that it was the 'World's Fastest Standard Motorcycle'. Originally launched in 1937, this 1949 model was one of the last to carry the initials of the legendary rider and maker Howard R. Davies. *National Motor Museum, Beaulieu*

Back cover top:
R. Weatherell is pictured astride one of his R. W. Scout machines at the 1921 Isle of Man TT. Weatherell's two motorcycle ventures typify the many short-lived marques in British motorcycle history. Both this and his subsequent 'Weatherell' marque came and went between 1920 and 1923. *Jim Boulton Collection*

Back cover bottom:
Motorcycling has never been solely a male preserve, as illustrated by this 1911 view of a smartly dressed Mrs C. C. Cook on a Bristol-registered Douglas. Combining speed with innovatory design, the Douglas was one of the most technically advanced machines then available. *Author's Collection*

Half-title:
Born out of one of Coventry's oldest bicycle firms, Premier made motorcycles between 908 and 1915. This fixed gear single is typical of their output, which also included powerful V-twins of up to 1,000cc. *VMCC*

Title page:
Introduced in September 1993, the Triumph T509 Speed Triple is gleaming proof that at least part of the British motorcycle industry has survived into its second century. *Triumph Motorcycles Ltd*

First published 1998

ISBN 0 7110 2490 1

Published by Ian Allan Publishing

an imprint of Ian Allan Publishing Ltd, Terminal House, Station Approach, Shepperton, Surrey TW17 8AS.
Printed by Ian Allan Printing Ltd, Riverdene Business Park, Molesey Road, Hersham, Surrey KT12 4RG.

Code: 9807/B1

Acknowledgements

In this section of a book it is usual to thank all of those people who have helped in its production, which I do below. But in a way I am also grateful to those unnamed organisations, whose excessive demands for reproduction fees on photographs caused me to approach and become re-acquainted with Jim Bolton, through whose kindness and generosity much of what you hold in your hands is owed.

I am also grateful to the following individuals and organisations without whose help and co-operation this book would not have been possible: Steve Bagley; Gillian Bardsley (British Motor Industry Heritage Trust); Barry Collins; Ray Cresswell and Brierley Office Products Ltd; Jim Davies; David Evans; Louise Hampson; Mellanie Hartland; Nick Hopkins (BSA Regal Group); Ray Hudson; Tessa Howard; Mike Jackson; Rod Laight (Redditch Manufacturers Association); Penny McKnight; Museum of British Road Transport, Coventry; Paul Richards (QB Motorcycles Ltd); Bruno Tagliaferri (Triumph Motorcycles Ltd); Vintage Motor Cycle Club Ltd, and Peter Waller, of Ian Allan Publishing Ltd, for all his patience and forbearance.

Paul Collins, MSc, MSocSc, PhD
Wollaston, Stourbridge, West Midlands

Above:
AJS's successes in the Isle of Man TT races of the early 1920s created a great demand for their machines. Here, waiting to take part in the 1923 Junior TT, is AJS team rider C.W. Hough. Hough's team-mate 'Curly' Harris came second in the race, which was won by Stanley Woods on a works Cotton. *Jim Boulton Collection*

Introduction

Much of the story of the British motorcycle since 1900 can be found within the histories of the individual marques that form the majority of this book. These 220 plus entries represent a personal selection from a larger database of some 639 marques compiled especially for this project. By immersing oneself in the history of so many individual motorcycle manufacturers, certain common themes and trends emerge from all of the expertise, frustrations, greed, hopes and aspirations, ingenuity, skills, stupidity and, ultimately, thwarted dreams that came to occupy this aspect of many people's lives in Britain during the first half of the 20th century.

As well as chronicling so many individual stories of motorcycle manufacturers, it would neither be practical nor prudent also to embark upon a detailed history of the industry. Instead, this section will tease out some of the common themes and trends referred to above, high-lighting along the way some of the major phases in the development of the British motorcycle and the industry that produced it.

Origins

Without the bicycle there would have been nothing to motorise. The history of the bicycle is to some extent a familiar one. With origins in France in the late 1770s, the next 50 years would see many developments and much rivalry as 'inventors' in that country, Britain and Germany vied with each other to 'improve' what was in

Below:
This device, looking like the result of an accident between a cable car and a perambulator, was patented by Harry J. Lawson on 27 September 1880 and said by the inventor to be the first petrol-driven motorcycle. *Author's Collection*

THE FIRST BRITISH MOTOR CAR (Petroleum),

A.D. 1880 27th September, No. 3913. HARRY JOHN LAWSON. "Improvements in Velocipedes and in the Application of Motive Power thereto, such Improvements being also Applicable to Tram Cars Traction Engines and other Road Locomotives"; and No. 2591, June 25th 1880.

essence a very simple device. Called, variously, the Célérifère, Céléripède, Dandy-horse, Hobby-horse or Vélocifère, each had two wheels suspended in line from a common beam or strut. The front wheel was steerable by the rider, who sat centrally between the wheels, the diameter of which was such that the rider's legs just touched the ground. By running on their toes, riders propelled the device forward, spreading their legs clear of the ground whenever its natural momentum, or a convenient gradient, allowed. In this way a speed of 7–8mph was possible, although the experience of riding a hobby-horse, especially for men, on the deeply pitted and rutted roads of the period, was often memorable in the extreme.

The same roads were also often muddy, and it was the desire of hobby-horse riders not to have to run in the mud that provided an imperative to devise a means of propelling the vehicles by other means. Two leaps forward were necessary to achieve this, one mechanical, one conceptual. The mechanical problem was that of coming up with a reliable means of translating the movement of a person's arms or feet into the motion of one of the wheels on a hobby-horse. One early solution to this was found by Kirkpatrick McMillan, a Dumfriesshire blacksmith, who developed a pedal-powered hobby-horse in which pedals on either side of the machine were connected to rods, which in turn were connected to cranks on either side of the rear wheel. Alternate movement of the left and right pedals propelled the machine forwards, or backwards. In an able demonstration of his creation, McMillan rode it the 70 miles to Glasgow over one night in June 1842. The conceptual leap forward required was the realisation that it was possible for a rider to balance on two wheels, thereby paving the way for larger diameter wheels that gave good ground clearance.

It took a further 35 years or so of claim and counter-claim, patent and rival patent from McMillan's time to perfect the bicycle — or more correctly the 'Safety' bicycle — that is still recognisable today. Amongst the most important of the 'movers-and-shakers' of this movement were Thomas Humber, Dan Rudge, George Singer, James Starley and Harry John Lawson — all Midlands people, the latter being from Coventry. That city had a difficult time of things during the 19th century. Its staple manufactures of ribbon and watches declined by the 1860s, and local people took the initiative in attracting new industries to the city. Thus, sewing machine manufacture was introduced, followed by bicycle production.

Credit for 'inventing' the first Safety Bicycle goes to Lawson, whose patent of 30 September 1879 shows a recognisable pedal-powered, rear-wheel, chain-driven bicycle, but with a larger front wheel, of what was termed 'Penny-ha'penny' style. Completing the picture was the development of the equal-wheel safety bicycle,

which was perfected by John Kemp Starley (James Starley's nephew) and William Sutton in a series of designs produced between 1884 and 1885, to which the name 'Rover' was applied.

The motorised bicycle

As with the motor car, the technology with which to produce a mechanically-driven bicycle had been available for some time. A German-built steam-driven vélocipède is shown in a drawing said to depict a trial of the machine in the Luxembourg Gardens, Paris, on 5 April 1818. Although similar drawings appeared during the 1820s and 1830s, no other evidence of these machines has survived, even though they pre-date more conventional forms of motorcycle by 50 years or more. Steam was the chosen motive power of later experimenters, notably in Britain, France and the United States. The first successful steam-powered bicycles appeared in the latter two countries in the late 1860s, but they suffered from the same problem as all other road-going vehicles driven in this way, the disadvantageous power to weight ratio of steam engines. Essentially, scale a steam engine down so that it is small and light enough to fit into a bicycle, and it will not provide sufficient power to drive it reliably, equip a bicycle with a steam engine that has sufficient power to drive it successfully, and it will be too heavy for practical use.

The solution to this problem came in 1883, when Gottlieb Daimler and Wilhelm Maybach perfected the high-speed internal combustion engine running on light petroleum spirit. These small, lightweight engines produced a disproportionately large amount of power because they relied upon the force of the explosion of pressurised petroleum vapour in a confined space. Applications of this technology to motorising the

bicycle came quickly, and included work by two now largely overlooked English pioneers, Edward Butler, who built his 'Petrol-Cycle' in 1887 and J. D. Roots, who developed a technologically advanced motor-tricycle in 1892; although Harry J. Lawson long-contended that his petrol-driven tricycle, patented on 27 September 1880 — a device that looked like the result of an accident between a cable car and a perambulator — should have the honour of being the first.

The beginnings of motorcycle manufacture

Ideas are one thing, but turning them into a reliable and saleable product that the public can be persuaded that they need, is another. The first motorcycle produced on a commercial basis was made in Germany. Brothers

Henry and Wilhelm Hildebrand, assisted by Alois Wolfmuller and Hans Greisenhof, developed their machine from 1892 and manufactured it from 1894 as the Hildebrand & Wolfmuller 'Motorrad', meaning Motor-cycle — the first use of the term.

A number of Hildebrand & Wolfmuller machines were imported into Britain, where motorcycles were also produced by Colonel H. Capel Holden, from 1897, and, from the same year, by the American, Edward Joel Pennington, whose flamboyant designs, and equally effusive claims for them, brightened both the infant motorcycle and motor car industries for a while. The design of two of these motorcycles is of note, because neither used the standard 'diamond' bicycle frame of the period as their bases. The Hildebrand & Wolfmuller machine was very like later designs of motor scooter, whilst Holden favoured a low-slung frame, anticipating a move away from the bicycle's diamond-frame that it would take later manufacturers over a quarter of a century to make.

The establishment of the British motorcycle industry

By 1900, at least 14 companies had tried their hand at motorcycle production in Britain. These included some of the most enduring names in the industry: Beeston, Clyde, Dennis, Eadie, Excelsior, Matchless, O.K., Pennington, Raleigh and Wolf. Each had a background in either bicycle manufacture or engine making, and were, for the most part, located in either the London or Midlands regions. The coming century would add to their number considerably, and would also establish the West Midlands as the most important motorcycle manufacturing region in the country.

From the sample of 639 marques collected for this book, the number of new motorcycle firms entering the business in the years 1900 to 1909 was:

1900	11	1905	16
1901	25	1906	10
1902	52	1907	7
1903	38	1908	6
1904	16	1909	11

a total of 192, of which just seven were 'one-year wonders', coming and going within one year. Moreover, two-thirds of the new companies (126), entered the business before 1904, showing what a boom period this was.

The development of the British motorcycle to 1916

The first British motorcycles accurately reflected their alternate name and description as 'motorised bicycles.' Most retained a (strengthened) bicycle 'diamond' frame, into which the mechanical parts were fitted, the majority going into the space between the main down tube and front fork. As a back-up, or auxiliary, bicycle pedals and a chain were fitted, the engine driving the rear wheel through a separate drive system, usually a belt. The machines did not have gearboxes as such. They were mostly of the fixed-speed kind, having no clutch, the rider having to push bike forward and run alongside to start it, and then jump aboard. This manoeuvre became difficult after the development of the sidecar, from 1903 onwards, and some manufacturers began to fit clutches, which proved to be a useful feature, as it permitted stationary starting, and also gave a 'free engine' facility — the ability to run the engine without the bike moving, favoured by the growing ranks of amateur mechanics.

Sporting uses were also found quickly for motorcycles. The machines had great attraction for some. It was a cheap and affordable sport, the basic skills for which were either held already or acquired quickly; it was also fast and dangerous. Manufacturers were quick to appreciate the advantages of participating in motorcycle sports events too. A win conferred instant prestige, especially for a new company, and the extremes of speed and riding conditions provided an excellent testing bed for mechanical reliability and innovation. A number of the bicycle-turned-motorcycle firms also had upwards of two or more decades' worth of experience from bicycle racing that they could bring to the sport.

The first motorcycle competitions took the form of endurance tests: 500-mile to 1,000-mile place-to-place tours of the country on public roads, interim distances to be covered in as short a time as possible. These were followed by reliability trials, hill climbs, speed trials, and scrambles, etc and, in May 1907, by the first Tourist Trophy (TT) races on the Isle of Man.

Most of the motorcycles built in the first few years of the 1900s would have had a four-stroke engine, probably of single-cylinder form. The four-stroke cycle is:

Below:
A Mr Mellerup, seen here, fitted an engine of his own design into this Dursley-Pedersen bicycle around 1905. This pattern of motorised bicycle was not uncommon in the early years of the 20th century. *Jim Boulton Collection*

1. Induction — inlet value open, piston moving down, air/petrol mixture drawn into cylinder;
2. Compression — both valves closed, piston moving up, air/petrol mixture under compression;
3. Power — both valves closed, air/petrol mixture ignited by spark, piston driven down;
4. Exhaust — exhaust valve open, piston moving up, burnt gases driven out.

This had inherent disadvantages, particularly in single-cylinder form in motorcycles. The most notable of these was that only one (the third) of the four strokes was powered, and that on the second, or compression, stroke the piston was both furthest from its last power stroke and encountering its maximum resistance. Without careful setting and adjustment of the valve timings, single cylinder four-stroke engines could run very erratically.

Two ways around these drawbacks were found. Firstly, by 1905 a variety of V-twin engines had been produced in Europe and the United States, and in that year these were joined by one such engine designed and manufactured by John A. Prestwich in Tottenham, North London. Vee- or V-twin engines have two cylinders, usually angled at something between 26° and 30° apart. By having one cylinder working two strokes ahead or behind the other, the engine as a whole runs on more power strokes than a single-cylinder unit, and thus more smoothly, as well as producing more power.

The other way around the drawbacks of a single-cylinder, four-stroke engine was the development of the two-stroke engine. An engine working to the two-stroke principle was developed by Sir Dugald Clerk in 1881, but this used two-cylinders, one to compress the mixture, and another in which it was exploded. Work to produce a single-cylinder two-stroke engine was undertaken by Alfred Angus Scott — founder of the Scott motorcycle company — in the years 1900 to 1908. Scott's basic principle, although improved by others, has remained the basis of the two-stroke engine ever since. By replacing valves with ports — openings in the cylinder wall sequentially covered and uncovered by the movement of the piston — Scott was able to eliminate the need for two of the four strokes in the latter cycle.

Thus, while the upstroke of the piston compressed its mixture, fresh mixture was let into the crankcase below, and compressed in there by the piston's downward movement on its power stroke following ignition. Then, as the piston returned upwards, it uncovered the openings of a transfer port, allowing the compressed mixture in the crankcase to jump to the head of the piston, also forcing out the exhaust gases from the previous power stroke. Two-stroke engines were used by Scott when he began to produce his own motorcycles from 1909, other early users of them being Butterfields Ltd, makers of Levis motorcycles, from 1910, and Veloce Ltd, makers of Velocette motorcycles, from 1912.

Sporting experience, especially in hill climbs, showed the value of different speed gears selected by the rider. Some of the first developments to this end took the form of adjustable pulley gears, of the kind introduced by Zenith on their 'Gradua' model in 1909, and by Rudge on their 'Multi' in 1911. Here the rider could operate a lever which varied the diameter of the engine and rear wheel (drive) pulleys, effectively giving an 'infinitely' variable gear ratio, usually between a fairly narrow range. More conventional two-speed gears became more widely fitted from around 1910, and by 1913 to 1914, three- and four-speed gear-boxes were provided by some manufacturers.

Another area of development in the early years of the British motorcycle industry was in the means of transmitting the power produced by the engine to the rear wheel. Early machines mostly used some form of belt-drive, and quite quickly the use of a 'V'-section flexible belt was adopted, although leather and composite materials were also tried. The problem with belts was that they were wont to stretch, slip, or break but they were still used into 1920s on single-gear, sports and light-weight machines. Some manufacturers favoured the use of drive chains, especially on twin cylinder models, where the extra power produced could cause belts to slip. The use of chain drive was favoured by P&M, Royal Enfield, James, Scott, Clyno and Sunbeam, more or less from their start of manufacture. A compromise used by many manufacturers on motorcycles fitted with gearboxes was the so-called 'chain-cum-belt' drive. Here the (primary) drive from the engine would be by drive chain, whilst the (secondary) drive from the gearbox to the rear wheel would be by belt. Thus the drive with the most torque had a chain, and was therefore less likely to slip.

Initially, World War 1 did little to halt the production of motorcycles in Britain. Some companies, like Triumph, made despatch rider machines for military use, in addition to their domestic production. The massive and wasteful losses from the opening day of the Battle of the Somme, on 1 July 1916, onwards changed all of this. As more and more people were drawn into the war the National Government suspended the production of motorcycles for the domestic market late in 1916, to free up manufacturing capacity for aircraft and munitions work, plus other war-related production.

The distribution of the British motor-cycle industry

Although individual makes could be found throughout the country, the British motorcycle industry was concentrated in the centres of bicycle production — the West Midlands and London. Considering all makes and periods, of the 639 marques studied, 238 (37%) were based in the West Midlands, in Birmingham (128), Coventry (79) and Wolverhampton (31), with 187 (29%) being based in the London area and 18 (2%) in Manchester. The industry was also very English, with only seven Scottish makes, six Welsh ones, and two each on the Isle of Man and Guernsey.

In the 20th century, the British motorcycle industry declined after 1929. The number of firms having their origins in each decade (for whom information is available) is as follows:

pre-1900	14	1940s	8
1900s	192	1950s	32
1910s	176	1960s	10
1920s	164	1970s	2
1930s	19	1980s	1

The later development of the British motorcycle industry

Domestic motorcycle production resumed by 1919, and the 1920s would prove to be a remarkable decade for the industry. There was a major influx of new makers, only a few of which would survive until the 1930s; and also important technical developments, and styling changes.

Many service personnel, returning from the most traumatic war in human history then to date, had acquired both the skill of driving or riding a motorised vehicle, and the desire to own one of the things themselves. It was a boom time for anyone prepared to produce cars or motorcycles, and many of the marques that appeared during the early part of the 1920s were formed specifically to meet this demand. Assembling motorcycles from proprietary parts, and adding little but their labour and a tank transfer, many of them were short-lived concerns. Of the 164 firms noted above, 60 were 'one-year wonders', 39 of these coming and going

before 1924. In addition there were a further 35 'two-year wonders', 32 of which had gone by 1924. Therefore, by the close of the 1920s, there had been 95 one- or two-year wonders, 71 of which had not survived into 1924.

Despite this massive turnover, the 1920s also saw changes to the design and specification of British motorcycles. During the decade there was a progressive move away from use of the symmetrical 'diamond' bicycle-style frame, to a more elongated, low-built style, with the saddle set further back and nearer to the ground. With this change came a related one, to the use of saddle petrol tanks, mounted on top of the frame, directly in front of the saddle; as opposed to being suspended beneath the top tube of the frame. Motorcycle transmissions progressed too. Veloce Ltd introduced the first foot-operated gear change for the 1925 Velocette range, setting a trend that most manufacturers would eventually follow; the decade also saw a progressive adoption of all-chain drive by most makers.

The marketing of motorcycles also began to change in the 1920s. As competition grew, manufacturers became increasingly aware of the power of advertising and of the need to make their machines more appealing to potential buyers. One way of achieving this was to give them names, a trend that began in the mid-1920s, but which gained pace from around 1928. Thus makers that had formerly been content to produce a 'Model 7', in 'Standard' or 'De Luxe' versions, were now making a 'Big Twin Export', 'Speed Chief' or a 'Super Sports', etc. Replicas of motorcycles that had enjoyed success in races and trials were also produced in the late 1920s, as were machines for use in the imported sport of speedway.

By the end of the 1920s Britain was entering a period of economic recession, one of the longer-term consequences of the war in the previous decade. In the British motorcycle industry fewer and fewer of the new ephemeral makes were formed, and all of the established firms experienced difficulties. A number went under and others had to pare and pare down their costs and prices just to remain in business. Some makes introduced budget models, such as Cotton, and others reduced their model ranges drastically and somehow managed to lop a few pounds off the price of their remaining models each year.

Above left:
Motorcycle sport took place almost anywhere, even on the public highway. Here, Flt Sub Lt L. P. Openshaw, of the Royal Flying Corps, rides his Zenith-Gradua at Hints Hill, on the A5 near Tamworth, on 17 May 1913. *Jim Boulton Collection*

Left:
One of the most successful of the variable ratio transmission systems was that used on the Rudge-Multi. Competitor No 137 in the 1913 Isle of Man TT was Frank Bateman, seen here on one such machine. The long lever just behind his hands is the variable ratio changing device. *Jim Boulton Collection*

Consolidation and decline

By the time that the economic recession bottomed out in the early 1930s, serious, and ultimately fatal, damage had been done to the British motorcycle industry. There would be great models and glories to come, but the course that would led inevitably towards the disasters of the 1960s and 1970s had already been set.

The first move was innocent enough. Colliers, makers of the Matchless motorcycles and proprietary engines, acquired the rights to the failed Wolverhampton marque AJS in 1931. In 1938 they also acquired that town's Sunbeam marque, and around the same time they were reformed as Associated Motor Cycles Ltd (AMC). The industry had begun to consolidate; engineering became a business, marques mere brand names. By the early 1960s, AMC had also acquired Francis-Barnett (1947), James (1952), Norton (1953) and Brockhouse Engineering (1959).

Fewer new firms appeared too. In the 1930s there were just 19, as opposed to the 164 that had been formed during the 1920s. Likewise in the 1940s, even allowing for the war, there were just eight new motorcycle firms started. The 1950s looked brighter, although in the early years there was still an air of austerity, and the rationing of certain things lingered. Nonetheless, there was a growing demand for personal motorised transport, and a number of companies were formed specifically to meet this. The decade would see some 32 companies embark upon motorcycle production for the first time:

1950	8	1955	4
1951	4	1956	1
1952	2	1957	3
1953	2	1958	1
1954	5	1959	2

A majority of these companies (21), began motorcycle production before 1954, eight of them would prove to be one year wonders, and nine would last just two years; the decade's only enduring marque being Greeves. The early 1950s saw a revival of the clip-on, an attachment to motorise an ordinary bicycle that had enjoyed its first spell of popularity in the early years of the century. Its contemporaries were autocycles and mopeds, but as the 1950s progressed a number of firms introduced their own make of scooter in response to the popularity of the imported Italian Lambrettas and Vespas. But, whilst the latter had style and were lightweight, a number of the British scooters were heavily engineered and far from handsome. Some also came onto the market too late: those interested in buying a scooter probably already had one; others were being tempted away to four-wheeled motoring.

Popular motoring only became established in Britain from the early 1960s, and the single most important factor in this was the launch of the Austin Seven and Morris Mini Minor by the British Motor Corporation in 1959. Motorcycling has, and always had, its loyal adherents, whom nothing would tempt off two-wheels; but those who turned to motorcycles because they were

Above:
This view, of the lightweight section of the 1934 Motorcycle Show, reflects the confidence of the British motorcycle industry after surviving a tough recession. Sadly, history now shows that the industry had peaked in the 1920s and that marques, already declining, would never be so numerous or varied again. *Jim Boulton Collection*

all they could afford were fickle in their affections. This was particularly true for people with families. By the late 1950s the cost of an ordinary motorcycle was fast approaching £200; more for a sidecar combination, and the standard of accommodation and comfort provided, especially by the latter, paled a little when compared to a £400 mini.

The 1960s would see just 10 firms comprise the British motorcycle industry, most of whom made trails machines, often sold in kit form, and few would survive into the 1970s. But it was the business machinations and ramifications of the decade that would prove most lasting. The collapse of AMC in the summer of 1966 and the formation of Norton Villiers from the ashes was the death knell of this once great industry. Two years later the withholding of Villiers engines from independent motorcycle makers dealt fatal blows to their precarious existences.

Whilst all of this was going on, imports of foreign motorcycles, notably from Japan, were making great inroads into the remaining domestic market. Generally offering a greater specification for the same or less money than the closest British-built machines, where these were available, the Japanese and other imported motorcycles were generally more reliable mechanically. Various attempts have been made to revive the British motorcycle industry, most notably the Hesketh débâcle of the early 1980s. Its lesson was simple: yes, there is still a demand for a prestigious British motorcycle, but if you are going to ask several thousand pounds for one, it had better be good. In the late 1990s, having celebrated the motor industry's 100th anniversary, the increasing success of Triumph and BSA's revival show that the British motorcycle industry is far from dead, but only time will tell its future.

Reviewing the British motorcycle industry from the 20th century's close, raises the question of its future prospects. Essentially little has changed from the viewpoint of the actual or aspiring motorcyclist. Produce a well-engineered, keenly priced motorcycle that's fun to ride, and it'll sell — that's the challenge.

ABC

ABC Motors Ltd/ABC Motors (1920) Ltd
Hersham, Walton-on-Thames, Surrey
Jarvis & Sons Ltd
Wimbledon, London SW19

The All British (Engine) Company was founded for the manufacture of internal combustion engines for use in aircraft, cyclecars and motorcycles. Through the interest and efforts of Granville Bradshaw, the company's founder and engineer, the firm quickly diversified into motorcycle production, producing its first machine in 1913. A low, streamlined design, the cycle had brazed tubular frame and leaf spring rear suspension. The engine was a 3.5hp 500cc two-cylinder unit, the cylinders being horizontally opposed, fore and aft. Power was transmitted through a four-speed hub gearbox. Finished in black and silver, the ABC sold for £72.

Production continued into 1914, but was discontinued upon the outbreak of war, the company turning to the supply of engines for aircraft and a variety of other war-related uses, including powering pumps to drain water from the trenches on the Western Front.

With the end of the war, the aircraft maker T.O.M. Sopwith approached Granville Bradshaw with a proposition to design a motorcycle, which the former would manufacture using the surplus workshop capacity and employees he had following the end of military contracts. On a wager, Bradshaw agreed to produce a design and prototype within three weeks, actually doing

Above:
Granville Bradshaw produced both the design and a prototype of this low and compact four-speed motor cycle for ABC in just 11 days during 1919. A 398cc horizontally opposed two-cylinder engine was fitted sideways into a full-loop frame, which had rear suspension, and gave protection to the rider's legs in front and below. Unfortunately, the company needed to charge around £300 for each one if they were to make any profit. *VMCC*

Below:
An ABC 'Scootamota' of 1919. Its almost skeletal design in tubular steel was in marked contrast to the luxury of ABC's Granville Bradshaw designed machine of the same year. Taking-up the luggage space is the 125cc engine.
Jim Boulton Collection

this in just 11 days! Retaining the principal elements of his prewar design, Bradshaw produced a revolutionary machine. Low and compact, the cycle had a full-loop frame into which a 398cc horizontally opposed two-cylinder engine was fitted sideways. Innovatory rear suspension, and protection for the rider's legs both in front and beneath, produced a comfortable ride.

Priced at a prewar level of around £70, manufacturing to Bradshaw's high standard soon showed that something just under £200 was more realistic, or nearer £300 if any profit was to be made. So, despite large order books, less expensive designs were produced, including the 'Scootamota' — a 125cc rear-engined, skeletal scooter, whose engine position ruled out the carrying of any baggage. But, even so, production of ABC motor cycles at Sopwith's factory ended in 1921. The bulk of the spares were bought by Jarvis & Sons Ltd of Wimbledon, who sold both these and complete cycles for a few years. Meanwhile, ABC re-formed in 1920 and produced cars until 1927 at a factory in Victoria Crescent, Walton-on-Thames, Surrey.

Aberdale; Bown

Aberdale Ltd
Bridport Rd, Edmonton, London
Bown Cycle Co Ltd
Llwynypia, Tonypandy, Glamorgan

The Aberdale autocycle fed the postwar demand for cheap personal transport. Introduced in 1947, the cycle had a tubular frame and was powered by a 98cc Villiers

Below:
'Abingdon' motorcycles were produced from 1903 to 1925, but when production resumed in 1927 they were branded 'AKD' an abbreviation of the parent company's trade mark. Produced for only five years, this Model 90 Sports was from the 1930 range, and used the company's own 248cc engine. It sold for just £39 18s 6d. VMCC

engine. Production was undertaken by the Bown company at their works in Wales, and the machines continued to be branded 'Aberdale' until 1949. From the following year Bown assumed both the production and the credit for the cycles, when, with a new 99cc Villiers engine, the Aberdale reappeared as the 'Bown Auto Roadster'.

In 1951 Bown also introduced a conventional motorcycle, again using a 99cc Villiers engine; a second, more powerful model being introduced the following year. Production of all the Bown models continued until 1954, but the make resurfaced in 1956 with a moped, which remained in production until 1957.

Abingdon King Dick; AKD

Coxeter & Sons
Abingdon, Berkshire
Abingdon Ecco Ltd
Shadwell St, Tyseley, Birmingham 25
Abingdon Tools & King Dick Spanners/Abingdon Works Ltd/ Abingdon Works (1931) Ltd
Kings Rd, Tyseley, Birmingham 25

Anyone wandering around the manufacturing district of Tyseley in Birmingham is likely to be surprised or even startled to see a large sign bearing the legend 'KING DICK'. Far from a proud boast, or the seat of a Plantagenet revival, it is the home of a remarkable company: Abingdon Tools & King Dick Spanners.

Founded to make hand tools, the company's most famous branded product was the 'King Dick' spanner, but during and after World War 1 the company also made motorcycles. The 'Abingdon' marque had its origins in the Berkshire town of that name, where Coxeter & Sons had made motorcycles using Fafnir, Minerva and MMC engines from 1903.

After a few years production was moved to Tyseley in Birmingham. Early versions were known as the 'Abingdon King Dick.' Four models were produced,

based around either a one- or two-cylinder engine of the company's own manufacture. Top of the range was a V-twin-cylinder model, with a three-speed gearbox, a chain-cum-belt drive and kick start, which sold for £82; almost the same configuration was available with a single-cylinder engine, for just £69 5s. There was also another a twin-cylinder model, with a fixed single gear and belt drive, the same being offered with a single-cylinder engine.

Production of Abingdon motorcycles ceased before the end of the war. In 1922 the firm dabbled in car making, with an overpriced light car that didn't sell well, and in 1925 they returned their attention to motorcycles, which were produced from 1927. Now branded the plainer 'AKD', these cycles were again based around the company's own engines, all single-cylinder units. By 1929 six models were offered, ranging from the 175cc 1.74hp 19 to the 300cc 3hp 49, which was also available with a sidecar. Prices ranged from £30 12s 6d for the 19 to £37 12s 6d for the 49, the combination selling for £50 12s.

The company hit financial trouble in 1930 and re-formed the following year. The most noticeable effect this had on its cycles was a change from model numbers to names; thus the 1931 range featured the Comet, Jupiter, Orion, Polar, Neptune and Mercury. For 1932 the model range was reduced, with the dropping of the Comet and Neptune, and revised, with the introduction of the 175cc 1.75hp Mercury Super Sports. This was to be the last year of manufacture for the AKD, the firm continuing, to the present, to make hand tools.

ABJ

A. B. Jackson Cycles Ltd
300 Icknield Port Rd, Birmingham 1
Jackson Cycles Ltd
109-111 Pope St, Birmingham 1

The ABJ had a good pedigree. It was named after the company chairman, A.B. Jackson, who had a long involvement with two-wheeled transport. First and foremost a bicycle manufacturer, before World War 2

Jackson had also made the 'Raynal' autocycle from 1937 to 1940, and again from 1947 to 1950.

Setting up under his own name in 1950, Jackson continued to produce autocycles and bicycles. Power was provided by a 98cc Villiers engine and two models were offered. Both the 'Autocycle' and 'Motorcycle' had a motorcycle look despite their tubular frames. They remained in production until 1952. That year Jackson also launched a cyclemotor clip-on device — the Auto Minor — housed above the front wheel of a conventional ABJ bicycle. The Auto Minor was also made in 1953, but production ceased in the face of the growing scooter and moped market. Jackson remained undaunted, and continued to produce his own brand and design of bicycles for a number of years.

Acme; Rex; Rex-Acme

Acme: Acme Motor Co Ltd
(before) 6 Lincoln St, Coventry 1
Rex: Birmingham Motor Manufacturing & Supply Co Ltd/Rex Motor Manufacturing Co Ltd
222 Osborne Rd, Coventry 1,
Stoney Stanton Rd, Earlsdon, Coventry 6
Rex-Acme: Rex Acme Motor Co Ltd
Stoney Stanton Rd, Coventry
Mills Fulford Ltd
Progress Works, Stoney Stanton Rd, Coventry

Now better known as the second part of the Rex-Acme marque, the Acme Motor Co Ltd had a separate existence as a low-volume motorcycle manufacturer. Founded in June 1902 to make cycles and engines, the company produced motorcycles, with interruptions, thereafter until its merger with Rex.

A slightly older concern, Rex had begun in 1900 as the Birmingham Motor Manufacturing & Supply Co Ltd, in Birmingham. It had a short existence, merging in June 1902 with Allard & Co, a Coventry bicycle firm founded in 1891. The resultant company, the Rex Motor Manufacturing Co Ltd, continued to make motorcycles, adding cars to its production too, until 1911. Its machines had a good reputation for reliability, something the company exploited in its advertising,

Left:
Between 1950 and 1954, Birmingham bicycle manufacturer A. B. Jackson produced lightweight motorcycles branded under his own initials. This is his Autocycle of 1950; it was powered by a 98cc Villiers 2F engine but retained many bicycle features, including pedals and a tool kit. *VMCC*

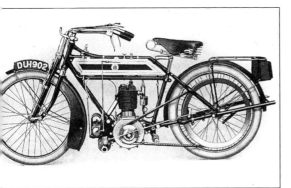

boasting of Land's End–John O'Groats runs (886 miles) in 48hr 30min etc. Further experiments with car designs continued until 1914, but by this time motorcycles had become the company's mainstay. Before production was interrupted by World War 1, Rex were producing two basic models, both based around their own V-twin-cylinder engine, offered with either a three- or two-speed gearbox, kick start, and a chain or belt drive, selling for £65 and £72 10s respectively.

Rex merged with Acme in 1922 and produced a wide range of mostly single-cylinder engined cycles until 1933. In addition to their own Rex-Acme engines the company also used Aza, Blackburne, J.A.P, Rudge, S.A. and Villiers single-cylinder units, together with J.A.P. twins. Early models bore only numbers, but from 1928 the names 'Junior', 'TT' and 'Junior DeLuxe' were used, together with letter/number combinations like B8; M8, etc. Prices ranged from 1929's V9A for £37 to that year's E/9 J.A.P.-powered twin for £72 10s. Sidecars were also offered as an extra from £13 to £25.

1931 was the last full year of Rex-Acme production; it saw the introduction of the £80 499cc J.A.P.-powered Speedway machine — the most expensive cycle the firm had produced. The year was also the company's last, although it was taken over by its sidecar supplier, Mills Fulford Ltd (established in 1899), who produced just two models — the 012 and R12 — both with J.A.P. engines, for just under a further year.

Advance

Advance Motor Manufacturing Co Ltd
Louise Rd, Northampton

Advance were one of a number of engine makers who became established in towns away from the main motorcycle producing areas of London and the West Midlands. Like many of their fellows, Advance tried their hand at cycle production, but this lasted only briefly between 1906 and 1908.

AEB; De Luxe; Motorite

A.E. Bradford
Sweetman St, Wolverhampton
Motorites (A.E. Bradford)
Vane St, Wolverhampton

A.E. Bradford was a Wolverhampton schoolmaster with a great passion for motorcycles. In 1912 he began to produce his own machines under his initials 'A.E.B.' in premises in Sweetman Street, Wolverhampton. Only a few machines were made there between 1912 and 1913. After World War 1, Bradford returned to motorcycle production with the 'De Luxe', another short run of machines that made good use of stock left over from the A.E.B.s, combined with bought-in components. The De Luxe was produced during 1919 and 1920. In later years Bradford established a motor engineering business — Motorites — on Vane Street in Wolverhampton, from where he produced a kit assembly motorcycle called, appropriately enough, the Motorite.

Above:
Wolverhampton schoolmaster A.E. Bradford had produced the 'A.E.B.' before World War 1, and afterwards he returned to motorcycle production with the 'De Luxe', seen here with a fashionable lady rider. This was a short run of machines, produced during 1919 and 1920, that made use of stock left over from the A.E.B.s, combined with bought-in components. *Jim Boulton Collection*

Right:
A plan view of a 6hp AJS Model 'D' motor cycle of 1914 showing the layout of the design and controls. *Jim Boulton Collection*

AER — see Reynolds' Special Scott

AJS

J. Stevens & Co
Tempest St, Wolverhampton
The Stevens Motor Manufacturing Co Ltd/A. J. Stevens Ltd
Pelham St/Retreat St, Wolverhampton
A. J. Stevens (1914) Ltd
Graiseley House, Graiseley Hill, Penn Rd, Wolverhampton
Matchless Motorcycles (Colliers) Ltd/Associated Motorcycles Ltd
44-45 Plumstead Rd, Woolwich, London SE18

In the 1880s, Joe Stevens was a screw and rivet maker in Wednesfield, Wolverhampton. He had five sons, and as each became old enough they went to work for their father. By 1896 Joe Stevens had a business: J. Stevens & Son, with premises in Tempest Street, in the Snow Hill area of Wolverhampton. The sons brought new skills to their father's business, which diversified into the production of press tools. Strongly 'mechanically minded', the Stevens brothers became fascinated by motor vehicles, and as early as 1894 had motorised a BSA bicycle using an engine of their own design and making.

The knowledge and notoriety of this motorcycle, and particularly of its engine, spread far and wide. Requests, orders even, from cycle makers and other manufacturers who wished to use it in their own motorcycles were at first rebuffed, but then acceded to. Branded as 'Stevens' engines, production of them soon outgrew their father's premises in Tempest Street, and so four of the brothers: George, Harry, Jack, and Joe Jr, set up a new company — The Stevens Motor Manufacturing Co Ltd — and moved to new premises in Pelham Street, Wolverhampton, around 1900.

Stevens sold engines to a number of motorcycle manufacturers, including the local Wearwell firm, makers of the Wolf and Wulfruna marques, and the Northampton-based concern, Clyno. Experiments were also conducted with powered vehicles: a forecar being made in 1903, and a design of ladies' motorcycle, with

Plan View of 6 h.p. PASSENGER Motorcycle, Model D

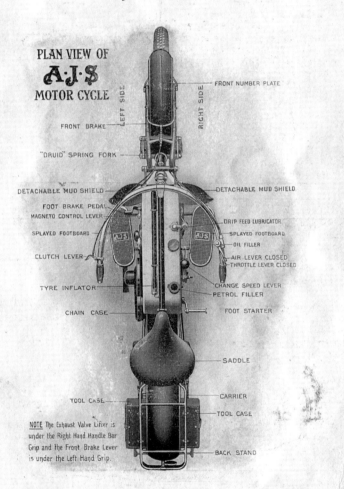

PLAN VIEW OF
A·J·S
MOTOR CYCLE

LEFT SIDE — RIGHT SIDE

FRONT NUMBER PLATE

FRONT BRAKE

"DRUID" SPRING FORK

DETACHABLE MUD SHIELD — DETACHABLE MUD SHIELD

FOOT BRAKE PEDAL
MAGNETO CONTROL LEVER

SPLAYED FOOTBOARD — DRIP FEED LUBRICATOR
SPLAYED FOOTBOARD
OIL FILLER

CLUTCH LEVER — AIR LEVER CLOSED
THROTTLE LEVER CLOSED

TYRE INFLATOR — CHANGE SPEED LEVER
PETROL FILLER

CHAIN CASE — FOOT STARTER

SADDLE

TOOL CASE — CARRIER
TOOL CASE

NOTE The Exhaust Valve Lifter is
under the Right Hand Handle Bar
Grip and the Front Brake Lever
is under the Left Hand Grip.

BACK STAND

—note its symmetrical build, its perfect balance, its possession of every device and refinement for perfect Motorcycling

6 H.P. 3 SPEED A·J·S
MODEL D.

| RIGHT-SIDE ILLUSTRATION | LEFT-SIDE ILLUSTRATION |

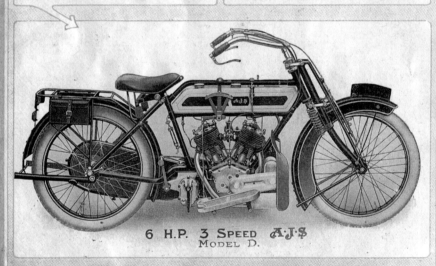

6 H.P. 3 SPEED A·J·S
MODEL D.

THIS is the famous "A.J.S. Model D." incorporating our pioneer features of
ALL-ENCASED WEATHERPROOF CHAIN DRIVE,
6 H.P. TWIN-CYLINDER ENGINE, HAND-CONTROLLED
CLUTCH, THREE-SPEED COUNTERSHAFT GEAR, PATENT
GATE CHANGE, AND KICK-STARTER. Suitable for
Solo use if desired. Patent Detachable Wheels fitted to order

6

Left and right side illustrations of a 6hp AJS Model 'D' motor cycle of 1914. *Jim Boulton Collection*

Below:
As well as testing components and parts before assembly, AJS also tested their completed motorcycles on the road. Here a group of six AJS testers pose outside one of the shops at the company's Graiseley Hill works before hitting the streets of Wolverhampton. *VMCC*

an open frame, also being produced. None was exploited commercially, although motorcycle manufacture remained a long-term ambition of the brothers. In the meantime, the engine-making side of the business prospered, and around 1908 the company moved to larger premises in Retreat Street, Wolverhampton, just over the Penn Road from John Marston's 'Sunbeamland'; Clyno moving into the former Pelham Street works. This move gave the Stevens the room they needed to develop their motorcycle making ambitions.

A name was needed for the motorcycles. As the engine-making business was to continue, the use of the family name was ruled out, and so they opted for 'AJS' — the initials of the eldest brother: Albert Jack Stevens. A separate company — A.J. Stevens & Co Ltd — was formed, and the first motorcycles appeared in 1910. Two models were made, both using a Stevens 2.5hp engine, and were belt-driven. The 'A' had a fixed gear and sold for £38 17s; the 'B' had a two-speed gearbox and sold for £44 2s. AJS machines were entered in the 1911 Isle of Man TT and, despite middling success, orders grew. They skipped the 1912 TT, but returned in 1913, and the following year won the Junior TT, held on 9 May, also taking 2nd, 4th, 6th and 29th places, and winning four Gold Medals. They consolidated this success by winning the Brooklands Junior TT on 13 June 1914, causing the motorcycling press to trip over themselves praising the team's 'reliability and regular running', and their 'phenomenally brilliant' performance.

The model range sold off the back of this success included the 'D', a 748cc 6hp V-twin (£73 10s); the 349cc 2.75hp 'B', sold as either a three-speed (£52 10s), or a two-speed (£49 7s); the 'Sporting B', with 'TT Racing Type' handlebars, footrests, a chain case and an 'Extra Large Exhaust Pipe' (same gearbox variants and prices).

This escalating success and demand for the

company's machines necessitated yet another move, further along the Penn Road, out of Wolverhampton, to a new factory erected in the grounds of Graiseley House, Graiseley Hill. The company was also reformed as A. J. Stevens (1914) Ltd. At the new site the house became the company offices, and production was housed in a single shop, 260ft by 80ft, which was completed and equipped early in 1915. By this time AJS were also undertaking war-related work, producing precision aircraft components; motorcycle production being halted in 1916.

When the war ended, the company set about developing its Graiseley works. Three large additions were made to the site in 1919, including a repair shop and stores, and a new fitting shop, allowing the original 1915 building to become a dedicated machine shop. These were built up from the brick bases of temporary corrugated iron buildings erected for war work.

AJS's post-World War 1 models were entirely new and not just the revamped versions of prewar ones produced by other firms. Top of the range was a £142, 6hp, sidecar combination, the latter being exceptionally sturdy, with a steel-panel body and large springs. With the resumption of TT racing in 1920, AJS took part once more. In 1921, Eric Williams won the Senior TT, so long the province of Wolverhampton rivals Sunbeam, in record time, re-establishing AJS and creating still more demand for their machines. Road-going TT replica models were produced, that for 1923 also reflecting the company's development of overhead valve engines by being fitted with a new 349cc 'Big Port' unit, selling for £87.

Racing success in the Isle of Man TT dwindled through the 1920s, but AJS engine development continued apace with the development, in 1926/7, of an overhead camshaft engine, first offered to the public in the 1928 model range. Styling also changed, the then current fashion for saddle tanks being adopted for 1929. A new 'R' range was announced for 1930, featuring four models, with single-cylinder engines sloped forward in the frame, plus a 996cc twin — the latter for only £63. Models were announced for 1931, but shortly after the firm's team had competed in that year's Isle of Man TT, with the tragic death of one rider, the company's bank called in all loans and overdrafts.

Debts were settled fully, the Stevens brothers returning to their old Retreat Street works and remaining in engineering. The motorcycle business was acquired by Matchless Motor Cycles (Colliers) Ltd, and production was transferred to their massive works at Woolwich. AJS's racing tradition was maintained after the move, but the machines themselves began to become diluted products, with, for example, the twin having a 990cc Matchless engine fitted to it.

Hereafter, things were done under the name of AJS, but owed more to the activities of a large manufacturer, which, upon acquiring Wolverhampton's Sunbeam marque in 1938, was renamed Associated Motor Cycles Ltd. This is not to say that some excellent machines badged as AJSs were not produced. The 1937 range boasted 12 models alone, from the 246cc single Model 37/12 at £42, to the 990cc V-twin Export Model 37/2A at £76 13s. After World War 2 one of the most significant machines badged as an AJS was the uninspiringly-named '7R', introduced in 1949. A 349cc overhead cam single, this was quickly nicknamed the 'Porcupine', after its heavily-finned cylinder head, later becoming known as the 'Boy Racer'. As the catalogues boasted: 'Each Model 7R is individually produced in the Works Racing Department.'

The 'interbreeding' at AMC became worse as the company acquired more and more marques, finally

adding Norton to its roster in mid-1962. Everything hit the fan in the summer of 1966, the AJS name being revived by the successors to AMC — Norton-Villiers — on a two-stroke machine, later being used on a limited production of trials and scrambler machines — all a far cry from the pioneering efforts of the Stevens brothers 70 years before.

AJW

Arthur John Wheaton/The AJW Motor Co
Frierhay St, Exeter
AJW Motor Co
Seabourne Rd, Bournemouth, Dorset
J. O. Ball
Mill Lane, Pilford Heath, Wimborne, Dorset

Motorcycling's other AJ, Arthur John Wheaton, worked in publishing before embarking upon cycle production. Under his own initials he planned to produce cycles from 1926, the first models appearing for the 1928 sales season. All two-cylinder machines, the AJW's used either J.A.P. or Rudge engines of between 680cc and 994cc, selling for £89 and £170 respectively, the latter being sold 'fully equipped'. All machines were also available with sidecar combinations for roughly £20 extra.

Wheaton had an obvious affection for foxes, or at least thought the name applicable to his machines, for from the 1930 model range onwards all machines were named, mostly using variants on this name: Black Fox, Silver Fox, Flying Fox, Vixenette, Red Fox, Flying Vixen, etc. The years also saw the addition of Anzani and Villiers engines to the J.A.P. and Rudge units used to date.

Production continued into the early months of the war, but ended in 1940. After the war the company was bought by Jack Ball, who moved it to a factory at Pilford Heath in Wimborne, Dorset. Material and

engine supply problems delayed a resumption of AJW production until 1948, when the J.A.P. engined road — Grey Fox — and speedway — Speed Fox — machines were launched. Engine supply problems persisted, and production of road machines ceased in 1952, but the speedway ones were still made.

The marque was rekindled in 1958 when it was applied to the Fox Cub, based around an imported moped-like machine. Production of this and other similar models allowed the AJW name to continue until 1964.

Alldays; Allon

Alldays & Onions Pneumatic Engineering Co Ltd
Matchless Works, Fallows Rd, Sparkbrook, Birmingham 11
Allon (from 1915): New Alldays & Onions Co Ltd
Great Western Works, Small Heath, Birmingham

One of the country's longest established engineering business, Alldays & Onions could trace their origins back to 1650. In 1898 they began to produce cars, and these were followed in 1903 by motorcycles. At the heart of all of the company's early machines was its own make of engine, a single-cylinder two-stroke, which was offered in a variety of fixed gear/three-speed and chain-cum-belt/belt drive models. Sold as being 'Fast on Hills, Low on Bills', the company proclaimed its machines to be 'The Best Lightweight Manufactured'.

Production continued until 1915, and for that season the firm's two-stroke machines were sold under the 'Allon' name, typically for between £32 and £42. Production was suspended due to wartime contracts, but did not resume immediately thereafter. When the name was revived it was in new premises, in Small Heath in Birmingham, as part of a restructured company, the New Alldays & Onions Co Ltd. For 1925 and 1926 the new Allons used a 292cc Alldays & Onions single-cylinder engine, but in 1927, their last year of production, a Dorman single and J.A.P. twin were used. The latter was of 680cc and fitted to a machine that sold for £75.

Ambassador

Ambassador Motor Cycles Ltd
Pontiac Works, Fernbank Rd, Ascot, Berkshire
DMW Motor Cycles (Wolverhampton) Ltd
Valley Rd, Sedgley, nr Wolverhampton

Motorcycle firms founded by ex-riders tend to suffer mixed fortunes, but one of the more successful was Ambassador. Kaye Don had ridden and driven at Brooklands before World War 2, and in 1947 he formed his own company, Ambassador Motor Cycles, to make lightweight machines. Established in a factory in Ascot, the cycles were sold as 'The Machine for the Connoisseur', and the names given to them (from 1951 onwards), reflected this theme: Embassy; Courier; Supreme, etc.

Villiers engines were used, and the range was slowly improved through the addition of new features, such as a self-starter on the Supreme (1953) and a four-speed gearbox on the Embassy (1955). That same year Ambassador also became concessionaires for Zundapp scooters, mopeds, light motorcycles and motorcycles, which were made in Nuremberg, Germany. Later Ambassadors adopted the heavy mudguards and sheet metal cladding in vogue at that time.

Always a hands-on company boss, when Kaye Don retired in 1962 the Ascot works closed before the year was out. The company's assets and name were bought by DMW Motor Cycles of Sedgley, near Wolverhampton, which also owned Metal Profiles Ltd, the suppliers of most of the Ambassador model's forks. Production resumed at Sedgley in July 1963, but the new Ambassadors bore more than a passing resemblance to an equivalent DMW model — the Dolomite II M. Production of this 'new' machine continued for two years, until the last badged Ambassadors were produced in September 1965.

AMC — see AJS

Argson Invalid Tricycle

Stanley Engineering Co Ltd
Egham, Surrey

Despite employing motorcycle mechanical parts, and sold and advertised with motorcycles, invalid carriages like the Argson are often overlooked in studies of the industry. The Argson was the product of the Stanley Engineering Co Ltd of Egham, Surrey. Production began in the late 1920s, and for the first few years the carriages used an engine of the company's own manufacture, a 170cc single. From 1933 this was replaced by a 147cc Villiers unit. Selling for between £58 and £70, Argson carriages continued to be produced throughout the 1930s.

Ariel

Ariel Motorcycles Ltd
Dale Rd & Grange Rd, Bournbrook, Birmingham 29

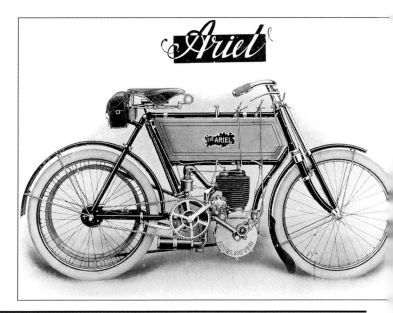

Right:
Innovative publicity stunts and sales promotions could not overcome the major problem with the early Ariel motorcycles — they were overpriced. Using its own engines, made under licence from White & Poppe, the bicycle origins of the machines were obvious.
VMCC

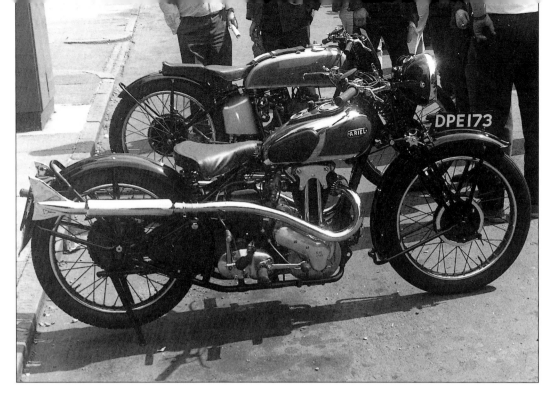

Above:
A 1936 Ariel 'Red Hunter' 250, seen on an Owners' Club tour of Birmingham in 1970. Introduced in 1933, the 250 Red Hunters continued in production into World War 2.
Jim Boulton Collection

Ariel began as a company called Components Ltd, makers of bicycle wheels, run by Charles Sangster. After experimenting with the production of a motor tricycle in 1898, they made the first Ariel motorcycle in 1902, using a Kerry engine. To promote the new machine it was sent on publicity grabbing proving runs, such as that between John O'Groats and Land's End. Ariel also began to make their own engines, in the 2hp to 3.5hp range, under licence from the Coventry engine-builders White & Poppe.

Unfortunately, sales were poor. The high price of the machines may have been an important factor, the range beginning at £35 for the basic 2hp model, up to £50 for the top 3.5hp one. To encourage customers, in 1905 Ariel introduced a sales promotion offer of a £25 cash-back allowance on any last year's model when traded in part exchange for a new Ariel — generous indeed, but buyers still had to have an almost new motorcycle to begin with! Despite such schemes, sales remained poor and the number and range of models offered by the company declined until 1913, when there just two, both based around a 498cc 3.5hp single-cylinder engine, with a fixed gear and belt drive (£45), and a three-speed gearbox and chain-cum-belt drive (£50). Two models with a 669cc long-stroke twin-cylinder engine were added for 1914 (at £76 10s and £93 10s), followed by a two-speed 349cc single in 1915 (for £42).

After World War 1, John Young 'Jack' Sangster, Charles' son, came into the business, but his main interest at that time was a light car the company also produced. The Ariel motorcycles of the period used the company's own make of single-cylinder engines, plus V-twins by proprietary firms such as M.A.G., but seemed stuck in the doldrums. Its fortunes were not revived until 1925, through the efforts of Victor Moles, the newly appointed sales manager. He engaged Valentine 'Val' Page, an ex-J.A.P. technician, and together they redesigned the motorcycle range.

A new range of 550cc side valve and 500cc overhead valve models were introduced, competitively priced and with exhilarating 80mph performance. Saddle tanks and cradle frames were introduced for 1927, followed in 1928 by two-port engines and a triangulated sidecar chassis. By 1929 production was running at 1,000 machines a week. Publicity was always to the fore. In August 1929 an Ariel on floats, with a paddle instead of a rear wheel, crossed the Channel in 3hr 50min, and returned even more quickly! Ariels were also photographed with well-known personalities — sales responded.

For 1931 Ariel introduced the first in a series of 'Square Four' machines, with four-cylinder engines of, at first, 499cc, followed by ones of 597cc and 995cc. Quickly nick-named the 'Squariel', the 499cc Square Four was introduced on a machine costing £70; the 597cc version in 1932 on a machine costing £78 5s. Another change was towards the use of inclined engines on the single-cylinder models, with the engine leaning forward (and sometimes backwards), by 30° or

60°, making the machines lower and appear more streamlined.

The early 1930s was a difficult period for the Ariel. They hit financial problems during 1932, upon which Jack Sangster took full control of affairs, re-forming the company as 'Ariel Motors (J.S.) Ltd' to save it from bankruptcy. In another blow that year, Val Page left to join Triumph (but would return in 1939). The troubled year had also seen the introduction of a new 499cc upright-engine, single-cylinder model called the 'Red Hunter', which sold for £48 15s. This set the pattern of Ariel motorcycle production for the rest of the decade. The singles were of the Red Hunter kind, with either 248cc, 346cc or 499cc engines, and the Squariels continued, bolstered by the addition of a 995cc overhead valve model in 1937.

On the business side, Jack Sangster bought the ailing Triumph motorcycle concern in Coventry for £28,000 in mid-1936. Re-formed as the Triumph Engineering Co Ltd, Jack Sangster appointed his chief designer at Ariel — Edward Turner — as General Manager and Chief Designer in Coventry. Back at Selly Oak, the Ariel range continued as above until 1940 when production was switched to war work and to making military versions of the 346cc single.

Jack Sangster approached BSA in 1943, with a view to selling the company to them. Striking a deal took until December 1944; the business was to retain its identity and to remain in Birmingham. Sangster left Ariel in 1947, to concentrate upon his Triumph interests. The marque continued, and at first such developments as there were could be counted as improvements. One was a move towards the use of alloy engine cast-

ings on the Squariels and Red Hunters from 1949/1950, but from 1954 replacement models used BSA engines, ranging from the 198cc Colt to the 647cc Huntsmaster.

No fundamentally new Ariel models appeared until 1958, when the fruit of several years' worth of development was announced as the Leader. Using unit construction, and with all its mechanicals enclosed behind steel panels, the Leader used a 247cc two-cylinder two-stroke engine, mounted onto an integral crankcase and gearbox casting. Fitted with a windshield and fairings, the Leader aped the style of the scooters then all the rage. Flushed with the successful launch of the Leader, BSA decided to drop the remaining Ariel four-stroke machines in its range in 1959, and in 1960 they substituted a sports version of the Leader — the Arrow — which was just the former with its clothes (or fairings) off!

Although an engineering success, the Leader/Arrow, and later Golden Arrow, fared less well commercially. An old Ariel problem — the price — came back to haunt the marque. At just over £200 for a Leader, prospective buyers had the choice of a scooter (cheaper to buy and run), or a Mini (more expensive, but could take the whole family); and motorcycle enthusiasts could invest a few extra pounds and get a more powerful machine, such as a Triumph 500 Twin, for under £250. BSA panicked and moved the remaining Ariel production to Small Heath in 1963, where it continued until 1965.

That should have been the end of the marque, but, unlike others sadly swallowed into larger concerns, it wasn't. In 1971, in the midst of its death throes, BSA launched a 50cc three-wheeled moped — the Ariel 3.

This remained in production almost until the demise of BSA's Small Heath plant, which closed officially on 15 December 1975.

Ascot-Pullin

Ascot Motor & Mfg Co Ltd
Phœnix Works, Pixmore Ave, Letchworth, Hertfordshire

Few factories have had a more varied life than the Phœnix Works in Letchworth, for in the mid-1920s it was home to no less than three makes of car: the Phœnix; Arab and Ascot, plus a motorcycle. Built for the Phœnix Motor Co in 1910, the works was designed in the 'Garden City' idiom of much that surrounded it. From the failure of the Phœnix company in 1926 the factory became (briefly) the home of the Arab light car, followed by the Ascot. The latter was designed by Cyril Pullin, who had also produced the Ascot-Pullin motorcycle.

Production of both vehicles was centred in the Phœnix Works at Letchworth from 1928 until the whole enterprise collapsed into bankruptcy on 31 October 1929. In that short period a number of Ascot-Pullin cycles were completed. These were notable both for their advanced design and for the luxuries they offered the potential customer/rider. Power was provided by a 497cc single-cylinder engine of the company's own manufacture, mounted into a pressed steel frame. Front and rear wheels were easily removed and interchangeable, and a capacious 4-gallon petrol tank was provided. Luxuries included an instrument panel, windscreen and wiper, plus protective fairings, and a passenger seat.

The full price of this magnificent machine was £78 15s, or £98 10s if bought as a combination. Sadly, this high price, plus steering problems, and generally being the wrong model in the wrong market at the wrong time, put paid to this great venture.

Aurora

Aurora Motor Manufacturing Co Ltd
22 Norfolk St, Coventry 1

Occupying a former watchmakers' house and workshop, the Aurora Motor Manufacturing Co Ltd was established in 1903. They began by making engines and then diversified into the production of motorcycles that used their own engine. Unfortunately, despite some technical excellence, the Aurora failed to become established in what was a far from stable motorcycle market, and was produced only during 1903 and 1904.

BAC; Bond

BAC: Bond Aircraft & Engineering Co Ltd
Gosford Street Works, Ribbleton Lane, Preston, Lancashire
Bond: Sharps Commercials Ltd/Bond Cars Ltd
Gosford Street Works, Ribbleton Lane, Preston, Lancashire
(from 1958) India Mill, Newhall Lane, Preston, Lancashire

The above ventures all share the involvement of one person: Lawrence 'Laurie' Bond. Sharps Commercials Ltd was founded in 1938, but had its origins in a firm formed in 1922. They serviced commercial vehicles, and were bought out as part of a venture to import, assemble and distribute Chevrolet trucks in advance of the coming war. With the war, and the need for larger premises, the venture was moved to an old rope works in Ribbleton Lane, Preston.

It was here that Laurie Bond came with the designs for his now famous three-wheeler, which was produced by Sharps from 1949. The following year Bond produced another startling vehicle, a motorcycle designed around a tapered oval section alloy tube from which the Villiers engine was suspended. With almost fully enclosed front and rear wheels, the Bond had a distinctly unusual appearance.

Other product developments at Preston required production of the Bond motorcycle to be undertaken by Ellis & Co Ltd of Leeds from 1951. In part this was to make way for the BAC (Bond Aircraft & Engineering Co) Lilliput, followed in 1952 by a scooter, the BAC Gazelle. Almost skeletal in design, this too used a Villiers engine.

For five years, from 1953 to 1958, production of the Gazelle was transferred to Projects & Developments Ltd in Blackburn, due, in part, to the need to make room for production of the ever popular three-wheelers. A move was inevitable, and in 1958 the company, now called Bond Cars Ltd, moved to a nearby former cotton mill: India Mill in Newhall Lane, Preston. Here scooter production was resumed and continued until 1962.

Baker

Baker Motor Cycles Ltd
Alvechurch Rd, Northfield, Birmingham 31
Tomey Rd, Greet, Birmingham 11

Dominating half of Tomey Road was the massive James motorcycle factory, something with which Frank

Below:
Frank E. Baker was the person behind Precision engines and Beardmore motorcycles before he tried his hand at motorcycle production from 1927. This is one of his early machines, which was fitted with a 172cc Villiers single-cylinder engine and a twin straight-through silencer — all for £39 10s. *VMCC*

E. Baker, the owner and founder of Baker Motor Cycles Ltd, was probably all too familiar. Baker was an engine manufacturer, who had previously tried motorcycle production under the Precision marque. By the late 1920s he was offering a range of six to seven models, all based around Villiers single-cylinder engines of between 147cc and 342cc, selling for between £25 and £37 10s.

The introduction of a model using a four-stroke 249cc James engine early in 1930 possibly began a dialogue that resulted later that same year in Frank Baker selling out to James, who continued to use his designs well into the 1930s.

BAT; BAT-Martinsyde

BAT: BAT Motor Manufacturing Co Ltd
2 Kingswood Rd, Penge, London
Martinsyde: Helmuth Paul Martin & George Harris
Handasyde/Martinsyde Ltd
Brooklands, Byfleet, Surrey

Motorcycling folklore has come to suggest that the BAT's name comes from the phrase 'Best After Tests.' Sadly, the truth is somewhat more prosaic; the BAT being named after Samuel Robert BATson, the original owner of the company that produced them. Founded in 1902, Batson's motorcycle designs were revolutionary for their time, featuring sprung frames that offered both greater comfort and increased road holding. Samuel Batson sold his motorcycle interests to T.H. Tessier in 1904, who continued to use Batson's designs in conjunction with J.A.P. engines. Also a rider, Tessier took part in the first ever Isle of Man TT in 1907, on a BAT.

By 1914 no fewer than 14 models of BAT were being offered, all using J.A.P. engines and with a variety of fixed gear, two- and three-speed gearboxes,

Above:
Although BAT also produced single-cylindered machines in the years up to World War 1, it was for V-twin models such as the 2a that they were best known. In this shot the J.A.P. engine and frame-springing are well to view; but a number of other makers might well have disputed the immodest claim for its supremacy. *VMCC*

chain-cum-belt, chain and belt drives. Top of the range was a V-twin-cylinder model with a three-speed gearbox and chain drive, selling for £75. Production declined during World War 1, but revived afterwards.

In 1923 BAT took over Martinsyde Ltd, a former aircraft maker, founded by Helmuth Paul Martin and George Harris Handasyde, and based at Brooklands in Byfleet, Surrey. From that point on the firm produced its cycles under the BAT-Martinsyde name, but not for long. Financial problems hit the company in 1925 and it folded in 1926. Ironically, Samuel Batson had remained in business, diversifying into the production of office equipment in 1902, which his company did with great success for many years.

Baughan

Baughan Motors
Tyburn Lane, Harrow, Middlesex
(from 1921) Lower St, Stroud, Gloucestershire

Henry Baughan established a general engineering business in Harrow in the early years of the 20th century. Quite quickly he had diversified into motorcycle production. In 1920 the company also began to make cyclecars, using the same gearboxes, chain drives, wheels, and either J.A.P. or Blackburne V-twin engines, as his motorcycles. Combining this with motorcycle production proved a strain and the company

moved to new premises, in Lower Street, Stroud, Gloucestershire. Production of both types of vehicle continued until cyclecar manufacture was abandoned in 1929.

The Baughan motorcycles of this period exclusively used single-cylinder Blackburne engines, ranging in capacity from 200cc to 550cc and selling for between £35 and £87 10s. A major change came about in 1931 with the exclusive use of Sturmey-Archer engines, which continued for the 1932 model season. The following year saw a partial return to Blackburne engines, plus some of the company's own manufacture. Production levels were low, as few as 10-15 machines being completed in a year, and as a consequence the operation became uneconomic. The last Baughan motorcycles were made in 1936.

Beau Ideal

Richards' Beau Ideal Cycle Co Ltd
Frederick St, Heath Town, Wolverhampton
Gresham Chambers, Lichfield St, Wolverhampton

Charles Richards founded his Beau Ideal Cycle Co in the Heath Town area of Wolverhampton in 1880. At the turn of the 19th century the company began to show an interest in producing a motorcycle. This may have coincided with their move to a larger works and showrooms in Lichfield Street, a grand street in the centre of the town created out of a notorious area of slum housing in the 1880s.

Some years of experimentation culminated in the exhibition of three motorcycles on the company's stand at the 1904 Stanley Show — the cycling world's equivalent of today's motor show. Each used Fafnir engines, imported from Germany, and was a single-speed fixed gear machine which, unusually, had all of the rider's

controls on the right-hand side of the handlebar. A three-wheeled tricar was also projected, but not produced, and only a few Beau Ideal motorcycles were made before the company returned to making only bicycles.

Blackburne

Burney & Blackburne Ltd
Tongham, Surrey

Burney & Blackburne have an assured place in motorcycle history as one of the major manufacturers of proprietary engines, which were sold under the Blackburne name. They also enjoyed an 11-year spell as a motorcycle manufacturer between 1915 and 1926, although more of their work in the early part of this period was directed towards wartime production. The company was established in May 1914 to manufacture engines and motorcycles. All of the early Blackburnes used the company's own single-cylinder 3.5hp engine and were available with either a chain or a belt drive. Both the 1915 and 1916 models were sold for £66 17s 6d.

Production continued until 1926, when Burney & Blackburne returned to their core business of engine manufacture. The rights to produce the Blackburne motorcycle were acquired by the Osborn Engineering Co Ltd, makers of the OEC, and production continued for that year only. A range of OEC engines, from 350cc single up to an 1,100cc twin, were used, the machines being branded as OEC Blackburnes.

Black Prince

Black Prince Motors Ltd
Thorngate Mill, Thorngate, Barnard Castle, Co Durham

Thorngate Mill was used as both a corn and woollen mill during the 19th century. In 1919 it was occupied by Black Prince Motors Ltd, a new company established that year by Herbert G. Wright to build cyclecars and motorcycles. Cars and motorcycles were assembled side-by-side, and, as with the then current trend for cyclecars, also shared many common components. These included the engine, which was a Union 2.75hp air-cooled model.

The production facilities were far from ideal. Vehicles were assembled on the first floor of the mill and rolled down a ramp to street level, before setting off for a test run around Thorngate and up the bank to the Market Cross. Concerns like Black Prince Motors often had a perilous financial structure, and the company hit difficulties in 1922 and ceased trading. Thorngate Mill reverted to woollen and worsted production, and is now a bookshop.

Bond — see BAC

Bown — see Aberdale

Bradbury

Bradbury & Co Ltd
Wellington Works, Wellington St, Oldham, Lancashire

Bradbury & Co were established on 5 May 1874. The Bradbury was one of the first British motorcycles, the earliest models appearing in 1902. Power was provided by the company's own make of engine, which, for the first years of manufacture, was a square (equal cylinder bore and stroke) 550cc single-cylinder model delivering

4hp. Machines were available with either a single-, two- or three-speed gearbox and ranged in price from £47 to £60. In 1914 a 750cc 6hp V-twin-cylinder model was introduced, which sold for £75. Bradburys were produced on into the early 1920s, but their manufacture ceased in 1925.

Britax

Britax Ltd
115-129 Carlton Vale London NW6

A name more familiar from the world of car accessories, Britax, established in May 1939, also dabbled in motorcycle production in the 1950s. All of their machines used four-stroke Ducati engines, imported from the manufacturers in Italy. The first Britax was a clip-on cycle attachment, which the company sold from late 1949 onwards. In 1953 this was joined by a complete motorcycle and in 1955 by a scooter, again all using Ducati engines. A racing machine was also tried, but the whole motorcycle venture was shelved in 1956.

Above left:
Learning his craft through trials, Henry Baughan also began to make his own motorcycles. First using Blackburne engines, in 1931 he switched to Sturmey-Archer units, this model costing £49 10s and having a prominent bulb horn. *VMCC*

Below:
Produced by an engineering company established in 1874, 'The Bradbury' motorcycle first appeared in 1902. For the first few years the company produced only single-cylindered models, of which this 3.5hp one was top of the range at £60. *VMCC*

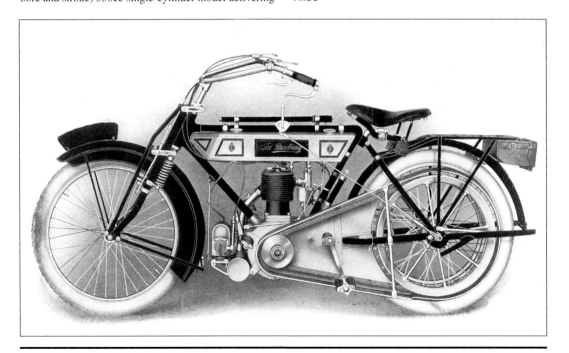

Brough

W. E. Brough & Co
129 Vernon Rd, Old Basford, Nottingham

William Brough was a colliery electrician. In 1895 he built a small works at the rear of his house at 129 Vernon Road, Old Basford, Nottingham. Here he experimented with building both a small car and a motor tricycle, before turning his attention to motorcycles in 1902. Prototypes gave way to production models, which were noted for their technical excellence, particularly of the engines. In 1914, Brough introduced a 3.5hp 500cc two-cylinder engine of an advanced design that featured high crankshaft speeds and high specific power output. This was incorporated into three designs of cycle, identified by the letters HTT, HS and HC, of which the latter was top of the range, selling for £66 5s.

Brough had two sons, William Jr and George, both of whom joined him in the business. William enjoyed much success racing his father's machines, but George

Left:
A drawing emphasising the lines of the Brough Superior SS80. Powered by a 981cc J.A.P. V-twin engine, the machine was one of the staples from a maker who also specialised in producing specials for the annual Motor Cycle Show. *Museum of British Road Transport, Coventry*

Below:
This rear three-quarter view of a 1937 model Brough Superior SS100 is dominated by the company's characteristic twin 'fish-tail' exhausts. For the 1936 range, Brough Superior had changed from using J.A.P. engines in favour of Matchless units. *VMCC*

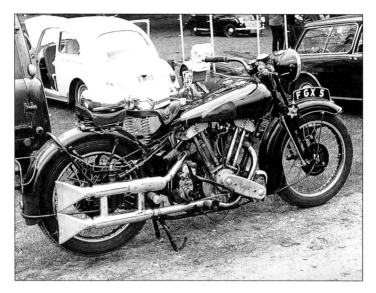

had ambitions to make his own motorcycle, one that would be superior to all other makes. Accordingly, in 1921 he left to set up on his own, leaving the Williams (father and son) to continue the business alone, which they did with some success until the mid-1920s.

Brough Superior

George Brough
Haydn Rd, Sherwood, Nottingham
(from 1934): 129 Vernon Rd, Old Basford, Nottingham

The son of William Brough, George Brough was born in Nottingham in 1890. He needed little coercion to follow his father's mechanical interests in the design of motor cars and motorcycles, and in 1906, at the age of 16, George Brough rode one of his father's machines in a Land's End to John O'Groats trial. The event was won by George's elder brother, William Jr. George finished three days after the rest of the competitors!

Although he entered into partnership with his father, George Brough had different aims and ambitions in the motorcycle market. He pursued a dream of producing a machine that was to be 'superior' to all others, and in 1919 he left to set up on his own. Later that year George Brough produced the first of his 'Brough Superior' motorcycles. It used a massive 967cc 8hp J.A.P. V-twin engine, and its 'superior' features included heavy rust-preventing plating and a special exhaust and silencer system. Styling was also unusual, with a bulbous-nosed tank.

In the days of genuine 'unsolicited testimonials', one proud owner of an early Brough Superior wrote to the company praising the machine, saying that it was 'the Rolls-Royce of motorcycles' — the phrase was used, and stuck. But during the early 1920s George Brough was his own best publicity machine, for he continued to compete in endurance trials, races and other motor

cycling competitions — all on a Brough Superior — with great success. Among the most successful of the early Brough Superiors were the SS100s, introduced in 1924. Each one was sold with a guarantee that it had been timed at over 100mph before sale!

A string of innovations were introduced in the Brough Superior range throughout the 1920s and early 1930s. 'Castle' forks, incorporating parallel tubes and bottom links to good shock absorbing effect, were introduced on all models in 1925, in 1928 the firm began to use a Bentley & Draper sprung frame, and 1929's Black Alpine 680 model had a hand-operated gear change.

The power for all of these machines came from J.A.P. V-twin engines of between 680cc and 976cc, producing a range of motorcycles selling for between £115 and £170. One exception came in 1929 with the introduction of a Straight Four, using an own-build 900cc engine, selling for £200. A break with 'tradition' came in 1931 with the introduction of a 'Baby' Brough, powered by a 500cc J.A.P. V-twin and selling for just £105. Only nine were built, and the model did not appear amongst the 1932 range. From that time the trend was towards larger Broughs, including a 1,150cc model introduced in 1933.

After his father's death, George returned to the former's Old Basford works in 1935, from where he continued to produce variations upon his luxury designs. During 1938 he embarked upon a project to build an ultimate luxury motorcycle that was to be the epitome of power and smoothness. Christened the 'Golden Dream', it used a 997cc four-cylinder engine. Shown at the 1938 Motorcycle Show, it would have sold for £250, but the outbreak of war the following year effectively killed the project.

The last Broughs were produced in the first weeks of World War 2, during which the company manufactured precision aircraft components, and they would remain in precision engineering when peace returned.

Brown

Brown Brothers Ltd
23-34 Great Eastern St, London EC

Browns is one of the longest established firms of motor factors in the country, supplying components and accessories to the trade. In the early years of the 20th century they were also a motor manufacturer, producing both a three-wheeled 'forecar', and motorcycles. By 1905 two cycles were in production, using, respectively, a 2.75hp and a 3.5hp engine. Very bicycle-like in design, the Browns boasted a number of innovatory features, including interchangeable inlet and exhaust valves, 'so that only one spare valve need be carried', extra large flywheels and an 'absolutely oiltight' crank case. Final drive was by means of a Duco V-shaped belt.

The 2.75hp model sold for £34 and the 3.5hp one for £37. Browns were produced until c1909, when the company returned to its core business of being motor factors.

BSA

BSA Cycles Ltd
Armoury Rd, Small Heath, Birmingham 11
BSA Company Ltd
Blockley, Gloucestershire
BSA Regal Group Ltd
Speedwell House, West Quay Road, Southampton

Below:
Bicycle makers since c1880, BSA were late entrants into motorcycle manufacture, spending a number of years making components for others. BSA's first machine was based around one of the company's bicycles and used its own make of 3.5hp engine, selling for £50. *VMCC*

Britain's largest motorcycle manufacturer had its origins in the Birmingham gun trade of the 18th century. Towards the end of that century a group of local gun makers formed an association called the Birmingham Small Arms Trade Association, the descendants of which went on to form the Birmingham Small Arms (BSA) Co in 1861.

Around 1880 the company branched out into the production of bicycles, which continued into the 20th century. Some early attempts were made to motorise one of these bicycles using an Otto engine, but this was not exploited commercially. From the beginning of the new century, BSA produced motorcycle components for other manufacturers, and it was not until 1910 that they produced their own complete machine. It had a 3.5hp engine and sold for £50.

By World War 1 just three basic models were being produced: two three-speed machines using a 556cc single-cylinder engine, for £59 15s and £63, and a 499cc fixed-gear single for £48 10s. Production continued throughout World War 1, supplying the needs of the British Expeditionary Force on the Western and other fronts. After the war, in 1924 the company secured a contract to supply the GPO with motorcycles for use by its newly introduced Telegram Delivery Service. This was followed in later years by massive orders from the AA, Police and more for the Army during World War 2.

BSA had a very clear market in mind for their motorcycles. They were suppliers of personal mobility to the masses, makers of soundly-built, basic, no frills, reliable machines, whose owners might dream of winning the TT, but for whom getting to and from work safely and dependably was more important. The company even made a virtue of this 'market awareness' in its brochures: 'The wide range of BSA models is the result of many years' experience of the varying requirements

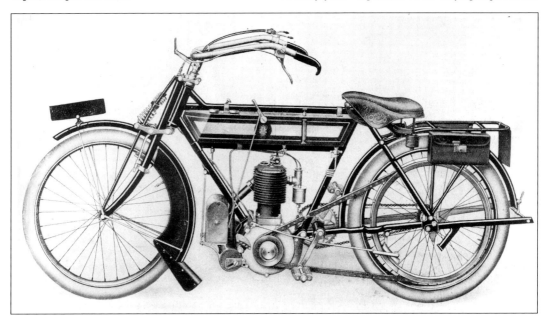

of the thousands of riders and prospective riders... We hope that the points to which we call attention may not be without interest even to the experienced rider, inasmuch as they embody the knowledge of practical riders who have had experience with our models.'

The excellence of the BSA machines was, as ever, demonstrated through their exploits in endurance and trials events. They also took part in special publicity stunts, such as one in 1924, when four BSAs climbed Mount Snowdon in less than 25min!; or in 1926, when two intrepid riders on BSAs completed a journey around the world in 18 months.

That year the range comprised six models and their variants: the 249cc B26, available as a two-speed (£36) or three-speed De Luxe (£37 10s); the 349cc L26, available in Standard (£41 15s) or De Luxe (£47) versions; the 493cc S26 (Standard £44 15s, De Luxe £48 15s); the 557cc H26 (Standard £55, De Luxe £60); the 770cc V-twin E26 (Standard £63, De Luxe £69) and the 986cc V-twin G26, available as a Standard (£64), De Luxe (£70), or Colonial model (£70).

In 1927 BSA introduced its 'Sloper' motorcycles, with sloping engines, seen first on the 'S27' series of 493cc machines. By 1930 the range had reached a peak

The BEEZA

A BRILLIANT NEW BSA SCOOTER!

of 16 models, starting with a 174cc single for £28 10s, and going up to a 986cc twin for £69 10s. Thereafter it was cut-back, as the economic tide turned nationally and internationally. Models were simplified to keep costs down, but as the recession lifted, improvements were made. For 1933 two 348cc and 499cc singles were named 'Blue Star', and from 1934 an electrical lighting kit, previously only a £7 15s option, was fitted as standard. Later, in 1937, the range of single-cylinder machines was simplified to a single design, produced in two ranges: the 'B', for 249cc and 348cc engines, and the 'M', for 349cc, 496cc and 596cc units.

During World War 2 BSA turned to war production, making, in addition to weaponry, 126,354 496cc singles for military use. The company also grew, by taking over some famous marques: Sunbeam in 1943, Ariel in 1944 and New Hudson before the war's end. Other concerns might have become big-headed over such expansion, but BSA resisted the temptation to call themselves 'Amalgamated British Motorcycles', or some such; also, in some instances, leaving the taken-over companies to get on with things, at least in the short term.

BSA resumed domestic motorcycle production in the latter part of 1945, reintroducing prewar models, including a mufti-version of the military model, plus a new 348cc single. One of the most famous of the postwar BSAs, the 'Bantam', was launched in June

1948. A 123cc two-stroke single, the designs for which had been acquired from the East German DKW factory, at Zschopau in Saxony, as war reparations. The following year saw the launch of the Gold Star, a 348cc single based on the prewar 'B' range, but using an alloy engine. Triumph were added to the BSA stable in 1951, although their operation continued at Meriden, safe from Small Heath's clutches for a while.

In 1953 motorcycle production was hived off under a separate concern — BSA Motorcycles Ltd. By the mid-1950s, the BSA Group, as it now was, had built up an impressive range of 12 motorcycles, promoted in full-colour, fold-out brochures that made excellent posters to adorn the walls of many an aspiring motorcyclist. Starting with two Bantams, the D1 125cc and the D3 150cc Major (£68 to £82), the range included a pair of 250cc machines, a 350cc, and four 500cc motorcycles, plus a 600cc model and a 650cc twin, 'the Golden Flash', for £191 10s.

Behind the scenes there were tensions within the large BSA Group, and changes at management level. The company also 'wobbled' badly over its model policy; the clearest signs of this being the débâcle that resulted from the attempted introduction of two light-weight machines: the 75cc two-stroke 'Dandy' (a motorcycle) and the 198cc four-stroke 'Beeza' (a scooter). The Dandy was underpowered and overheated easily, being withdrawn soon after its October 1956 launch; the Beeza didn't even get that far. Announced in November 1955, it was a shaft-driven, four-speed, four-stroke boasting a wide range of features, including a 'Thief-proof steering lock'. All this could have been bought for £204 12s, but the plug was pulled on it, a victim of a growing Triumph versus BSA management feud in which the former were gaining the upper hand.

Triumph's hold on the company grew in 1957 when their Edward Turner was appointed Head of the BSA Automotive Division. Unsurprisingly, the only major new BSA model in the late 1950s — the unit construction 247cc C15 single — was a thinly disguised Triumph Cub, originally introduced for their 1954 range.

To the public in the 1960s the BSA-Triumph story was a resounding success, but behind the scenes the dramas of the 1950s continued. Many lines of communication within the BSA Group hadn't so much broken down, as never existed in the first place. The management was a mess, and the production side needed new models to compete with both the better organised British manufacturers and the very-much-together foreign ones, notably the Japanese. One hope came with the appointment of Harry Sturgeon as Managing

Director. With a background in the aircraft industry, Sturgeon also proved himself to be an excellent salesman, sending the BSA Group's motorcycle exports rocketing, especially those to the USA. Queen's Awards were won, and capital invested in new plant at Small Heath. There were new models too, and BSA once again produced large-engined machines, including 1965's 441cc Victor. But Sturgeon's tenure was tragically brief; illness forced his retirement early in 1966.

Sturgeon's replacement knew management much better than he knew motorcycles. There was a new machine in 1968 — the 750cc Rocket 3 — with a three-cylinder engine. Sold first in the USA, it was launched on the domestic market in 1969, and was generally well-received. Problems remained with the company though, and these grew. The profits of the late 1960s turned to a loss in 1971, and strong measures were proposed that October, including the closure of the main BSA works at Small Heath, all motorcycles now to be made at Meriden.

This decision was overturned, but terminal decay had set in. Events too complex to relate here led to the sale of the BSA Group to Norton Villiers, to form Norton-Villiers-Triumph Ltd, on 17 July 1973, and within two months their Chairman, Dennis Poore, announced a reversal of the previous policy, namely that Meriden would close, and that production would be concentrated at the former BSA plant at Small Heath. This sparked off the Meriden sit-in and Co-operative, a mess that would drag on for 10 years. It also marked the effective end of BSA motorcycles as they had been known. The company's former Small Heath plant closed officially on 15 December 1975, actually producing its last machine on Christmas Eve that year.

Left over following the cessation of motorcycle production were a mass of parts, which were used to form the basis of a spares operation, based in a former Norton assembly plant at Andover. Through a series of management buy-outs, by people involved in this and the NVT operation at Shenstone, the rights to the BSA name were acquired in 1979, and a new BSA company was set-up in Blockley, Gloucestershire. Acquired too was the right to manufacture machines up to 175cc for sale in the UK, and a series of Yamaha-engined trials and off-road machines were made, many of which went for export. Army motorcycles were made too, using Rotax engines. In 1991 the new BSA was merged with the Andover Norton concern to form a new BSA Group.

History then repeated itself. This new BSA Group hit trouble, and was taken over in 1994 by the Southampton-based firm Regal Engineering, a long-established family engineering company, which took the opportunity to bring its diverse interests in 12 companies together on one site, and acquired a former transport and warehousing depot in Southampton for this purpose. In January 1997 a new BSA motorcycle appeared, based around the Yamaha SR400. The company receives a donor machine, from which the engine, forks, and other major components, are stripped. These are then added to an own-build chassis and other parts to produce a motorcycle retro-styled to evoke a 1960s BSA. Made on a batch production system, and employing only five to six people directly in their manufacture, some 200 machines have been made so far, and plans are well advanced for the introduction of a more powerful model — the Gold SR500. So, in a small but growing way, one of Britain's most famous motorcycle marques lives on.

Calcott

Calcott Bros. Ltd
XL Works, Far Gosford St, Coventry 1

The Calcott brothers established themselves as bicycle manufacturers in 1886. In 1905 they also began to produce a motorcycle, and in 1913 went on to produce cars too. The motorcycles were typical of their period, but their manufacture had increasingly to take a back seat to car production, which had come to dominate the firm's activities by World War 1. When peacetime production resumed it was of cars only. Great success was enjoyed until the death of one of the brothers, William, in 1924, from when the firm began to flounder, being taken over by Singer in 1926.

Calthorpe; Calthorpe Lightweights

Minstrel & Rea Cycle Co Ltd/
Calthorpe Motor Cycle Co Ltd
16-17 Barn St, Bordesley Green, Birmingham 5

Like many motorcycles, the Calthorpe marque began as a bicycle. It was the creation of George W. Hands; he established his cycle business in the Bordesley area, by the River Rea, to the southwest of Birmingham city centre, around 1890. Experiments with car manufacture began in 1904, and with motorcycles in 1910. The full production of motorcycles began in 1911, and soon created overcrowding problems that were only resolved when car production was transferred to a new factory in Cherrywood Road, Bordesley Green, in 1912. Thus, the Barn Street works was left clear for bicycle and motorcycle production.

Before World War 1, the company's motorcycles were known as Calthorpe Lightweights and exclusively featured J.A.P. engines. Most were single-cylindered 292cc 2.5hp or 242cc 2.75hp models, with either a single, fixed or two-speed gearbox and a chain-cum-belt drive. The range also featured a Ladies' machine and a two-cylinder combination, prices starting at £30 15s, for the 2.5hp fixed gear model and ending with £68 5s for the two-cylinder version.

Car production withered from 1927 onwards, but motorcycles continued to be made at Barn Street. In addition to their own make of engines, most notably a 348cc overhead valve single introduced in 1926, those by Blackburne, J.A.P. and Villiers were also used. The motorcycle range was also given a facelift in the late 1920s. Model names were introduced, such as the Super Sports, instead of the letter/number codes D6,

G1, D9S, etc, that had been used before. Perhaps the greatest change of all came in 1929, when the model range was out-shopped with a white petrol tank and mudguards, a striking contrast to the all-black finish used on most makes. This led to Calthorpe cycles being called 'Ivories', something reflected in the model names from 1932 onwards, when the Ivory Minor, Ivory III, Ivory Major, etc appeared.

Keen attention was paid to prices, and these actually reduced as the 1930s progressed: the equivalent to a 498cc model that had cost £75 in 1928 cost only £46 4s in 1934. Despite the excellence of their engines and production generally, Calthorpe hit difficulties in the late 1930s and went into receivership in 1938. The factory and company assets were sold to Bruce Douglas, a member of the Bristol-based motorcycle family, who planned a range of Calthorpes for 1939, but the war stymied this. A further attempt to revive the marque in 1947, by the Black Country-based DMW company, also came to nothing, despite the construction of a prototype.

Campion

Campion Cycle Co Ltd
Robin Hood St, Nottingham

Campion were a Nottingham-based cycle firm who also produced motor cycles from 1901. Just before World War 1 they were using Villiers single-cylinder and J.A.P. V-twin engines in a range of five cycles that offered either fixed, two-, three- or four-speed gearboxes and chain-cum-belt drive. Bottom of the range was a 2.5hp fixed-gear single which sold for £28 in 1914; top of the range being an 8hp V-twin for £75. Model ranges were produced for 1914 and 1915, and after the war until 1925. Their last design was a 1,000cc V-twin machine similar to Nottingham's Brough Superior.

Carfield

The Carfield Motor Co/Carfield Ltd
Windmill Lane, Smethwick

Carfield were another firm that sprang up to meet the immediate postwar demand for personal motorised transport that grew just after World War 1. Founded in 1919, the company was based in Windmill Lane, off Cape Hill in Smethwick. At first just two models were offered, both using a 2.5hp Villiers two-stroke engine and belt drive, one featuring a kick start and two-speed gearbox; the other a single, fixed drive. These sold for £65 and £50 10s respectively.

In 1921 the choice of engines was widened to include Coventry Victor and J.A.P. units, the former being a flat-twin, used in a £90 cycle that did not sell well. Two years later a 1.5hp budget model, the Carfield Baby, was introduced, selling for just £29. Success in endurance trials followed, but, despite revisions to the model range and a keen eye on prices, the Carfield venture folded in 1928.

Cedos

Cedos Motor Cycles Ltd
Brunswick Place, Kettering Rd, Northampton

Like the Advance before it, and the Hesketh afterwards, the Cedos proved that motorcycle production and Northamptonshire just did not seemed destined for each other. Cedos used a combination of their own design together with Blackburne, Bradshaw, J.A.P, and Villiers engines, to make a range of up to nine single-cylinder cycles. For 1927 the range began with the Model 15, a Cedos engined 247cc 2.5hp machine, selling for just £25, and extended to the Model 21, a Bradshaw engined 350cc 2.75hp cycle, for £55 10s. For 1928 and 1929 the range was reduced to just four machines, using either a J.A.P. or Villiers engine, but this proved to be the last season for Cedos production, although stocks of cycles were sold on into the early 1930s.

Chater; Chater-Lea

Chater-Lea Ltd
78-84 Golden Lane, Aldersgate, London EC
(from 1928) New Icknield Way, Letchworth, Hertfordshire

Chater-Lea Ltd was founded in 1900 to manufacture bicycle components. Situated almost in the heart of London, their first interest in motorcycles came through being asked to make frames and forks for other firms, and by the mid-1900s the company were experimenting with clip-on attachments to motorise bicycles. This in turn led to a decision to enter into full motorcycle manufacture, and by the turn of 1909 a V-twin machine was ready for sale. A variety of proprietary engines were tried, mainly imported French units such as the Antoine, de Dion Bouton, Minerva and Peugeot.

Chater-Lea were also experimenting with car manufacture, and to accommodate both this and motorcycle production, plus their cycle component work, a new nine-storey factory was built, coming into use around 1912. The motorcycles were noted for being powerful, using 770cc and 1,000cc J.A.P. V-twin engines, and for incorporating technical innovations, such as telescopic spring forks, fitted to some models from 1910 onwards. Another feature was a low body frame, giving the machines a low centre of gravity and thus greater stability. They performed particularly well when used in a sidecar combination. By the early 1910s the standard model had become an 8hp V-twin square-engined cycle which sold for £78 15s.

Production was halted during most of World War 1, but resumed thereafter with the prewar models. Blackburne, J.A.P. and Villiers engines were used for a few years but by 1926 Chater-Lea had perfected their own 348cc single-cylinder camshaft engine that would form the basis of most of the cycles the company would go on to make.

In 1928 Chater-Lea moved to a new factory on New

Icknield Way in Letchworth, Hertfordshire, and by 1930 they had produced a simplified range of motorcycles powered by their own engines. These had either the proven 348cc camshaft unit, or a 545cc single which was fitted to the 'Sports' model. The latter was also sold with a sidecar, for £72 10s, and found particular favour with the AA, whose motorcycle patrols were ever on the increase at the time.

Chater-Lea had continued to manufacture components alongside their motorcycles, and over the 1935 to 1936 period they gradually withdrew from producing the latter.

Cheetah

Cheetah Engineering Ltd
Denmead, Hampshire

The Cheetah was an all-British trials machine produced by Bob Gollner and Mick Whitlock. Expertise from engineer Peter Barge made their dreams reality in 1966, the first machine being prepared in February 1967. Appearances at trials led to orders from fellow riders and to production being commenced on a commercial basis. Villiers engines were used at first, but once these became scarce in 1968, imported units were tried. Sold in kit form for £249, the Cheetah was sold under the slogan: 'Some Cheapa — None Beata Cheetah!!' Sadly, this promising marque petered out within a few years.

Chell

Chell Motor Co, Moorfield Rd, Wolverhampton

The Chell was one of many prototypes that were announced to the motorcycle press, never to see the light of day as a production machine. In the case of the Chell this may have been due to the war, as it was launched during the early months of 1939. Two models were proposed, using 98cc and 125cc Villiers two-stroke engines, at a predicted price of £21 10s.

Clyde

Wait & Co Ltd
London Rd, Leicester
Clyde Motor Co Ltd
Queen St, Leicester

Beginning motorcycle manufacture in 1898, G. H. Wait was one of the pioneers of the industry in Britain. Based in Leicester, Clyde motorcycles initially used Wait's own engines, but later switched to proprietary J.A.P. units. The company was in production for just a few years after World War 1. By 1926 there were just two motorcycles in the range: a 490cc single-cylinder 4hp, that sold for £45, and a 980cc twin-cylinder 8hp, available for £72. similar models were offered for 1927, but 1928 saw just a 350cc single, selling for £38, which proved to be the last of the Clydes.

Clyno

Clyno Engineering Co Ltd/Clyno Engineering Co (1922) Ltd
Pelham St, Wolverhampton

In the early 1900s two Northamptonshire cousins, Frank and Alwyn Smith, designed a pulley with a variable drive ratio for belt-driven motorcycles. They termed this device an 'inclined pulley', which, over time, became abbreviated to 'clined and eventually became immortalised in the name of their company: The Clyno Engineering Co Ltd. This was founded in November 1909, and in 1910 they moved into a factory in Pelham Street, Wolverhampton, recently vacated by Stevens Brothers, manufacturers of the AJS motorcycle.

Two models of Clyno motorcycles had been exhibited at the 1909 Stanley Show, and these were put into production at Pelham Street. Both machines used Stevens engines. Gradually a model range was developed, starting with a fixed-gear single, which sold for £32, and extending up to a 746cc twin-cylinder cycle, with a three-speed gearbox, that sold for £75. The latter also formed the basis of a combination that sold for £91. Other models were developed, including an open frame ladies' version, which had its engine and all of its working parts totally enclosed.

Things were going well for Clyno, and then World War 1 intervened. The big twin had proved to be a rugged design and it was ordered in quantity for use as a machine gun carrier, doing admirable service on all battle fronts. Aero-engines were also produced, which left no room to make motorcycles for domestic use.

Left:
Clyde's founder, G. H. Wait, pioneered the use of loop frames, seen to good advantage in his 2.75hp model. The engines were also Wait's design, using forward facing valves and carburettor, being made under licence from F. R. Simms, who had brought the Daimler patent internal combustion engine to Britain in 1893. *VMCC*

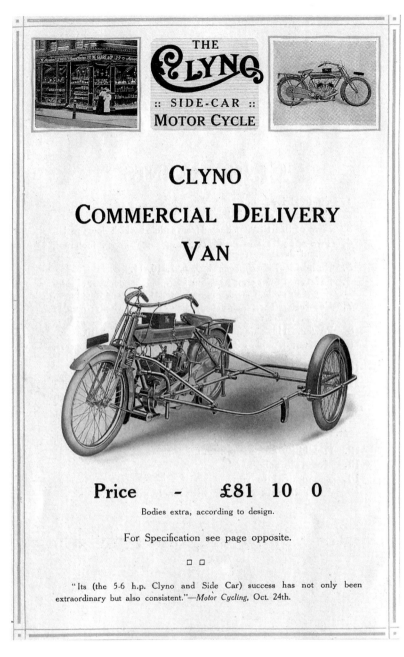

THE CLYNO
:: SIDE-CAR ::
MOTOR CYCLE

CLYNO COMMERCIAL DELIVERY VAN

Price - £81 10 0

Bodies extra, according to design.

For Specification see page opposite.

□ □

"Its (the 5-6 h.p. Clyno and Side Car) success has not only been extraordinary but also consistent."—*Motor Cycling*, Oct. 24th.

Left:
Before World War 1, Clyno sold their machines under the tag of being the 'Side-Car Motor Cycle.' This 'Commercial Delivery Van' version is taken from the company's 1912 catalogue.
Jim Boulton Collection

Right:
Some of the Clyno staff line-up near to the works in Pelham Street, before setting off on an outing to Stourport in 1915. The Smith cousins, who founded the business, are both in the photograph: Frank is on the left in a Peugeot, Alwyn on the right in a Panhard.
Jim Boulton Collection

Production did resume after the war, but despite the favourable circumstances occasioned by it not having been entirely suspended for the duration, Clyno hit difficulties.

A new model, the Spring 8, was launched at the 1919 show at Olympia, but production models took a further three years to appear. Technologically advanced, the Spring 8 won a rave review from the motorcycling press, but Clyno already had their sights set upon car production, their ultimate downfall, and no more motorcycles were made after 1922.

Connaught

The Bordesley Engineering Co Ltd
New Bond St, Bordesley, Birmingham
The Connaught Engineering Works
York Mills, Witton Lane, Aston, Birmingham

The Connaught was a lightweight motorcycle produced over a 13-year period in two engineering works around Birmingham. First listed in 1913, early Connaughts used a 293cc single-cylinder 2.5hp two-stroke engine, a basic model selling for £26 5s, one with more refine-

ments costing £33 10s. Production was interrupted by World War 1 and when it resumed it was under a new company name and in another works, in Witton Lane, by the Aston Villa football ground.

Using a mixture of their own make, Blackburne, Bradshaw and J.A.P. engines, Connaught produced a series of cycles that were distinguished only by a single letter: the A, B, C, D, E, F, G, K and M. The most powerful was the G, with a 490cc Connaught engine delivering 4.9hp; the most expensive was the K, with a 348cc Blackburne engine giving 2.75hp, costing £57 10s. Listed each year up to 1929, no Connaughts appeared for 1930.

Corgi

Brockhouse Engineering Co Ltd
Crossens, Southport, Lancashire

A collapsible motorcycle, to assist the movement of parachutists dropped behind enemy lines, was developed during World War 2. Called the 'Welbike', it was made by the Excelsior company at Tyseley in Birmingham. Sensing a civilian market for the cycle after the war, its production was taken over by Brockhouse Engineering Ltd, of Southport, which had been established in 1936 as an engineering and sheet metalworking business. The first machines were available for sale in 1948. Power came from a 98cc two-stroke engine, built under licence from Excelsior.

Although exceedingly basic, the Corgi, as the cycle was called, proved popular for getting to work, shopping, etc. Refinements, such as a kickstart, enclosed body, windshield, etc, were added as production continued, until manufacture ceased in 1954.

Coronet

Coronet Motor Co Ltd
83-87 Far Gosford St, Coventry 1

The Coronet Motor Co Ltd was established in 1903 to produce motorcycles, although the following year it also began to make cars. Occupying the former cycle factory of Townend Brothers, built in 1891, Coronet had Walter Iden as its chief engineer, late of Coventry's Motor Manufacturing Company. Neither venture had much of an opportunity to prosper, as early in 1906 the company was taken over by Humber.

Cotton

The Cotton Motor Co/E Cotton (Motorcycles) Ltd
Vulcan Works, Quay St, Gloucester
(from 1970): Stratton Rd, Gloucester
later at Cheltenham and Bolton

Ostensibly, Cotton motorcycles appear to have been produced from 1913 to 1980, but closer inspection shows that something nearer 1920 to 1970, with interruptions, is probably more accurate.

The machines and the company that made them took their name from Frank Willoughby Cotton, affectionately known as 'Bill'. Just before World War 1 he was a law student, with a passion for motorcycles. Those of the day often gave an unsatisfactory ride, something Cotton ascribed to their frames, which still showed their bicycle parentage, but were contorted to accommodate the mechanical components. As a result, Cotton thought, motorcycle frames were not acting in a fully mechanical fashion, the stresses and strains produced during use were not being fully dissipated, other than

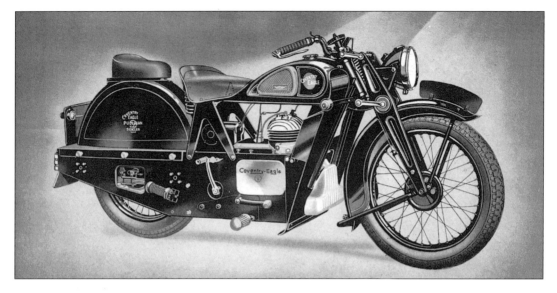

Above:
The Coventry-Eagle Silent Pullman Two-Seater of 1936 was a remarkable machine, full of advanced features for its day. These included: a rigid chassis, an enclosed engine, and rear-wheel suspension by means of exposed leaf-springs, plus a rear bumper. A 'Pullman Folder', available on application, included a cartoon showing two lady pillion passengers. One just off a-n-other motorcycle complains: 'Ooh! My Back', whilst another, still on a Coventry-Eagle Pullman, sighs: 'I Never Thought It Could Be So Comfortable.' *Author's Collection*

through the rider's seat, or manifested in fracture or failure. The answer lay in fully triangulating all the forces at work within and upon a motorcycle frame, for which all the tubes making up the frame needed to be straight, and only subjected either to compression or tension, not to torque or any other form of distortion.

Putting this theory into practice produced a motorcycle frame that was both stronger and lighter than its contemporaries. Cotton asked the Levis company to make one of his frames up, but had the sense to keep control of their production by establishing his own company: The Cotton Motor Co at Vulcan Works, Quay Street in Gloucester in 1920.

Early Cotton motorcycles were single-cylinder machines, using proprietary engines from J.A.P., Sturmey Archer, Villiers, but predominantly from Burney & Blackburne. Each year during the 1920s a range of between seven and nine models was offered, ranging from a Blackburne engined 250cc for £47 15s to a J.A.P.-engined 350cc model for £81 10s. The predominant use of Blackburne engines gave way to J.A.P., Rudge and Villiers units from 1931, but production levels dropped progressively throughout the decade. Liquidation was stared in the face in 1940, but reversed upon receipt of a large military contract. Limited civilian production resumed briefly after the war, but the factory closed in 1946.

In 1953 two Cotton enthusiasts, Monty Denley and

Pat Onions, persuaded Bill Cotton to allow them to start up the factory again and revive the marque. This they did, production resuming in 1954, but of Cottons in name only, devoid of the triangulated frame and other innovations of their prewar namesakes. None the less, the cycles sold well and enjoyed success in trials and races. The Quay Street factory was demolished in the 1960s, precipitating the first of several moves to new premises. Those in Stratton Road, Gloucester provided a much needed bolt hole, but before too long the company was on the move again, first to Cheltenham and then to Bolton, where the protracted second death of the marque took place in 1980.

Coventry-Eagle

Coventry Eagle Cycle Co/
Coventry Eagle Cycle & Motor Co Ltd
Bishopgate Green Works, 201 Foleshill Road,
Coventry 1 & 6
Lincoln Street Works, Lincoln St, Coventry 1

Many of Coventry's bicycle firms turned their attention to motorcycles, and Coventry-Eagle were amongst the first to do so. Founded in 1890, their first motorcycle appeared in 1901, the machines being built alongside ordinary bicycles, which they closely resembled. Models are listed up to 1916, when singles using Villiers and J.A.P. engines, and a twin using an Abingdon unit, appear. The basic model cost £36 15s and used a 269cc Villiers engine with a fixed single gear; the top of the range was an Abingdon engined twin with a three-speed gearbox for £75 10s.

Motorcycle production resumed after World War 1, most of the models using J.A.P. engines, until 1928, when Villiers, and later Sturmey Archer, and the company's own designs, were also featured. All tastes and pockets were catered for, the 1930 model range extending from a 147cc 1.5hp Villiers-powered cycle for £24 15s, to the Flying 8, with a 988cc 9.8hp J.A.P. twin engine, costing £120.

With the recession-torn 1930s the company wisely dropped its more expensive models, but still produced some very stylish motorcycles, most notably the Silent Pullman Two-Seater of 1936. These boasted some remarkable features for their day, including a rigid chassis, and an enclosed engine, plus rear wheel suspension by means of exposed leaf-springs, as on a car, plus a rear bumper. The price was £44 2s, but those who just wanted to know more were invited to 'Write now for a Pullman Folder.'

Coventry-Eagle continued producing motor cycles into the war, acquiring an additional factory in Lincoln Street from Singer on 2 August 1937. They introduced an autocycle in 1940, well suited to conditions of austerity and petrol rationing, but, despite this keen 'market-awareness', the model did not enter production. Coventry-Eagle relocated to a new factory in Duggin's Lane, Tile Hill, in Coventry after the war. They continued to produce bicycles, but their motor cycle manufacturing days were over.

Coventry-Premier; Premier

The Premier Cycle Co/Coventry-Premier Ltd
1-7 Read St, Coventry 1
8 Lincoln St, Coventry 1

Coventry-Premier was one of that city's oldest bicycle firms, having been founded in 1879 as the Hillman, Herbert & Cooper Cycle Co, by William Hillman, later to form his own car company. The firm became the Premier Cycle Co in 1890 and Coventry-Premier in 1914.

Motorcycle production began in 1908, and in 1912 a three-wheeled cyclecar was produced, using many of the firm's motorcycle components. Catalogue evidence suggests that the motorcycles were also sold as Premiers, and that production of some models continued into 1915. Both single- and two-cylinder models were made, the cheapest having a 2.5hp engine and a single, fixed gear, for £36, the most expensive being a three-speed twin at £80.

Only car production resumed in 1919, the firm being taken over by their neighbours, Singer & Co Ltd, in September 1920.

Coventry-Victor

The Coventry Victor Motor Co Ltd
137-139 Cox St, Coventry

Coventry-Victor began by making proprietary flat-twin engines in 1911. Their Cox Street works lay in the shadow of one part of the massive Triumph motorcycle works in Priory Street. The company embarked upon motorcycle manufacture in 1919, and have the distinction of only having used their own engines in their motorcycles and other vehicles for the duration of production.

Three-wheeled cars were also produced from 1926 onwards, by which time the motorcycle range consisted of two basic models: the Colonial and the Super Six. Both used a 688cc flat-twin engine and costed £67 10s and £82 12s 6d respectively. A Silent Six followed in 1929, together with a 499cc Dirt Track model at £65. These models remained in production until 1933, and the following year the company listed three models — all three-wheelers — which remained in production until 1937.

Coventry-Victor produced a prototype four-wheeled car in 1949, but a return to motorcycle production was not envisaged. The company still survives, under the style A. N. Weaver (Coventry-Victor) Ltd.

Cyclaid

British Salmson Aero Engines Ltd
Raynes Park, London SW20

Another of the postwar clip-on attachments used to power ordinary bicycles. This one was made by the British Salmson Aero Engine company at their works in Raynes Park, and was appropriately well-engineered. Attached over the rear wheel, the drive was via a belt, power being provided by a 31cc two-stroke engine. The Cyclaid was produced between 1950 and 1955.

Cyclemaster

EMI Factories Ltd
Dawley Works, Hayes, Middlesex

Below:
Another company quick to respond to the Speedway craze was Coventry-Victor. This is their 'Dirt Track Racing Model', introduced for 1929. The 499cc flat-twin engine was tuned to give: 'even torque which is a vital factor of success in Broadsiding.'
Jim Boulton Collection

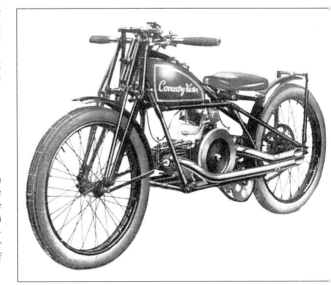

The Cyclemaster's history is strikingly similar to that of the Cyclaid. It too appeared in 1950, and was manufactured by a large company with no previous experience in the motorcycle business; in this case the massive EMI factory at Hayes, more used to making gramophones, radiograms and pressing records. The Cyclemaster also drove the bicycle's rear wheel, but came as a complete unit that replaced the wheel, with the 33cc engine at the hub. A complete powered cycle was produced in 1953, followed two years later by the Cyclemate, a moped-like hybrid of the bicycle and autocycles then available. Both the Cyclemaster and the Cyclemate remained in production until 1960.

Cymota

Cymo Ltd
364/366 Kensington High St, London W14

The postwar demand for any form of motorised transport breathed fresh life into the clip-on trade. One such was the 'Cymota', manufactured by Cymo Ltd. To be located on the front forks of an ordinary bicycle, the unit contained a 45cc two-stroke engine driving a roller which turned the front wheel, secured behind an attractive 'bonnet'. Introduced in 1950, the stylish Cymota faded from the scene by the end of 1951.

Dayton

Dayton Cycle Co Ltd
Dayton Works, Park Royal Rd, North Acton, London NW10

Dayton were bicycle makers, founded in 1905. In 1955 they decided to take on the Italian scooter firms by launching a luxury model to which they gave the rather unfortunate name of the 'Albatross'. Using an all-steel construction, the 'secret of its strength' was a tubular frame, power being provided by a Villiers 225cc two-stroke engine. A four-speed Villiers gearbox was used, and much was made of the comfort and protection afforded to the rider and passenger. Selling at just over £200, in 1957 the 'Single' was joined by the 'Twin', which used a 250cc Villiers vertical-twin two-stroke engine and sold for £235. Changes were made to the models for each new season. Those for 1959 shared a new body and frame developed jointly with Panther and Sun, and were given a more exciting name — the Flamenco. But all of this was to little avail, the Dayton scooter did not appear for 1961.

De Luxe — see AEB

Dennis

Dennis Bros Ltd
Rodboro' Buildings, Bridge St, Guildford, Surrey

John Dennis started making bicycles in the back of his cycle shop near Guildford Bridge in 1895. Joined in a new company by his brother Raymond, they moved to a redundant barracks nearby, from where they produced motor tricycles and quadricycles in and around 1900. The following year the firm moved again, this time to a purpose-built car factory — possibly the first in England — the Rodboro' Buildings in Bridge Street, Guildford. This is as far as the brothers' motorcycle making ambitions extended. From 1901 to 1913 they produced cars, but abandoned these in favour of buses, lorries, fire engines and other commercial vehicles; a line of business in which Dennis Specialist Vehicles Ltd still continues.

Diamond

The D.H.&S. Diamond Cycle Co
Sedgley St, Wolverhampton
Dorset, Ford & Mee (DF&M) Engineering Co Ltd
(from 1908): Sedgley St, Wolverhampton
(from 1919): Diamond Works, Vane St, Wolverhampton
(from 1930): St James's Square, Wolverhampton
(from 1935): Upper Villiers St, Wolverhampton

The D.H.&S. Diamond Cycle Co were bicycle makers in Sedgley Street, Wolverhampton, during the 1890s. A restructuring of the company to form Dorsett, Ford & Mee (DF&M) Engineering Co Ltd in 1908, corresponded with the addition of motorcycles to the company's product range. Production levels were low, but the cycles were of an advanced design that enclosed almost all the working parts. The engine was 2.75hp, and worked through a two-speed gearbox, the cycles selling for £52 10s.

Production of this motorcycle ceased with the outbreak of World War 1, but the company continued to produce simpler machines, powered by a variety of proprietary engines, until 1916. After the war motorcycle production resumed in new premises in Vane Street, where two models were made, one with a 2.75hp J.A.P. engine, the other with a 2.5hp Villiers unit. As the 1920s progressed the Diamond motorcycle range was reduced from a peak of nine models in 1923, down to just five or four by 1926–27. The smaller engines used, up to 342cc, were all supplied by Villiers, whilst the larger ones, up to 496cc, came from J.A.P.

Production at Vane Street ceased in 1928, but resumed two years later in workshops off St James's Square, in the centre of Wolverhampton, with the production of just one model, a three-speed single, using a 247cc Villiers engine, selling for £36 15s. This became the mainstay of the last two years of Diamond production, although four cycles were offered in all, the top of the range being a 3.5hp 496cc J.A.P.-engined single — the Sports — which sold for £54 12s. Diamond motorcycles were advertised for 1932, but not thereafter, and production may have ceased the year before. This was not the end of the company though. They moved to the former Villiers foundry in Upper Villiers Street, Wolverhampton, where they made trailers and electric milk floats.

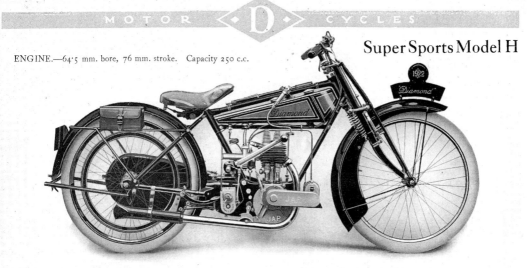

M O T O R ◈ D ◈ C Y C L E S

Super Sports Model H

ENGINE.—64·5 mm. bore, 76 mm. stroke. Capacity 250 c.c.

Two-speed All Chain Drive   -   -   -   **75** gns.   *Code Word*—SPORTOH.
If fitted with Three-speed   -   -   -   **4** gns. extra.

metal case.   These cases are entirely weatherproof and easily detachable.   A standard type of carrier can be fitted if required.   The Engine shown on this page is a replica of that which during the past season was so successful in SPEED and RELIABILITY, capturing the premier awards in its class.

DKR

DKR Scooters
Neachels Lane, Willenhall

The DKR was a motor scooter, the brainchild of Cyril Kieft, a sometime sports car designer and manufacturer. Kieft also imported motor scooters, and felt that he could produce a domestic version that was every bit as good. Around 1956, he approached Barry Day, the managing director of the Willenhall Motor Radiator Co, and Noah Robinson, a director of the same firm, with his plans. The scooter was formed out of ten main pressings, which the Willenhall firm were able to produce, and powered by a Villiers 147cc two-stroke engine. Production was agreed, and the scooter was named after the surnames of the three principal partners: Day, Kieft and Robinson — DKR.

The first DKR model — the Dove — appeared in 1957. It had the 147cc Villiers engine, a three-speed

Left:
Although DKR Scooters Ltd was run from Pendeford Airport in Wolverhampton, production of the machines was undertaken at the Willenhall Motor Radiator Co's works in Neachels Lane, Willenhall. Inside there in 1957 two lines of 147cc DKR 'Dove' scooters can be seen in the course of construction. *Jim Boulton Collection*

gearbox and was painted two-tone blue. One unusual feature was a very bulbous front, the fuel tank being accommodated above the front wheel! Priced at £162 15s, the Dove sold well, and was followed by the Pegasus, Defiant and Manx, the latter having a two-cylinder 249cc engine and selling for £229.

DKRs sold well and enjoyed considerable success in competitions and endurance trials. The model range was revised for 1960. Out went the bulbous nose and the new 'Capella' machines took on a more conventional scooter-like appearance. Although well designed and built, the DKRs were undercut on price by foreign imports, production coming to an end in 1966.

DMW

Dawson's Motor Works/DMW Motor Cycles
(Wolverhampton) Ltd
Valley Road Works, Valley Rd, Sedgley

DMW stands for Dawson's Motor Works, the name of a garage business conducted in the 1930s by Leslie 'Smokey' Dawson, a well-known local grass-track motorcycle rider. Dawson repaired motorcycles as well as building ones for his own use in competition. An innovator, Dawson developed both front and rear suspension systems for his motorcycles, and, but for the war, would have put these into production. When the war ended, Dawson returned to building grass-track bikes incorporating his suspension systems, and enlisted the financial and technical help of a local businessman, Harold Nock, the owner and founder of Metal Profiles Ltd.

Housed in a former steam tram depot in Valley Road, Sedgley, near Wolverhampton, Metal Profiles was the logical place to manufacture motorcycles to Dawson's design. Unfortunately, Dawson was only interested in producing grass-track machines, and Nock, sensing that there would not be a sufficient market for these, had tried to steer him towards the design and production of a road machine instead. Dawson was not interested in this idea and sold out to Nock before emigrating to

Canada. As a result of this, a new company — DMW Motor Cycles (Wolverhampton) Ltd was formed late in 1945, and housed in part of Nock's Valley Road Works.

Having retained only Dawson's initial, Nock was in need of a new designer and hired Mick Riley, a former development engineer with BSA, to fill this role. Working throughout 1946, Riley's first design was for a lightweight roadster, powered by a 125cc Villiers engine. A prototype appeared in 1947, but did not enter production until 1950, well-spent time being expended in off-road competitions around the country in the meantime.

A range of cycles was introduced for 1951, all using Villiers engines and available in both standard and de luxe versions. The latter were distinguished by their use of a frame made from square-section tubing, which offered a considerable strength advantage. This was made available at just a £10 additional cost over the standard models: the 122cc version cost £97 (standard) and £107 12s (de luxe); whilst the 197cc was £106 (standard) and £116 (de luxe). By 1954 the company was producing the 'Dolomite', a 250cc machine with a top speed of 72mph, for £240. This was quickly followed by a road-racer, the 'Hornet', with a 125cc engine and a £363 10s 6d price tag.

As the 1950s progressed, DMW took account of the popularity of motor scooters. A prototype had been produced in 1955, which entered production as the 'Bambi', powered by a 98cc Villiers engine, in 1957. The 'Disney' theme was also followed for the unfortunately named 'Dumbo', a cross between a motorcycle and scooter, which did not enter production, but was dropped when naming a strikingly similar machine — the 'Deemster' — which appeared in 1962.

That year, Harold Nock bought the failed Ambassador Motor Cycle concern in Ascot, moving production of their machines to Sedgley, although they quickly became 'badge-engineered' DMWs. Roadster production faded out after 1966, and the manufacture of other machines withered in the face of dwindling supplies of Villiers engines. When Harold Nock retired

Above:
Noted for their conventional motorcycles, DMW was also tempted to produce a scooter. Christened the 'Bambi', it was introduced in 1957, and stood-out from the scooter crowd with its rather large wheels. A trio of Bambis are seen at Upper Green, Tettenhall, Wolverhampton, in this maker's leaflet view from 1958. *Jim Boulton Collection*

in 1971, his successors acquired stock, patterns and jigs from Villiers, by then part of Norton-Villiers, who were moving into industrial engine production. This move had longer-term consequences for the company. Limited motorcycle production continued through the 1970s, but DMW became a gold mine for those seeking Villiers engine spares.

DOT

H. Reed & Co
38 Ellesmere St, Hulme, Manchester
DOT Motors Ltd
69a Market St, Manchester
DOT Motors (1926) Ltd/DOT Cycle & Motor
Manufacturing Co Ltd
Arundel St, Hulme, Manchester 15

Founded in 1903 by pioneer rider Harry Reed, the origins of the DOT name are obscure. In later years the company adopted the slogan 'Devoid-of-Trouble', but which came first? Others say that the name derives

from the affectionate form of Dorothy, but which Dorothy?

The pattern of DOT production before World War 1 is unclear. Harry Reed first had premises at 38 Ellesmere Street, Hulme; later moving to 69a Market Street in the city. His machines used imported Minerva and Peugeot engines, before the use of J.A.P. units was adopted. Reed also entered and won many races riding his own machines, including the early Isle of Man TTs, but retailers' lists from 1911 onwards do not refer to DOTs.

The postwar picture is clearer. Production resumed at Market Street, but after the company was restructured, in 1926, it was transferred to Arundel Street, back in Hulme, where it would remain. Each year thereafter a range of five or six models was offered, using J.A.P. or Bradshaw engines. The entry level model used a J.A.P. 300cc 2.5hp single-cylinder engine, and sold for £38 10s. Top of the range were a 680cc J.A.P. powered twin (£60), and a 350cc single at £80. The 1928 range featured seven models, with engines from Villiers, Dorman, Bradshaw and J.A.P., and prices from £37 10s to £51; the 1929 models continuing in this vein.

With the 1930s came problems for DOT. It announced no new models that year, and when its 1931 range was launched it contained just three cycles, two with Villiers engines and one with a Bradshaw unit. The following year saw yet another revamp, again with just three basic named models — the Midget, Minor and Major — using Villiers 98cc; 147cc, and 148cc engines, and drastically reduced prices — £17 17s, £22

Above:
Salvation for DOT came in the form of its 'Motor Truck', a
Villiers-engined three-wheeled delivery vehicle that offered
90mpg fuel consumption. Its success was assured when the
company secured an order to produce these in quantity for the
Ministry of Food during World War 2. *Ian Allan Library*

1s and £26 15s, respectively. This was to be DOT's last
year of motorcycle production before the World War 2,
the firm continuing with general engineering work
thereafter.

However, during the war, almost by chance, the
company secured an order to produce a Villiers
powered three-wheel delivery vehicle for the Ministry
of Food. This both buoyed the company's fortunes and
kept it involved with motorcycle technology.
Production of the vehicle continued after the war and,
in 1949, motorcycle manufacture was reintroduced.
Both road and trials machines were produced, but the
latter came to dominate, so much so that in between
1953 and 1955, no DOT road machines were made.

1956 saw the introduction of the Mancunian, a
Villiers-engined road bike, but the following year the
company began to import Vivi motorcycles from Turin,
assembling these at Manchester. Imports of Guazzoni
motorcycles also began in 1960, crowding out both the
need and space for DOT to make its own road
machines. Trails and special bikes were still produced,
but their production tailed-off through the 1970s as the
company returned to general engineering.

Douglas

Douglas Engineering Co Ltd/Douglas Motors
Ltd/Douglas Motors (1932) Ltd/Douglas (Kingswood)
Ltd/Douglas (Sales & Service) Ltd
Hanham Rd, Kingswood, Bristol

If proof were needed that innovative design and financial success are not synonymous in the motor industry,
then Douglas is a good case in point. The company,
which had been formed in 1882 to manufacture boot
making appliances, produced its first motorcycle in
1907. This used a horizontally opposed twin-cylinder
engine in which the pistons ran fore-aft, a design which

Joseph Barter had produced for the Fairy motorcycle in
1905. Douglas had produced castings for Barter, and
acquired the rights to the engine, which they developed
over the years.

By 1910 Douglas motorcycles featured a number of
innovations, including a two-speed gearbox, with a
selector lever on top of the petrol tank (this was nick-
named the 'tram driver', because its action aped that of
a tramcar motorman at the controls), and a roll-forward
starting system. The Douglases were also fast and
enjoyed much racing success in the years up to World
War 1. Motorcycle production was maintained
throughout the war due to large military contracts to
supply machines for dispatch riders. In the immediate
postwar period the company reconditioned many of
these ex-service machines, neatly bridging the gap
before production could resume.

New Douglases were produced from 1920 onwards,
all using the company's flat-twin engine. Indeed,
looking through a retail trade handbook, Douglas is one
of the few motorcycle firms for whom the 'Make of
Engine' column always reads 'Own', and the 'No of
Cylinders' one always contains a '2', at least until
1933. Yet, despite sound engineering, racing successes
and a growing market in supplying bikes for the new
sport of Speedway, Douglas hit financial trouble and
was sold by the family at the end of 1931.

Restructured under new management as Douglas
Motors (1932) Ltd, the two most obvious differences to

the motorcycling public were the adoption of model
names for the 1933 range: Bantam, Golden Star,
Standard, Bulldog, Greyhound, Mastiff and Powerflow,
and the use of a 148cc Villiers single-cylinder engine to
power the first of these. By 1934 the company was
producing its own 149cc single, but as the decade
progressed the company's model range was ever
reduced, until in 1939 it was making only a 585cc flat-
twin.

Defence contracts, producing aircraft components,
generators and small industrial trucks, sustained the
company through the war, and, once again, this also
provided the springboard for their postwar return to
motorcycles. The generators they had made during the
war had been powered by a 350cc transverse, square,
flat-twin engine, which was refined and used to power
the first postwar production Douglases that appeared in
1947. Unfortunately, the bikes were launched without
sufficient testing, and problems began to show. There
were also inadequacies in the materials available in the
period of postwar austerity and with the training standard of the workforce, who could find better paid jobs
elsewhere locally.

Matters came to a head late in 1948, when receivers
were appointed and the company was reformed as
Douglas (Sales & Service) Ltd. As a bolt-hole amidst
these difficulties, in 1951 the company took on
assembly of Vespa scooters, under licence from the
makers (Piaggio in Genoa). Conventional motorcycle
production continued too, but with little development of
the machines and heavy discounting had to be used to
sell them at all. As the 1950s wore on, Douglas became
ever more vulnerable, despite the introduction of
impressive machines like the 350cc, twin-cylinder,
'Dragonfly' in 1955. At the end of 1956 Douglas was
taken over by the Westinghouse Brake & Signal Co, of
Chippenham, Wiltshire, for whom motorcycle production was a far from a core business. In March 1957
motorcycle production ceased, although Vespa
assembly continued until 1960. Douglas also became
the UK sales franchisee for Gilera motorcycles,
enabling them to retain a link with the world of motorcycling until the middle of 1982.

Dunelt

Dunford & Elliot (Sheffield) Ltd
Bath St, Snow Hill, Birmingham 4
Dunford & Elliot (Sheffield) Ltd
Attercliffe Wharf Works, Sheffield
Dunelt Cycle Co Ltd
Rabone Lane, Smethwick, Birmingham 40

The firm of Dunford & Elliot (Sheffield) Ltd was
founded in February 1902 as a steel making business.
They entered motorcycle production in 1919, the
machines being built in Birmingham. In addition to
conventional motorcycles, the company also produced
a variety of delivery vehicles based around motorcycle
combinations, and up until 1929 listed a van, small van,
truck and box carrier amongst their range. Power came
from the firm's own 499cc single-cylinder engine, the
entire range selling for between £75 and £82.

From 1929 most of the combinations were dropped,
as was the use of the firm's proprietary engines the
following year, with Sturmey Archer and Villiers units
being substituted. Like many other firms, Dunelt intro-

Left:
Sheffield steelmakers Dunford & Elliot commenced 'Dunelt' motorcycle production in 1919. Until 1929 the company used its own make of two- and four-stroke engines, before switching to Sturmey-Archer, Villiers, and, later, Rudge units. Production was based in Birmingham until 1931. *VMCC*

duced model names for their motorcycles in the early 1930s, and so for 1931 prospective purchasers could choose from the Cygnet, Vulture, Drake and Heron. Production was also moved to Sheffield later that year.

Dunelts remained in production until 1935. The marque was revived briefly in 1957 on a moped that lasted just four months on the market.

Dunkley

Dunkleys Products Ltd
National Works, Bath Rd, Hounslow, Middlesex

Despite sharing the same name as the perambulator, motorcycle and car maker, this Dunkley had no connection with that well-known Birmingham firm. The Dunkley 'Whippet 60 Scooterette' was a rather austere scooter introduced in 1957, whose bodywork fitted into rather than around its tubular frame, giving it the appearance of one of those tubular-steel 'church hall' chairs that were so common at that time. Made by Dunkleys Products Ltd in Hounslow, the Popular used an own make of 61cc single-cylinder engine and a two-speed gearbox, which made it capable of 'comfortable cruising at 30mph'. The publicity material boasted of the machine's 'simplicity', for which read basic features, but at least the price was low. For 1958 a 64cc engine version was offered, and the following year a 49.6cc four-stroke 'Popular' model appeared, selling for £77 11s 1d. None of them carried forward into 1960.

Charles Edmund & Co

C. Edmund & Co (1920) Ltd
Crane Bank, Chester, Cheshire
C. Edmund & Co (1920) Ltd
Milton Works, Chester

Charles Edmund & Co produced motorcycles in Chester from 1907. The machines were notable for having adjustable leaf-spring frames, and production continued until 1916, by which time the company was producing just one model: a 254cc 2.5hp single-cylinder machine, with a chain drive and two-speed gearbox, selling for £46 5s. The firm was restructured after World War 1, and later moved to new premises elsewhere in Chester, but it made its last motorcycle in 1923.

EMC

Ehrlich Motor Co Ltd
Twyford Abbey Rd, Park Royal, London NW
Ehrlich Motor Cycles Ltd
Southall Lane, Heston, Middlesex

The EMC was another initial-bearing marque. Here the 'E' came from Josef Ehrlich, who fled Nazi tyranny in his native Austria and arrived in the UK in 1937. With an interest in engines, Ehrlich built one to his own design by 1939, and, but for the war, would have gone on to put it into production. His plans had to wait six years, but, with the war over, Josef Ehrlich formed the Ehrlich Motor Co Ltd to make complete motorcycles, using his own engine design, to be branded 'EMC' — a good choice given that Einstein's general theory of relativity was being well publicised at the time through atomic testing.

The first bikes were produced in 1947, using a 345cc two-stroke engine and a four-speed gearbox. In 1950 Ehrlich joined up with the Austrian firm Puch, incorporating their components into his machines. This link led, almost inevitably, to the idea of producing an EMC by 'badge-engineering' a Puch, but, in 1953, Josef Ehrlich moved on to other things before this could be developed further.

Enfield — see Royal Enfield

Excelsior

Bayliss, Thomas & Co/Bayliss, Thomas, & Co, Ltd
Excelsior Works, Lower Ford St, Coventry 1
Excelsior Motor Co Ltd
King's Rd, Tyseley, Birmingham 11

Bayliss and Thomas entered into partnership to make bicycles in 1874. They chose the name 'Excelsior' as their brand, and had premises in Lower Ford Street, Coventry. The business became a limited company on 21 July 1896, a move that also heralded a certain amount of restructuring. One change was to begin the production of motorcycles, making them one of the first firms to do so in the UK.

Another early involvement was in motorcycle racing, Excelsior teams being a regular feature of races from around 1900. By the end of the Edwardian period Bayliss, Thomas & Co was offering a range of six motorcycles, ranging from a 210cc 2.25hp two-stroke single for £30 15s, to a 488cc 8hp twin with chain-cum-belt drive for £78 15s — all engines being proprietary ones manufactured by J.A.P.

In 1910 the company was renamed the Excelsior Motor Co Ltd, and after World War 1 it was taken over by R. Walker & Son, one of its main suppliers of components. Motorcycle production was transferred to the Walker works in King's Road, Tyseley, where a large new industrial estate housed a number of car and motorcycle companies. Here, the number and range of cycles produced could, and did, expand. In 1926 the company produced just seven models, increasing to 10 in 1927 and 15 in 1929. The following year saw a reduction to 14 models, ranging from the 147cc 1.5hp Villiers-engined '0' for £20 1s, to the 245cc 2.5hp J.A.P.-engined '13' for £78. Subsequent model ranges gained a year letter, thus 1931's went from A2 to A14; 1932's from B0 to B14; 1933's from C0 to C14, etc.

Racing continued to play an important role in the company's plans, and experience here led to the development of its own design of engine — a 246cc four-valve unit which was built for Excelsior by Burney & Blackburne. The first production model to house this new engine was the D14 of 1934. Selling for £80, the cycle was more aptly described by the company as the 'Mechanical Marvel'. In 1935 Excelsior introduced two new models, both called 'Manxman', powered by 246cc and 349cc engines developed for the Mechanical Marvel unit.

Excelsior motorcycles were produced until 1940, when the company went over to war-related work. This included the manufacture of the 'Welbike' collapsible motorcycle designed for use by Allied paratroopers. After the war this was developed as the Corgi and built by Brockhouse Engineering in Southport. Domestic production resumed in 1946 and concentrated upon lightweight machines. A variety of names and configurations were tried, some for only a season or two. One of the more enduring was the two-stroke Talisman, which used a twin-cylinder 243cc Excelsior engine and had a four-speed gearbox.

Never ones to buck a trend, Excelsior had two ventures into the scooter market. The first was in 1957, with the 'Skutabyke', which was just what it sounds — a 98cc motorcycle (an Excelsior 'Consort'), enclosed in steel panels to ape the look of a scooter. A more conventional scooter — the Monarch — appeared in 1959. It used the same body panels as the DKR, but with Excelsior's own 147cc engine, and remained in production through 1960. By 1962 the company had reduced its range to just two models, and from 1963 these were sold in kit form only, remaining in production until 1965. From that time the company turned to make car and motorcycle accessories for Britax Ltd.

Federal; Federation

Co-operative Wholesale Society Ltd
Federal Works, King's Rd, Tyseley, Birmingham 25

It is perhaps surprising that a large organisation like the Co-operative Wholesale Society should ever become involved in producing motor vehicles. In fact they had a go at making cars, lorries and delivery vans, as well as motorcycles. The cars etc were produced from 1919 to 1926 at the former Bell works in Manchester; the motorcycles in the Federal Works on the large King's Road Estate in Tyseley, Birmingham.

Sold under both the 'Federal' and 'Federation' brands, the former was the shortest-lived, from 1928 until 1932. Engines were either J.A.P. or Villiers and the range went from the Model 1 of 1929, with a 172cc Villiers single-cylinder engine for £29 10s, to the 680cc twin, J.A.P.-engined GT/H of 1932 for £56 10s. The Federation range was slightly broader, but very similar to the Federals, with identical top and bottom models, but with some available as a combination. As the 1930s progressed, the Federation range became ever more reduced and vanished completely after 1937.

FEW

F.E.W. Patents & Engine Co Ltd
South Avenue, Kew Gardens, Surrey

Going by its specification, the FEW was a luxury bike. The product of the F.E.W. Patents & Engineering Co Ltd of South Avenue in Kew Gardens, London, the FEW is listed as being produced in 1927 and 1928, but may also have been made for a year or two before this. In 1927 two models were offered: the Special and the Duo, both with a 980cc twin-cylinder engine, selling for £130 and £138 respectively. For 1928 the makers changed tack completely, producing another Duo, this one having a 550cc single-cylinder engine and selling for £79 15s. This was the last of the FEW!

Firefly

The Firefly Motor Co
72 High St, Croydon, Surrey

Firefly were one of those ephemeral marques that came and went in the early years of motoring. They produced both cars and motorcycles, the former being based upon Renault chassis. Two motorcycles were listed for 1903: a two-speed chain-driven model and a single-gear chain-driven model.

Forward

The 'Forward' Cycle & Motor Co
7-9 Edmund St/Summer Row, Birmingham

Forward were yet another Birmingham bicycle maker who ventured into motorcycle production, beginning in 1909. By 1912 they were producing two lightweight models: the 'Standard', with a 349cc V-twin engine, for £39 18s and the 'Open Frame', with the same engine, for £44 2s. These struck quite a contrast. The Standard was as old-fashioned as the times allowed, whilst the Open Frame version was partially enclosed and predated the styling of many of the autocycles and early mopeds of decades to come. Light but powerful, Forwards enjoyed great success in their class at many trials and races. This inspired the company to produce a 'Dropped Top Tube TT' model for 1913, at £40 19s. Models with a 498cc V-twin engine were also produced, but the company ceased making motorcycles in 1915, never to return to them.

Below:
In six years, from 1909 to 1915, Forward produced light but powerful motorcycles that enjoyed great success in their class at many trials and races. This is the 'Open Frame' model, which was partially enclosed and whose style predated that of many autocycles and mopeds in decades to come.
Jim Boulton Collection

Francis-Barnett

Francis & Barnett Ltd
Lower Ford St, Coventry 1
(from 1962): Gough Rd, Greet, Birmingham 11

For such a once large industry, motorcycle manufacturing produced surprisingly few dynasties, eg the Broughs, the Sangsters of Ariel, the Stevens, father and sons. Another example was the Francis family: father Graham being the latter half of Lea-Francis, son Gordon becoming the first half of Francis-Barnett.

After World War 1, Gordon Francis, who had been in charge of motorcycle repairs in the Army, went into partnership with Arthur Barnett in 1919 to produce their own motorcycles. Both had ideas of producing an affordable means of transport for those who were not necessarily experienced with motorcycles.

Their first machines were built in the former Bayliss-Thomas 'Excelsior' works, where some of the first British motorcycles had been constructed. They were two-speed machines with 292cc J.A.P. engines and provided the rider with an unusually high degree of protection from the hazards of everyday road use. The mudguards were valanced, footboards replaced footrests and part of the chain drive was encased. Unfortunately, none of this came cheap, and the machines had a price tag of £84!

Gordon Francis set about trying to reduce the cost of his motorcycles, whilst at the same time improving them. His wartime experience had given Francis a great deal of practical knowledge about the weaknesses of contemporary motorcycle design, especially that of the frames. By 1923 he had developed a frame that took advantage of the basic strength of a triangle. Constructed from six pairs of straight tubes, plus one

The Reliable "Forward" Lightweight.

Open Frame Model, **42** Guineas, nett cash.

Francis-Barnett

Above:
A part of the growing AMC Group from June 1947, by the early 1950s the Francis-Barnett name was being used to produce a range of two-stroke lightweight motorcycles. One example was the 197cc 'Falcon 64' scrambles model of 1953, produced in both domestic and export versions. *Jim Boulton Collection*

especially formed pair, Francis' frame formed an inverted triangle beneath the fuel tank, another around that tank, and a third, upright, triangle for the frame extending down to the rear wheel hub.

There were other design innovations too. The wheels were mounted on spindles that allowed their easy removal and used just two sizes of nuts, thereby being easily dismantled using two spanners (supplied). A 147cc Villiers two-stroke engine powered the machine through a two-speed gearbox and belt drive. Because of their strong construction, Francis-Barnett sold these motorcycles under the slogan 'Built Like a Bridge', for just £25. The company also made larger-engined machines using 172cc, 250cc and 350cc engines.

In 1928 Francis-Barnett introduced their 'Pullman' motorcycles. These used a Villiers 344cc two-stroke twin-cylinder engine and sold for £65. A range of six motorcycles was offered each year, with very little change, until 1933. That January saw the launch of the 'Cruiser', a 250cc machine that took the company's initial idea of enclosing motorcycle mechanics several stages further. Here both the front and rear mudguards partly encased their respective wheels, the engine was cased and the rider was protected from road dirt by leg shields. All of these fairings were made from pressed steel by a subsidiary company. The Cruiser sold for just £34; the rest of the Francis-Barnett models that year gaining bird's names, there being two 'Lapwings', two 'Black Hawks', and a 'Falcon'.

In 1935 the company introduced the 'Stag', which had a four-stroke 247cc Burney & Blackburne engine and remained in production until the engine builders ceased their manufacture in 1938. Augmenting the range that year was the 'Snipe', a 98cc or 122cc Villiers-engined machine with a channel-section frame that was bolted together. This was aimed at the export market, particularly in Europe and Scandinavia, where limits on engine capacity and machine weight conferred tax advantages. Just before World War 2 Francis-Barnett also added the 'Powerbike', an autocycle with a 98cc engine, to their range, which went forward into 1940.

Francis-Barnett were bombed out in the Coventry blitz of 1940, but returned to making motorcycles in 1946. They were taken over by Associated Motor Cycles Ltd, of Woolwich, London, in June 1947. Production remained at Coventry, whose emerging modern cityscape the company exploited in its advertising. The range for 1957 comprised the Plover 78, a three-speed machine using a Villiers 147cc engine (price £122 17s 7d), the Falcon 81, a three-speed machine with a 197cc Villiers engine (price £159 13s 7d), and the Cruiser 80, a 250cc machine (price £185 5s).

By 1959 this range had been augmented by the Light Cruiser 79, a four-speed machine with a 175cc engine, the Cruiser 84, a partially enclosed 250cc motorcycle, the Scrambler 82, a 249cc competition machine introduced in 1957, and the Trials 83, another 249cc competition bike, developed from the Scrambler. Both the Cruiser 80 and 84 used engines designed by an Italian — Vincent Piatti — which proved difficult both to make and to run. One idea behind producing the engines had been to break from Villiers, but the new units proved so troublesome that the Wolverhampton maker had to be called in to build them properly.

AMC had made so many miscalculations by 1961 that they were in serious financial difficulty. In an attempt to cut costs by avoiding duplication, Francis-Barnett production was transferred to the James factory in Greet, Birmingham, in 1962. From there, motorcycles and mopeds with the Francis-Barnett name on them continued to be made by AMC, with an inevitable merging of the marque's products with those of James, with only the badge and paintwork colour (Francis-Barnett = Arden green; James = red) to distinguish them. The whole AMC débâcle came to a head on 4 August 1966, when the Francis-Barnett marque effectively died.

Greeves

Invacar Ltd/Greeves Notor Cycles
Church Rd, Thundersley, Benfleet, Essex

Although an enthusiastic motorcyclist, Bert Greeves came to produce machines bearing his name by a curious route. He had a cousin, Derry Preston Cobb, who had been paralysed from birth. Invited to help motorise Cobb's wheelchair, Greeves conceived the idea of producing powered invalid carriages on a commercial basis. Joined enthusiastically in the idea and then the venture by Cobb, Bert Greeves designed a vehicle and established a company — Invacar Ltd — taking premises in Church Road, Thundersley, near Benfleet in Essex.

Successful in gaining Government contracts to supply Invacars to soldiers disabled as a result of World War 2, Greeves and Cobb's company prospered. The Invacars used mainly motorcycle components, and, given the former's previous interest as a competitor, the idea of making a motorcycle was almost inevitable at some point. That point arrived in 1951, when work began on a scrambler, embodying a rubber suspension system like that used in the Invacars. Production models were launched in 1953, with two road and two competition versions, using either Villiers or British Anzani engines.

Another feature unique to Greeves machines was a one-piece light cast alloy main frame. Combined with the rubber suspension, this gave their motorcycles exceptional ride and handling. Unfortunately, these features also made the bikes very expensive to produce, and first the frame was replaced by a conventional tubular structure (1955), then the suspension by an hydraulically damped system (1957). None the less, trials and racing successes continued, and the continuous test-bed provided by this involvement fed back into the company's road models.

In 1964 Greeves introduced a new machine, the Challenger 250, which featured their own make of engine and in a racing form enjoyed many victories. Sadly, Greeves suffered for having survived into the 1960s, when so many had fallen away beforehand. The company therefore had to face the combined onslaught of imported Japanese bikes, plus the backlash of the problems then playing themselves out at Villiers, still

their main engine supplier. Supplies of Villiers engines began to dry up and Greeves suspended production of road machines in 1966, although some were produced for the Police. Competition bikes remained in production and continued after Invacar was taken over in 1973. A new model was in development in 1977 when fire destroyed part of the factory. What bikes that could be assembled were, the last leaving the factory in May 1978.

Grindlay-Peerless

Grindlay (Coventry) Ltd
Shakleton Rd, Coventry 5

Shakleton Road in Coventry is a quiet residential street which has, none the less, been the centre of production of two motor vehicles: the Aircraft car and the Grindlay-Peerless motorcycle. The latter began as sidecar manufacturers in 1918, first producing their own motorcycles in 1923. By 1926 the range totalled eight models, ranging from a single, with a 344cc 2.75hp Barr & Stroud engine, for £61, up to a twin, with a 998cc 8hp Barr & Stroud engine, for £110 as a cycle or £135 as a combination.

Thereafter the model range was reduced and expanded year-on-year: 1928 (9); 1929 (9); 1930 (13); 1931 (7); 1932 (3); 1933 (5) and 1934 (5), all with either J.A.P. or Villiers engines. Model names were introduced for 1932: Tiger Cub, Tiger and Tiger Chief, and augmented for 1933 by the Speed Cub and Speed Chief. Grindlay-Peerless now exclusively used Rudge Python engines, as they did for their 1934 range, the last the company produced. Top of this was the Racing 500, with a 499cc 5hp engine, for £65. This was not the end of the company though, which continued to make sidecars and general motor accessories.

GSD

G.S.D. Motors
Smithford St, Coventry 1

Marques with initials for their names often have curious origins. The GSD was named after the 'Grant Shaft Drive' developed by the company's founder R. E. D. Grant. Promoted as 'The only British motorcycle with car refinements throughout', it appeared in 1921, using a 350cc White & Poppe two-stroke engine, four-speed gearbox, with a lever shift just like in a car, plus the owner's shaft drive. The frame was of the duplex kind and claimed to be 'unbreakable'. Advanced though the concept and design were, it was also pricey at £85. For 1923 a 500cc Bradshaw flat-twin was tried, pushing the price up to £88. It was not a success and the GSD failed to appear for 1924.

HB

Hill Brothers
Walsall St, Wolverhampton

The HB is another example of a well-designed motorcycle that failed to take off due to a combination of circumstances, time, cost, recession being amongst them. Standing for Hill Brothers, Ronald, Tom and Walter Hill introduced the HB in 1919. It was belt-driven by a 2.75hp Blackburne engine and was made in a works in Walsall Street, Wolverhampton. Selling at £73 10s, the price rose quickly by £16 5s with postwar inflation, and by 1921 it stood at £99 15s! For the following year an ambitious range of five models was announced, but the brothers' small output allowed few economies, and the whole venture collapsed in 1923.

Healey

C.G. & T Healey
Washford Industrial Estate, Redditch, Worcestershire

In the 1960s, deep in the heart of Royal Enfield territory, brothers Geoff and Tim Healey set up a business to refurbish Ariel Square Fours. With some 'refurbs' almost constituting total rebuilds, somewhere along the line the idea of producing their own machines emerged. Work on the Healey 4s began around 1970. refurbished Squariel engines were fitted to purpose-built swinging arm frames, a development Ariel had pursued only on experimental machines. The Healey 4s looked smart and sturdy, and plans for a sprinter model were taken as far as a prototype, but abandoned when this blew up while on test. Like other low volume makers, the Healeys were plagued by parts supply problems, which eventually brought motorcycle production to a halt after only a few years. The Healeys then went their separate ways, Geoff into powder coatings and Tim into shot blasting.

Heldun

Heldun Engineering Ltd
26-28 Augusta St, Birmingham 18

With origins in Shropshire, Heldun made trials, racing and road machines from 1965, all powered by imported 49cc two-stroke engines. Sold in either complete or kit form, there was the 'Hammer' scrambler, the 'Husky' trials, the 'Hawk' racer and the 'Hurricane' sports roadster. All were five-speed models. Later a 75cc two-stroke trials model — the 'Harlequin' — was introduced, but in whatever form, few of the models sold, and Heldun had gone by 1969.

Below:
Bromsgrove brothers Geoff and Tim Healey began refurbishing Ariel Square Fours, but then produced their own machines, such as this very smart-looking 1000/4 from 1971, using Squariel engine fitted into a purpose-built swinging arm frame. Plagued by parts supply problems, the venture only lasted a few years. *Jim Davies*

Henley; New Henley

Henley Engineering Co
114 Spring Hill, Birmingham
Steward Works, 18 Doe St, Birmingham 4
17-18 Warstone Lane, Birmingham 18
New Henley Motors
Wellington Works, Park Rd, Oldham

Both the Henley and New Henley were made by the Henley Engineering Co. Established by the mid-1920s, the company assembled a range of one- and two-cylinder motorcycles using Blackburne, J.A.P. or Villiers engines, together with other bought-in components. The earliest available listing is for 1926 and shows eight models, named the Popular, Touring or Sports, in various combinations. Cheapest was the Popular, with its 300cc J.A.P. single-cylinder engine, at £39 10s; top of the range was the Sports, with a 680cc Blackburne two-cylinder engine, for £67 10s. For 1927 the range was down to six models (a Sports, a Semi Sports, and four Super Sports); whilst 1928's models were all Marks, from 1 to 9.

The company was no less susceptible to the vicissitudes of the motorcycle industry than any other of its time; a situation made worse by its move in the late 1920s to industrial Lancashire, far from the Midlands heart of the trade — all to no avail. No models are listed beyond 1930, that year's range being nine strong.

Hercules

The Hercules Cycle & Motor Co Ltd
Britannia Works, Rocky Lane, Aston, Birmingham 6

Like Forward, Hercules was a Birmingham bicycle maker which tried its corporate hand at producing motorcycles, but in its case it left it as late as 1955! Launched at the Motorcycle Show as the 'Eagerly-awaited Hercules Grey Wolf Mo-ped', this used a 49cc two-stroke J.A.P. engine and a two-speed gearbox. Echoes of the American prairies cut little ice in Britain and for later seasons the Grey Wolf became the 'Her-cu-motor'. When supplies of J.A.P. engines dried up in 1958, the company were forced to look elsewhere for power units. They chose the 50cc French Lavalette, which came with its own automatic single-speed transmission. Taking the Gallic air, Hercules christened the revamped moped the 'Corvette' and spoke of 'Continental flair PLUS first-class British workmanship'. Introduced in 1960 the Corvette sold for £56, but not all that well as it was withdrawn at the end of 1961.

Hesketh

Hesketh Motorcycles plc/Hesleydon Ltd
Daventry/Easton Neston, Towcester, Northamptonshire

Lord Hesketh first came to prominence through his involvement in Formula One motor racing. The

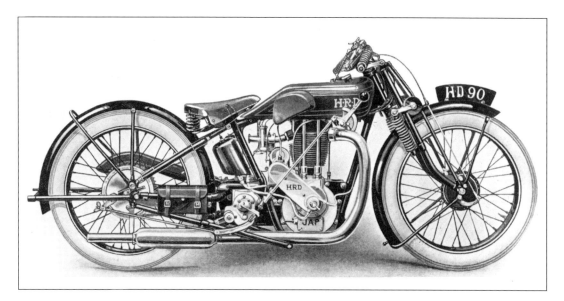

Hesketh car and team came on the scene in 1973 and enjoyed considerable success, mainly through the skill of their top driver, the late James Hunt.

With considerable workshop space and expertise at his disposal, Lord Hesketh nurtured his concern over the piteous state of the British motorcycle industry into a project to build his own machines. A brave attempt to rescue the dying Norton factory at Wolverhampton in late 1975 first associated Hesketh's name with motorcycles, but it was not until 1977 that plans were first developed for a Hesketh bike. Five frustrating years ensued, during which the machine was planned and backing sought for its production. A pre-production model was unveiled in April 1980, but it would take another 16 months before a Hesketh factory, in Daventry, could be opened on 11 August 1981.

There were problems from the start, from before it in fact. The bike — called the V1000 and selling at £4,500 — used a mix of components, some of which did not sit together easily, and there were all too evident problems as a result of this, some of which showed through on machines loaned to the motorcycle press. Spending was also out of hand and debts ballooned out of control. By the end of 1981 the company reported a loss of £623,000, and so things went on.

The first machines reached their patient customers in February 1982, but it wasn't long before they started to return to the factory to have such minor things as faulty engines replaced! Things couldn't go on this way, and they didn't. On 16 June 1982 Hesketh Motorcycles plc went into receivership. But this wasn't quite the end of the story. Despite an auction of stock in September 1982, that December Lord Hesketh established Hesleydon Ltd, a new company which was to produce the cycles at his home in Easton Neston, Towcester, Northamptonshire. A new workforce was assembled and the relaunched V1000 was announced at £5,647, to be joined by a £6,535 Grand Tourer called the Vampire. Heavily reliant upon export orders, few materialised, and what production work there was came to an end in January 1984.

Set up to restore pride in the British motorcycle, and to learn from the mistakes of the then recent past, the Hesketh failed the first and compounded the second.

HRD

HRD Motors Ltd
Fryer St, Wolverhampton

In the history of motorcycles, a number of current and former racers have tried their hand at manufacturing, with varying degrees of success and failure. Perhaps the most successful was Howard R. Davies, a one-time tester at Sunbeam in Wolverhampton and a competitor in the Isle of Man TT both sides of World War 1, in which he served in the Royal Flying Corps. In his postwar attempts Davies was on an AJS, for whom he

Left:
Basking in the sunshine, this carefully posed Hesketh V1000 gives little indication of the behind-the-scenes chaos that surrounded its launch and production. It took just over two years — from the unveiling of a pre-production model in April 1980 to the appointment of receivers on 16 June 1982 — for the Hesketh drama to be played out. Production began on 11 August 1981 but machines didn't reach their buyers until the following February, and pretty soon started to come back with faults. One of British motorcycling's great might-have-beens, and an object lesson in how not to do something.
Jim Boulton Collection

Above:
The short-lived but legendary HRDs were the product of former Sunbeam tester Howard R. Davies. One of his first production models in 1924 was the HRD90, which used a 500cc J.A.P. engine. Aimed at the sporting market, the HRD's downfall was its price: the 1926 version of this model selling for £102 18s.
VMCC

Above:
Howard Davies continued to compete in races on his own machines, winning the 1925 Senior TT. Here he is seen at right (stripy jumper; flat cap, and fag) preparing HRDs for competition, surrounded by helpers and packing cases. *VMCC*

rode. He won the Senior Race at 1921's TT on a 250cc machine, against competition mostly from 500cc cycles. Thereafter, race success eluded Davies, and things did not improve when he moved to OEC in 1924, where his rides were bedevilled by mechanical failures.

Convinced that he could build a better machine himself, Howard Davies took a small workshop in Heath Town, Wolverhampton in 1924, moving to larger premises in Fryer Street in the town before the year's end. Working round the clock, Davies had his first cycles ready for the 1924 Motor Cycle Show at Olympia. They caused a sensation, being the first to have saddle fuel tanks. The production models were the HRD 90, with a 500cc J.A.P. engine, the 80, with a 350cc engine, and the 70, for use in combinations, with a 500cc engine.

Davies's next triumph was winning the 1925 Isle of Man TT on his own machine — all excellent publicity. Production continued through 1926, 1927 and on into 1928, but the HRDs were becoming ever more expensive compared with even his nearest neighbours, and the one area Davies could not compete was on price. Production ended that year, but the company was bought by an Australian, Phil Vincent, who moved production to Stevenage, where the machines were known as Vincent-HRDs.

Humber

Humber & Co Ltd
Humber Road, Beeston, Nottingham
Humber Road, Stoke, Coventry 3

Thomas Humber established a bicycle business in Beeston, Nottinghamshire, in 1869 and in 1886 this became a limited company. By the 1890s it also had factories in Wolverhampton and Coventry. Experiments with internal combustion engines began in 1895, and a prototype motorcycle was produced the following year. Nothing came of this, and the company had become embroiled with the financial machinations of Harry J. Lawson, the force behind Daimler and the other car companies holed up in Coventry's Motor Mills.

Escape came in the form of a restructuring in 1900 under new management. Production of new designs of motorcycle began at Beeston in 1902. Two models were introduced, one driven by a Minerva engine, the other being a P&M built under licence from Phelon & Moore Ltd. These machines were built until 1905, when motorcycle production was suspended whilst the company's various operations were reorganised within its different sites. Now making bicycles, cars and motorcycles, Humber built a new factory in Folly Lane (renamed Humber Road), Stoke in Coventry, their main plant in the city, at 122 Lower Ford Street, having been hit by disastrous fires in both 1896 and 1906.

Humber's Beeston works closed in 1908, production being transferred to the company's new Stoke works. Motorcycle production resumed in 1909, with 2hp and 3.5hp belt-driven models. These were produced in great numbers and enjoyed some success in races and endurance trials. Production continued until 1916, when it was again suspended, this time to allow for the production of shells and field kitchens. Resuming in 1919, the company used a 4.5hp flat twin-cylinder engine, which became the staple of their motorcycles until 1924. From then, until the end of motorcycle production in 1930, the company used its own make of 349cc single-cylinder 3.49hp engine in a range of five variously named cycles.

In 1928 Humber bought out fellow car maker, and Stoke neighbours, Hillman, deciding to concentrate upon car production. The last Humber motorcycles were made in 1930, and, following a subsequent take-over of Humber-Hillman by Rootes Securities Ltd in 1932, Humber's bicycle interests were sold to Raleigh, thereby returning to where the business had begun: Nottingham.

Indian

Brockhouse Engineering (Southport) Ltd
Crossens, Southport

The Indian was an American motorcycle, produced by the Hendee Manufacturing Co of Springfield, Massachusetts since 1901. In 1947 the company president, Ralph Rogers, came to Britain to try and secure import rights for British bikes. On his visit he met John Brockhouse of Brockhouse Engineering, a company

Below:
Humber motorcycles were produced in great numbers and enjoyed some success in races and endurance trials. This competition model dates from 1913, the rider being Sam Wright. Production continued until 1916, when it was suspended to allow for the production of shells and field kitchens, resuming in 1919. In 1930 new owners — Rootes Securities — and a focus upon cars alone spelled the end of Humber motorcycles. *Jim Boulton Collection*

established in 1936 as engineers and sheet metal-workers. The firm had prospered during the war due to Government contracts, including production of the 'Welbike' parachutists collapsible motorcycle, which they still made as the Corgi.

Brockhouse agreed to invest in Indian, in return for a secure export base for his company's products. A new motorcycle — the Indian Brave — was developed and launched in the USA in 1951. It had a 248cc single-cylinder engine, and boasted of 'American styling', which amounted to little more than having the kick start, gear change and brake pedal positions reversed! Also plagued by reliability problems, the Brave fared badly in the USA. At the same time the American company all but ceased to exist, leaving what was left to be controlled from Southport. Launched in Britain in 1953, the Brave was overpriced, at £129, compared to its nearest rivals. It was also sluggish and suffered the same reliability problems of the earlier export version. All in all this was more than a little American exoticism could overcome, and Indians were not advertised after 1957, although limited production continued for a further two years. In 1959 Brockhouse sold the manufacturing rights to the Indian to AMC, who 'badge-engineered' some Royal Enfields thus, in an ill-judged attempt to break into the American market.

Invicta

A. Barnett & Co
58 West Orchard, Coventry

Invicta was the brand name of bicycles and motorcycles made by A. Barnett & Co in their works at 58 West Orchard, Coventry. Motorcycles were produced from 1914. Three models were made: two powered by a 269cc single-cylinder engine, one with a fixed gear (priced at £29 7s 6d), the other with a two-speed gearbox (priced at £36 15s); and one using a 499cc single, with a three-speed gearbox (priced at £60 17s 6d). Production was halted by the war in 1916, but did not resume thereafter.

Ivy

S. A. Newman Ltd
47-53 Lichfield Rd, Aston, Birmingham 6

Newman's Ivy is one of the lesser-known Birmingham makes, but his Ladies' and Gents' Popular range of single-cylinder motorcycles sold well in the late 1920s and early 1930s.

The engines were Newman's own make, and either 224cc or 249cc, combined with 499cc J.A.P. units. In 1926 the Populars, with the smaller Newman engine, were priced at £34 for the Gents' and £35 for the Ladies'. Completing the range was the M, with the larger Newman engine, for £49, or the J.A.P.-powered M5, at the same price as a cycle or at £64 15s in a combination. This basic range was offered until 1931, when it was slimmed to just three: the two Populars, plus the mysterious Model X, a J.A.P. 300cc-powered bike, selling for just £40. A clear sign of problems, from 1934 onwards the trade listings noted 'Manufacture suspended' against all Ivys.

Ixion

Whittall Engineering Co
Whittall St, Birmingham 4
Ixion Motor Manufacturing Co
35 Great Tindal St, Ladywood, Birmingham 16
15 Wellington Rd, Smethwick, Birmingham 41
New Hudson Cycle Co Ltd
132 Princip St, Birmingham 4

The exotically-named Ixion was actually made in Birmingham. The company began as Whittall Engineering, and produced a range of five single-cylinder motorcycles, three of which used a 269cc engine, the rest having different types of 349cc unit. In 1913 the cheapest cycle cost £26 5s; the top of the range being the 349cc 'Sidecarette' at £56. This basic range, which also included a 'Lady's' model, continued to be produced until 1916, when production was suspended due to the war.

The Ixions returned in 1919, with a restructured company — the Ixion Motor Manufacturing Co — and in a new works in Great Tindal Street, just off Monument Lane, Birmingham, later moving to Wellington Road, Smethwick. Ixion motorcycles were produced until 1928, when the company folded. Rights to use the name were acquired by the New Hudson Cycle Co Ltd, and put to poor use in 1930 when the company 'badge-engineered' a slow-selling stock of 249cc singles under the Ixion name. Once all were sold, the Ixion marque was finally laid to rest.

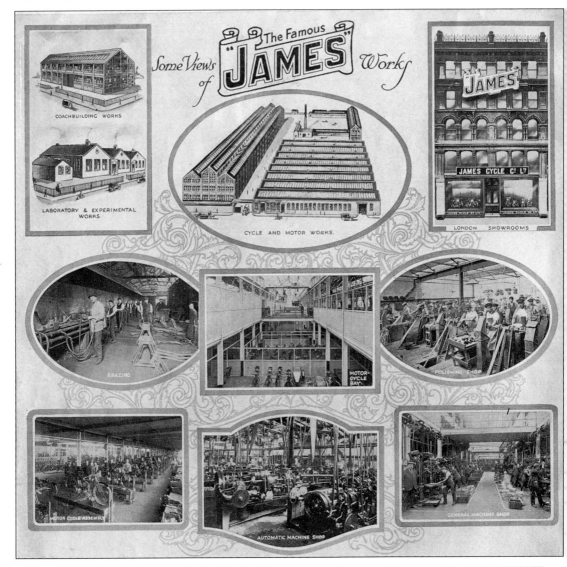

James

The James Cycle Co Ltd
James Works, Gough Rd, Greet, Birmingham 11

Harold James founded his eponymous cycle company in Sparkbrook, Birmingham, in 1870, but was to die before it produced its first motorcycle. His business grew through the 1880s and 1890s, and in 1897 the James Cycle Co Ltd was formed, whereupon Harold James duly retired.

The first James motorcycle appeared in 1902 and was designed by Frederick Kimberley, who had as much experience as anyone in those early days of the industry. Two models were produced. Both were essentially powered bicycles: the 'A' having a Minerva engine and being belt-driven; the 'B' having a Derby engine and being driven by a friction roller that rubbed against the rear tyre. Both cost £55.

In 1904 James introduced a loop frame to accommodate a Belgian F.N. engine, but shortly afterwards they began to build their own engines. James introduced a major innovation in 1908, in the form of the 'Safety' — a motorcycle designed by P.L. Renouf. It had an open

Left:
The Home of the 'Famous "James"', an illustration from inside the company's 1929 catalogue. *Jim Boulton Collection*

Below:
Also from the 1929 James catalogue, the No. A2 De Luxe 500cc Sports, from which 'a guaranteed speed of 65mph, in touring trim, is easily attainable'. 'Distinctive in Design — Dependable in Service' was the company's slogan; this model was available for £65. *Jim Boulton Collection*

frame, with running boards instead of pedals or footrests, its wheels being mounted on spindles that made changing them easier; the saddle was long and sprung, and power came from James' own design of four-stroke engine.

The company expanded further in 1911, by taking over the Osmond Motorcycle Co. By 1914 its range comprised just four models, from a two-speed 225cc single for £38 12s 6d to a 598cc three-speed single for £80 15s, and included a 495cc three-speed twin, for £66 5s.

During World War 1 the company produced motorcycles for the Belgian and Russian armies. Plans for the resumption of domestic production were interrupted by a fire at the works, which set things back until 1920. In the 1920s the company made 250cc and 350cc single-cylinder machines and 500cc V-twins. The 1929 catalogue shows ten models, ranging from the A9 Standard 196cc Utility Model (£26 15s) to the A10 OHV Special 500cc Speedway Model (£80), the back page being taken up with a closely printed list of the 'recent' (post 1924) 'successes achieved by the Famous James'.

In 1930 James took over the firm of Baker Motor Cycles Ltd, another Birmingham maker, who had made lightweight machines. Changes for 1931 included the adoption of model names for the company's two V-twin-cylinder models, which became the 'Flying Ace' and the 'Grey Ghost', but only the former continued on into 1932, being dropped altogether in 1936. From this point onwards James produced only two-stroke motorcycles, with engines from 98cc to 250cc, the former powering the 'Autocycle', introduced in 1938, which was based around a strengthened bicycle frame.

During World War 2 James made aircraft compo-

nents and munitions, plus over 6,000 especially adapted two-stroke autocycles, for use by the Allied Forces in invasions, and some 2,600 lightweight motorcycles adapted for military uses. The works was badly damaged during an air raid in November 1940, and full production was not resumed until 1943.

James hit financial difficulties in the early 1950s and were taken over by Associated Motor Cycles Ltd in 1951. There were initial benefits from this move as AMC personnel spent time at Greet and oversaw improvements to the range. At this time the models were the 99cc Comet, the 122cc Cadet, and the 197cc Captain, all available in Standard or De Luxe versions. Competition models were also built to order. A 99cc Commodore model was introduced in 1951, this being an enclosed version of the Comet, and the Autocycle continued in modified form. The following year the bespoke competition models went public as the 'Colonel Competition'.

In 1956 the first negative signs of AMC rule were seen as James became embroiled in the Piatti engine débâcle, detailed under Francis-Barnett. For a company who, like the latter, were so heavily tied to Villiers, this was not a smart move. Other changes in 1956 included a new frame for the Cadet, plus new models bearing the Comet and Commando names. More changes were announced for 1957, but the new models announced were 'badge-engineered' AMC-engined machines that appeared as either Francis-Barnetts or James.

A scooter bearing the James name was launched in May 1960. This had an AMC 149cc two-stroke engine, fixed into a duplex frame, and a four-speed gearbox. Less bulky than many British scooters, the James 150 remained in production until mid-1965. But by the 1960s the James marque had become just another brand-name in the AMC lexicon. The overall company had made so many mistakes by 1961 that they were in financial difficulty. Costs were cut by avoiding duplication, the James factory playing host to Francis-Barnett production from 1962. Motorcycles and mopeds with the Francis-Barnett and James names on them continued to be made at Greet by AMC, with both marques merging beneath the paint and badges. AMC collapsed on 4 August 1966 and the James name died.

J.A.P.

John A. Prestwich & Co Ltd
Northumberland Park, Tottenham, London N17

Some of the most famous initials in the history of British motorcycles relate to an engine builder rather than a make of bike. John Alfred Prestwich lived in Kensington, London. He became interested in internal combustion engines around the turn of the 20th century, and by 1901 had designed his first motorcycle engine. Prestwich established a company to produce his engines, which were sold under his initials J.A.P. The works was at Northumberland Park in Tottenham, North London.

The introduction of the J.A.P. engine gave the infant British motorcycle industry a great fillip, which had up to that point been highly dependent upon imported engines, mostly French de Dion Boutons or Belgian Minervas. In addition to its availability, the J.A.P. was a good engine, and established makers like Triumph, who had been using Minervas, soon switched to them. Prestwich was also an innovator, and by 1906 he had perfected a V-twin engine which was produced in capacities up to 1,000cc, as well as in a special 2,700cc 16hp version.

Many of the practices now considered standard in engine manufacture, such as grinding and machining parts to strict gauges, were introduced by Prestwich. His engines also found favour with aircraft makers, and the first Avro planes were powered by them.

It was perhaps inevitable that J.A.P. would have a go at producing their own motorcycle, which they experimented with during 1904 and 1905, before abandoning the idea. They also tried car making, but gave that idea up too. Their core business was too successful, and from 1908 onwards they were set on being manufacturers of motorcycle engines. Always abreast of innovations, J.A.P. benefited from the lessons learned from aero-engine development during World War 1, producing advanced overhead camshaft motorcycle engines in 1922. The Brough Superior that broke the world motorcycle speed record, with a 170mph run, was also J.A.P.-engined.

In 1956 J.A.P. merged with their great competitor Villiers and the Tottenham works was closed down. Some J.A.P. engines continued to be produced for a while at Villiers' Wolverhampton works.

JD

Bowden Wire Ltd
Victoria Rd, Willesden Junction, London NW10

The Bowden Wire Co were manufacturers of cycle accessories and, in particular, of cycle brakes and the wire cables that operated them. Adding motorcycle production to this list was therefore a logical progression. The machines were made at the company's works in Victoria Road, Willesden Junction, in northwest London. Called, for some reason, the JD, a single model — the Gents — was offered, powered by the company's own make of 116cc engine. Produced from the early 1920s, the last JD Gents was made in 1927, selling for only £20.

Left:
Between 1904 and 1908 the great builder of proprietary motorcycle engines, John Alfred Prestwich, tried his hand at making complete machines. Based on a bicycle, the J.A.P. engine was slung between the frame and front wheel, the main 'diamond' being filled by a thin petrol tank, which would also have contained a surface carburettor and the coil for the ignition.
VMCC

JES

J.E. Smith Motor Co Ltd
J.E.S. Motor Works, Worcester St, Gloucester
J.E.S. Motor Co (Gloucester) Ltd
York Mills, Witton Lane, Aston, Birmingham

The JES was produced by J.E. Smith, who established a motor works bearing his initials in Gloucester in 1909. JES motorcycles are listed from 1912. They used a 116cc single-cylinder engine, selling for just £20. By 1916, the price had risen to £24, but that year JES production became yet another casualty of the war effort. Resuming in 1919, the marque was bought by the Birmingham-based firm of Connaught in 1924, which did little with it.

JH

J.H. Motor Engineering Works
Castle Hill St, Mumps, Oldham

James Howarth, the proprietor of the J.H. Motor Engineering Works in Oldham, was late of Bradbury & Co, and used J.A.P., M.A.C. and Villiers engines in his range of 13 motorcycles, which were only listed from 1913 to 1916. Five used single-cylinder 2.5hp or 2.75hp Villiers engines, and were available with fixed, two- or three-speed gearboxes; prices ranged from £32 to £50. Four models had M.A.C. two-cylinder engines, with either fixed or three-speed gearboxes, ranging in price from £58 to £87, for an 8hp model. Completing the range were four J.A.P. two-cylinder cycles, which were identical in every other specification to the M.A.C.-powered models. Whether this impressive line-up was ever produced is unclear, but either way the JH did not survive World War 1.

Juckes

TC Juckes Engineering/The Efficient Engineering & Motor Co
Bilston Rd, Wolverhampton

The Juckes was another example of a motorcycle component maker trying its hand at making its own machine. TC Juckes Engineering, later renamed The Efficient Engineering & Motor Co, was established by T.C. Juckes at the turn of the 20th century, in premises on Bilston Road, Wolverhampton. Here the company made motorcycle gearboxes, including an early four-speed version, plus engines. Juckes also made motorcycles for his own use, and for friends and in 1912 entered limited production with a 4hp model.

Demand for gearboxes was high during World War 1, and this became the company's main product. But T.C. Juckes was always keen to have another go at making his own motorcycle, and in 1923 he introduced his model A and B machines. Belt-driven, by the same 2.75hp two-stroke engine, the A featured a fixed gear and a top speed of 50mph — all for £34, the B having a

four-speed gearbox and costing £49 10s. Production continued through 1924, and the following year saw the introduction of the GA 347cc four-stroke machine, capable of 80mph, and all for just £54.

Like many smaller makers, T.C. Juckes lived with and by precarious finances, but events overcame him later in 1925, and the company was declared bankrupt, the works and stock being auctioned off.

Kenilworth

Kenilworth Utility Motors Ltd/Booth Bros.
Much Park St, Coventry 1

The demand for cheap forms of motorised transport just after World War 1 produced a number of scooters. One such was the Kenilworth, built in Coventry from 1919. It had a tubular frame and was powered by a 143cc Norman engine, although later versions used both J.A.P. and Villiers units. The Kenilworth rode its wave until 1924, when production ceased.

Re T. C. Jukes.

MONDAY, NOVEMBER 2nd, 1925,

AT 11 A.M. PROMPT.

The Efficient Motor Cycle Engineering Co.,

East End Works,

BILSTON ROAD, WOLVERHAMPTON.

JOHN LAYTON, F.A.I.

Favoured by instructions of the Trustee in Bankruptcy (Edgar W. Page, Esq., Chartered Accountant), will submit for SALE BY AUCTION, on the premises as above, the VALUABLE

PATENT RIGHTS

relating to Motor Cycle Gear Boxes and Lubrication of Engines,

LOOSE WORKING PLANT & TOOLS

Finished and part finished Motor Cycles

and

STOCK-IN-TRADE

comprising Castings, Stampings, Forgings, Patterns, etc., and the

OFFICE FURNITURE

consisting of Desk, Typewriters, etc., etc., fully detailed in Catalogues to be obtained from the TRUSTEE IN BANKRUPTCY at his Offices, Lichfield Street, Wolverhampton, or from JOHN LAYTON, F.A.I, Machinery Auctioneer and Valuer, 6, Darlington Street, Wolverhampton. Telephone 358.

NOTE—The Freehold Works with Possession, together with the Fixed Plant will be submitted for Sale by order of the Mortgagee, at the Victoria Hotel, Wolverhampton, on Wednesday, October 28th, 1925, at 5 p.m. prompt.

Whitehead Bros. (Wolverhampton) Ltd.

Kerry

The East London Rubber Co Ltd
211 Shoreditch & 2, 4 & 8 Great Eastern St, London EC

The Kerry was purportedly manufactured by the East London Rubber Co Ltd in East London. In reality it may well have been a re-badged import. Either way, the machines were on offer to the British public in 1905. There were five cycles in the range, four singles and a twin, called the Popular Lightweight, two called Populars, and a single- and twin-cylinder Modele De Luxe. Prices ranged from £29 8s to £44 2s, but the machines were available for only a few years.

King

W. King & Co
Bridge Street Motor Garage, Bridge St, Cambridge

One of the early pioneers, King ran a motor garage in Cambridge and also made motor bicycles under his own name. These featured a modified bicycle frame that allowed room for the engine behind the main down strut of the frame, the final drive being by a chain. Judged the Highest Award in their class at the 1902 Crystal Palace Motor Show, for 1903 King motorcycles boasted a number of improvements, including a 'combined spring chain wheel, and a friction clutch'. Five models were produced, fitted with either a 2hp, 2.5hp or 2.75hp engine.

Kingsbury

Kingsbury Engineering Co Ltd
Kingsbury Works, Kingsbury, London NW9

Surplus production capacity after the end of World War 1 led a number of companies to produce motorcycles in the early 1920s. One such was the Kingsbury Engineering Co Ltd, the successor to Kingsbury Aviation Ltd, a subsidiary of Baringham Ltd, who were machine tool makers. Established to produce aero-engines, by 1918 the works site at Kingsbury, London, had grown to 109 acres (including an airfield) and employed 800.

What to do with all of this after the war was the big question. The mass production of both cars and motor-cycles was the reply, a few of each being made before the whole venture imploded into bankruptcy in 1921. After the dust settled, the site was bought by Henri Vanden Plas for use by his coachbuilding company, where they remained until their closure in 1979.

Lagonda

Lagonda Motor Co Ltd
The Chestnuts, The Causeway, Staines, Middlesex

Around the turn of the 19th century, an American by the name of Wilbur Gunn came to live in a house called The Chestnuts, off The Causeway in Staines, Middlesex. Gunn experimented with motor vehicles, and in 1906 he built a number of motorcycles in his greenhouse, followed by tricars and four-wheelers. Tinkering turned into manufacture not long afterwards and gradually took over the grounds of The Chestnuts. Gunn adopted the name Lagonda for his vehicles, but quite quickly came to concentrate upon making cars, so whether any of his motorcycles can properly be called by this name is perhaps debatable.

Lea-Francis

Lea & Francis Ltd
Lower Ford St, Coventry 1

The partnership of Richard Lea and Graham Francis in 1895 combined the skills of an irrepressible inventor and an engineer with wide commercial experience. They set up a small workshop in Days Lane, Coventry, to produce bicycles to compete with the likes of Humber and Sunbeam. Within a year their success necessitated a move to a two-storey workshop, with a converted house as offices, on two acres of land in Lower Ford Street, Coventry.

Their first venture into motorised transport was the production of cars in 1903, which continued until 1906. Motorcycles were not tried until 1911, the first having a 430cc J.A.P. twin-cylinder engine and two-speed gearbox. More models followed, using either a J.A.P. or M.A.G. engine.

The Lea-Francis machines had a number of unusual features. One was the use of footboards rather than rests, and protective mudshields, and a full casing for the chain. By 1914 their were three models on offer, all with two-cylinder engines of 430cc, 496cc and 749cc capacity. The 496cc model, for example, came with a three-speed gearbox for £73. Production came to a halt in 1916 whilst the company undertook Admiralty contracts. Motorcycle production resumed in 1919, with models very similar to their prewar counterparts.

Pressure of space at Lower Ford Street brought an end to motorcycle production in 1924, this being immediately followed by an expansion in car production.

Levis

Hughes, Butterfield Bros
Stechford, Birmingham 9
Butterfields Ltd
Levis Motor Works, Old Station Rd, Stechford,
Birmingham 9

Above:
Noted Coventry car makers Lea-Francis also produced motorcycles between 1911 and 1924. All V-twin machines, they had a number of characteristic features, including footboards instead of rests, protective mudshields, and chain casings. Engines were by J.A.P. or M.A.G., but space restrictions at the works forced production to cease in 1924. *VMCC*

Left:
The rider of this Coventry-registered Lea-Francis is taking no chances: his socks are pulled-up tight, cap secured, spare tyre stowed, and essential reading stashed in his jacket pocket. The machine is a J.A.P.-engined V-twin, probably the Sporting Model introduced for 1922. Two years later Lea-Francis dropped motorcycle production to concentrate upon making cars. *Museum of British Road Transport, Coventry*

Brothers William and Arthur Hughes Butterfield had a broad education that embraced the classics and the sciences, both of which were to come in useful when they became partners in business.

In 1906 the Butterfields set up in business as engineers. Like the Stevens brothers, they took an interest in the still new technology of the internal combustion engine. By 1910, William Butterfield had built his own two-stroke engine; the following year he and his brother became established as motorcycle makers. They were aided by Howard Newey, an engineer and keen motorcyclist, who worked on the design of the machines. As a name for their motorcycle the Butterfields chose 'Levis', from the Latin phrase *'Levis et Celer'* — Light and Quick — adopted as the firm's motto.

The prototype Levis motorcycle appeared in 1911. Based upon a bicycle frame, it had a 198cc single-cylinder, two-stroke engine and belt drive. The first production Levis was a modified version of the prototype, appearing later in 1911. It used a larger engine — 269cc — and sold for £35 10s. By 1913 the business was going well enough for the company to become incorporated under the style of Butterfields Ltd, with Howard Newey as Works Manager.

At any one time only two or three Levis models were on offer. Four two-stroke engines, of the company's own design and make, were used: 211cc, 269cc, 292cc and 349cc, and all but one model had a fixed, single-speed gear. In 1915 a wider range of machines was on offer, with the addition of a 349cc De Luxe model. This sold for £41, a 292cc model selling for £33 10s and a 211cc one for £28.

Production for the domestic market ended in 1916, but resumed after the end of World War 1, in 1919. Whilst other makers were coming to realise the potential of two-stroke engines for the lightweight machines that the market demanded, Levis had been there from

the start, and had therefore a 'natural' advantage in this field. This they allied to technical innovations, such as improved gearboxes and brakes, kick starters and mechanical oil pumps, and promoted their new models under a new slogan: 'The Master Two-Stroke'.

During the 1920s Levis consolidated their reputation through a very active involvement in racing, both at home and in Europe. Their most successful rider was Geoff Davison, who notched up a number of major triumphs in the 1922 to 1925 period. In 1924 Levis introduced their model 'K', a 250cc three-speed machine with chain drive, a first for a company that had almost always used belt drive from the beginning. The next year's model 'M' was a cheaper version of the 'K', and Levis were amongst the keenest of companies at both keeping down and reducing prices at a time of growing economic recession. This was reflected in the model range, which in 1926 was reduced to just two: the 'M' and 'K'.

New models were introduced for 1927: a 247cc 'O' for £39 18s and a 346cc 'A' for £54 12s, and the following year the range expanded to eight, with new 247cc machines, some of which were named. The basic model became the 'Levisette' and was reduced to £28 15s; there was also the 'M De Luxe' for £38 15s, the 'Six-Port' for £39 10s and the 'Z' for £36 10s. For the 1930s Levis revised their model range further, and prices rose again as the worst of the economic recession passed. A 498cc four-stroke engine was introduced in 1933 on the model 'D' (£57 10s), and 1937 saw the addition of a 591cc four-stroke.

When World War 2 began, the Levis factory turned to producing aircraft parts and motorcycle production did not resume when peace returned six years later.

LGC

The Leonard Gundle Motor Co
41-42 Smith St, Hockley, Birmingham 19

Leonard Gundle was a maker of butchers' cycles and ice-cream trikes, who added motorcycles to his output in the early 1920s. Called LGCs — after Leonard Gundle Co — the cycles all used J.A.P. single-cylinder engines of between 247cc and 350cc. Two or three models were offered each year, ranging in price from £42 to £51 17s 6d.

Gundle's also made sidecars, and all of its cycles were available as a combination for an additional £12 12s to £15. Unusually, the sidecars versions were named: Sidecar A, Sidecar B, Sidecar Sports, Touring; whilst the cycles themselves were not. Leonard Gundle's motorcycle venture just lasted into the 1930s, their manufacture being discontinued from 1931 as the company concentrated upon its main products.

Lloyd; LMC

W.A. Lloyd
Clyde Works, 7 Freeman St, Birmingham 5
Lloyd Motor Engineering Co Ltd
132 Monument Rd, Ladywood Birmingham 16

The fondness of Birmingham motorcycle makers for using initials as trade names was remarkable. Here LMC stood for Lloyd Motor Engineering Co Ltd, which produced engines at their works at 132 Monument Road, Ladywood. The Lloyd was W. A. Lloyd, a cycle fittings manufacturer, who had made motorcycles under his own surname from 1907 at his

Freeman Street works. Given this background, the production of motor cycles was a logical move for LMC, a decision it took around 1910.

At first just one model of LMC was produced, using a 499cc single-cylinder engine and having a fixed gear. This sold for £48 and was joined in 1915 by four other models, three 499cc singles and an 843cc twin, all but one of which had a three-speed gearbox and chain-cum-belt drive. The same range was offered for 1916, when the cheapest cost £52 10s and the top of the range twin was £79, but this was the last year of production, owing to the war.

Above:
The stylish office frontage to the Levis Motor Works in Old Station Road, Stechford, Birmingham. Incorporated as Butterfields Ltd in 1913, the firm began making its motorcycles, with the company's 'Master' two-stroke engines, in 1911. *VMCC*

Below:
Leonard Gundle made butchers' cycles and ice-cream trikes, adding motorcycles to his company's production in the early 1920s. In 1928 he offered this £49 Model TS/1, a 247cc Villiers single finished in black enamel. Three years later the company produced its last motorcycle. *VMCC*

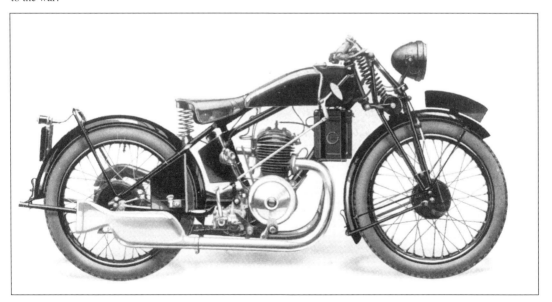

Martinshaw

Martinshaw Motors Ltd
Clarence Works, Park Rd, Teddington

Martinshaw motorcycles only appear in trade listings for 1926 and 1927. The origins of the marque are obscure, although a fairly obvious one stares out from the page! Technical details abound though, and from these it can be seen that the Martinshaw exclusively used Burney & Blackburne single-cylinder engines of between 350cc and 550cc. In 1926, three models were offered, two 350s and a 550, costing between £48 and £52. The following year just two models were listed, both 350s, at £53 10s and £68 10s, or £69 10s and £84 10s as a sidecar combination.

Massey; Massey-Arran

Massey-Arran Motor Co Ltd
Birmingham
Massey Motor Co Ltd
35 Mincing Lane, Blackburn, Lancashire

Like so many others, Massey-Arran started to produce motorcycles just after World War 1 and continued into the early 1930s. The firm began in Birmingham in 1920, and in five years it managed to occupy no fewer than six different sets of premises in the Bordesley, Highgate, Northfield, city centre and Smethwick districts of the city, before finding a more permanent home in Blackburn, Lancashire, around 1925. From that time onwards their range consisted of just four models, all singles, powered by Blackburne (appropriately enough), J.A.P. or Villiers engines, of 250cc, 293cc or 350cc, selling for between £35 and £47. This continued until 1928, when a reduced range of just two singles was offered, using a 172cc Villiers and a 350cc Blackburne engine. Finally, from 1929 until the end of production in 1931, just one model, the 172cc Villiers-engined single, was made, selling in its final year for £32 10s.

Matchless

H. Collier & Sons Ltd/Matchless Motor Cycles
(Colliers) Ltd/Associated Motor Cycles Ltd
44-45 Plumstead Rd, Woolwich, London SE 18

Harry H. Collier and his brother, Charles R. Collier, were bicycle manufacturers and amongst the earliest firms to produce motorcycles in Britain. Their bicycle business was founded in 1878 and they produced their first motorcycle in 1899. This was very much a motorised bicycle, complete with chain and pedals, the engine being located between the saddle tube and the rear wheel. The brand-name 'Matchless' was adopted by the Colliers for their motorcycles, and production was based in a small factory, destined to grow much larger, on Plumstead Road in Woolwich, in the shadow of the massive and historic Royal Arsenal West there.

For 1903 Matchless motorcycles had their engines relocated to behind the front wheel, proud of the frame. The following year saw the introduction of a Matchless tricar, which was a conventional motorcycle with its front wheel replaced by a passenger seat on two-wheels. When the Isle of Man TT races began in 1907 the Colliers entered their own machines, with great success, winning their class and recording the then fastest lap times.

In 1913 the Colliers produced a three-wheeled cyclecar which used a J.A.P. engine and had the advanced feature of independent suspension for the two front wheels. Production of the cyclecar ceased in 1914 but resumed after World War 1. In 1923 it was joined by a four-wheeled car — the Tourer — but production of both was hit by the mass production and low cost of Morris cars, both models not being made past 1924.

The pre-World War 1 motorcycles were all twins, using either a 964cc or 992cc engine. They were also expensive, a 1913 964cc belt-driven model, with two-speed hub gear, costing £89 5s and a 1916 992cc chain-driven model, with three-speed gearbox and detachable wheels, being £97 12s 6d. Domestic production ceased in 1916 and resumed after the Armistice, marking the

beginning of a period of massive growth for Colliers. Their Woolwich site was expanded and more and more workers were taken on to meet the demand for both their motorcycles and engines. These ranged from a 246cc single to a 1,000cc V-twin, which were sold in proprietary form to other motorcycle manufacturers, including Brough Superior, Calthorpe, Coventry-Eagle and OEC, and to Morgan for use in their three-wheelers.

By 1928, Colliers had stopped using other makers' proprietary engines in their own machines, becoming self-sufficient in terms of engine production. In the years up to this time they had been using 996cc M.A.G. and 980cc J.A.P. V-twins, the latter in their £120 top of the range model H sidecar combination.

Colliers entered the 1930s with a comprehensive range of motorcycles to suit most tastes and pockets. The range included seven singles and three twins, from the 246cc 'R7' single (£37 10s) to the 990cc 'XR2' twin (£62 10s). But they were also as capable as any other manufacturer of misjudging the market, and in 1930 announced a model that did just that. Called the

'Silver Arrow', its distinctive feature was the engine: a 397cc unit which, as the trade catalogues noted, was a 'Monobloc — Twin engine with cylinders at an angle of 26°'. The narrowness of the 'V' may have taken up less room, but the engine itself, whilst quiet-running, was low-powered. Even with a £55 price tag, sales were unimpressive. In a similar vein was the 'Silver Hawk', announced at the same time. This had a 593cc four-cylinder engine, with the cylinders set in the same, narrow 26° angle. Noisy in use, and pricey — £75 — at a time of economic recession, the Silver Hawk ran on until 1934, one year longer than the Arrow.

In 1931 Colliers took over the Wolverhampton marque AJS, moving production of the machines to Woolwich. They also acquired Wolverhampton's Sunbeam marque in 1938, whereupon the company was renamed Associated Motor Cycles Ltd (AMC).

During the 1930s the Matchless range was revised to keep pace with trends and developments in the motorcycle field. The single-cylinder machines were redesigned, adopting the inclined-engine pattern then in vogue. Typical was the 'Sports 250', or model 34/F, which was chain-driven, with a 246cc engine and three-speed gearbox, selling for £36 15s. By 1937 the models on offer had been developed into three distinct ranges: the 'Clubman', which used 246cc, 347cc and 498cc single-cylinder engines; the 'Clubman Specials', which were scrambles and trials versions of the Clubmans; and the 'Tourist' range, an eclectic mix of 246cc, 498cc singles and 990cc V-twin powered machines. Prices began at £41 10s for the '250 Clubman' and reached £72 10s for the '990 Sports Tourist'.

Although a model range was announced for 1940, during the war AMC were engaged in war-related production, including that of a 347cc single motorcycle, modified for military use. In 1943 the Sunbeam name was sold on to BSA, and after the end of the war AMC acquired Francis-Barnett (in 1947), James (in 1952), Norton (also in 1952) and Brockhouse Engineering (in 1959). For the most part, production of the absorbed marques continued at their original factories, the Woolwich works being fully engaged in the production of its Matchless and AJS machines.

By 1951 AMC's Woolwich factory was one of the largest motorcycle plants in the world, employing over 1,000 people and producing more than 400 machines each week. As the 1950s progressed there was an inevitable blending or merging of the various marques owned by AMC; this being most noticeable between the AJS and Matchless ranges. Under the latter name, between eight and 13 models were offered each year during the 1950s. For example, that for 1957 comprised eight models: six singles and two twins. Bottom of the range was the G3/LS, a 347cc single which sold for £211 8s 5d, the top of the range being the G45, a 498cc vertical-twin selling for £403.

AMC took over Norton in 1956, production at the latter's Bracebridge Street factory in Birmingham ceasing in 1962 when everything was transferred to Woolwich. This was to be AMC's last acquisition. Beset by financial and other problems, the company collapsed on 4 August 1966, the remnants forming the kernel of the Norton-Villiers Group. In 1973 this became Norton-Villiers-Triumph, formed by Dennis

Poore, whose Manganese Bronze Holdings had bought the assets. Motorcycle production ceased at the former Matchless works in Woolwich in 1969, although it remained open to provide a spares service until 1971.

Max

W. Claude Johnson
The Studio, Westbourne St, Lancaster Gate, London W

Who decided that motorcycle riders should sit down? Certainly not W. Claude Johnson, the designer of the 'Max', whose curious little machine required the rider to 'assume a standing position on footplates which are within a few inches of the ground'. To accommodate this posture the motorcycle had an extremely short wheelbase and a near triangular form. All that survives of the make is a leaflet of c1906, with two photographs, each of a different machine! A belt drive can be seen, but all particulars could be had from a Mr Louis Burn, at the above address, who is probably long gone.

McEvoy

McEvoy Motor Cycles (1926) Ltd
Leaper St, Duffield, Derbyshire

Part of the 1920s boom in motorcycle production, McEvoy had been manufacturing their machines since the end of World War 1, but had suffered financially

Below:
Taken from the cover of an advance publicity leaflet, dated 2 September 1925, issued by McEvoy Motor Cycles, this was an early McEvoy machine, powered by a 994cc V-twin British Anzani engine. The leaflet bears the slogan 'Quality is Economy' and urges inquiries, because 'every point, however small, will have the **personal** consideration of Mr McEVOY'. So did the price, marked down in pen inside the brochure, from £145 guineas (£152 5s) to £130, but still vastly expensive for the time, even for a machine that would top 100mph.
Jim Boulton Collection

around 1925, re-forming with the tell-tale date in the company name one year later.

For a comparatively small maker, McEvoy produced quite a large range of machines, using quite a variety of different proprietary engines in the process, including units by Blackburne, British Anzani, J.A.P., their own make, Rudge and Villiers. The range expanded each year, from three in 1926 to no fewer than 17 in 1929. This included nine singles, six twins and two four-cylinder models. The latter were unusual for their time and used a McEvoy 986cc engine, selling for between £140 and £150 a time. Sadly, these machines were offered for only one year, 1929 being the company's last as a motorcycle manufacturer.

Mercury

Mercury Industries (Birmingham) Ltd
Dock Lane, Dudley, Worcestershire

Mercury made bicycles, but ventured into lightweight motorcycle and moped production in 1956. Their first models were the 48cc two-speed 'Mercette' moped and the 49cc two-speed 'Hermes' scooter. For 1957 these were joined by the 99cc Villiers-powered 'Grey Streak' motorcycle (£85 5s) plus a new scooter — the 'Dolphin' — and an enlarged Mercette, now called the 'Whippet 60'. All but one of these new models did not appear for 1958, and Mercury had only the Mercette, Grey Streak, plus yet another new scooter — the 'Pippin' — to offer in what was to be their third and last year as a motorcycle producer.

Metro

Metro Manufacturing & Engineering Co Ltd
15 Francis St/Adderley Rd, Saltley, Birmingham 8

The Metro Manufacturing & Engineering Co Ltd was registered in June 1916. That same year they announced a range of four motor belt-driven cycles, all based around a 269cc single-cylinder engine. These included a Ladies' model, and the machines were offered with either a fixed speed or two-speed gearbox. Prices ranged from £28 10s to £36 10s, but production was halted by the needs of the war before it had had much of a chance to become established.

Monopole

Monopole Cycle & Motor Co Ltd
Foleshill Rd, Coventry 1

Founded in 1890 as the Monopole Cycle and Carriage Co, this company originally had premises at Great Heath in Coventry. They resisted the temptation to follow their rivals into motorcycle production for a long time, then took the plunge, twice. On the last occasion it was arguably a little too late.

The first Monopole's are listed in 1916: two models, both using a 269cc single-cylinder engine, one with a fixed gear and belt drive, the other with a two-speed gearbox and chain-cum-belt drive. Production was then suspended for the duration of the rest of World War 1 and resumed around 1920. By 1926 the company was still producing just two models, with curiously lavatorial names: the Ladies and the No 2 (unfortunate if there was more than one seen together)! The Ladies had a 150cc Aza engine and sold for £28; the No 2 used a 350cc J.A.P. engine and cost £50. Fortunately, the public were spared any further names the company might have come up with: 1927 was the last year of production for the Monopole motorcycle. The company survived, moving to a new site at 6 Little Park Street in Coventry, from where they produced bicycles and carrier cycles.

Montgomery

W. Montgomery & Co
Bury St Edmunds, Suffolk
139 Much Park St, Coventry 1
Montgomery Motors Ltd
Gosford St, Coventry 1
Leicester Causeway, Coventry 1
Butts Works, Walsgrave Rd, Coventry 2

Montgomery was a durable marque that produced a wide range of motorcycles assembled from proprietary parts. The company began at Bury St Edmunds in 1894, moving to Coventry in 1913. By the 1920s it was also makers of remanufactured machine tools and motorcycle sidecars. At the heart of the Montgomery motorcycles was the company's own design of frame, which was noted for its strength. Into this a variety of engines was placed, including Aza, Bradshaw, Villiers, but, predominantly J.A.P.

The works was destroyed by fire during 1925, but the operation recovered, and for 1926 there were 11 models — eight singles and three twins — ranging from an unnamed 175cc Aza powered single for £28, to a 980cc J.A.P. powered twin for £140. Six of the machines were also available as combinations. The following year the company hit difficulties following a fire at its works, which also disrupted production of P&P motorcycles, produced there since 1922. Trade lists show a blank 'No particulars' against the Montgomery marque for 1927, but these problems were weathered, and 1928 saw a smaller range of eight machines offered.

For a proprietary producer, Montgomery managed to make a good range of motorcycles for all pockets during the 1930s, and its model ranges take up every bit as much room in the trade listings as larger makes such as Brough, Cotton or Douglas. The company also kept a keen eye on the market, adjusting its range and prices accordingly. By the mid-1930s gone were the £100+ models, with the top of the range now being a J.A.P.-engined 750cc twin at £66 10s. Model names were introduced in 1933, with the uninspiring 'Standard' and the more appropriate 'Greyhound', 'Bulldog' and 'Twin'. Production continued until 1940, when the demands of the war and a shortage of proprietary parts, on which Montgomery depended, forced its suspension; never to be resumed.

Morton-Adam

Morton Adam Motor Co
6 Matlock Rd, Coventry 1

One of Coventry's shorter-lived motorcycles was the Morton-Adam, produced by the Morton Adam Motor Co at 6 Matlock Road. This venture began to produce its own machines in 1923, having been established a few years earlier to produce engines. One of these, a 246cc single, provided the power for the Morton-Adam motorcycles. The range was modest, just five models, costing from £29 10s to £50, with the costliest two machines also being available in a combination for £63 or £68. There were just four seasons of Morton-Adams motorcycles, the last being 1926. Thereafter trade catalogues simply noted 'Manufacture ceased' against this marque.

Motorite — see AEB

Mountaineer

Mountaineer Motor Co
Manchester Rd, Marsden, Yorkshire

The story of the Mountaineer is strikingly similar to that of the Morton-Adam above. Both companies were founded at around the same time in the early 1920s, and both used one version of an engine of their own manufacture in a limited range of motorcycles. In Mountaineer's case, this was four machines. Each was powered by the Mountaineer 269cc single-cylinder engine, which produced 2.75hp. None of the machines was named, the cheapest being sold for £29, the dearest for £37, with this and a £34 10s model also being available as a combination. The similarity with Morton-Adam has one final twist too — Mountaineer also went out of production in 1926!

NER-A-CAR

Sheffield Simplex Ltd
Tinsley, Sheffield, Yorkshire
Canbury Park Rd, Kingston-on-Thames, Surrey
F.W. Lane
236 Norwood Rd, London SE27

The 1920s saw the production of a number of vehicles that crossed the divide between cars and motorcycles. There were of course cyclecars, which used proprietary motorcycle parts, and bikes that offered some of the features of a car. The aptly-named Ner-a-Car was one such, although its name was also a pun on the surname of its American designer: J. Neracher. Its most noticeable feature was a low-slung frame, built from channel steel, and clad to protect the rider. Indeed, one of the Ner-a-Car's selling points was that riders did not need special clothing, they could: 'Go just as you are on your Ner-A-Car.'

Produced first in Syracuse, New York, the British rights were acquired by Sheffield Simplex, and production began in 1922. A range of four Ner-a-Cars was developed, one using the company's own 285cc single-cylinder engine, the remainder having a Burney & Blackburne 349cc single. Prices ranged from £39 10s, to £85 for the De Luxe, which boasted such features as an electric light, a speedometer and a windshield. The manufacturers hit trouble 1926, forcing the production of a limited range of just two models in 1927, one with its own engine, the other with a Blackburne unit. Sadly, this was not enough and later that year the firm went into liquidation. Enough Ner-a-Cars had been sold for a spares operation to begin to support them, and this was operated by F. W. Lane from 236 Norwood Road in southeast London.

New Comet

A. H. Haden
Princip Works, Princip St, Birmingham 4

Princip Street, to the northwest of Birmingham city centre, was home to no less than three cycle and motorcycle manufacturers, all of whom had the word 'New' in their names: New Hudson, New Imperial and, here, the New Comet.

The first New Comet motorcycles appeared just before World War 1. They were made by A.H. Haden, a motorcycle components supplier, in his Princip Works. Production continued until 1916, and for this short period, five models were produced. The cheapest sold for £26 10s and used a 211cc single-cylinder engine, the top of the range being a 771cc two-cylinder machine, costing £75 7s 6d. Production was suspended until 1919.

The New Comets of the 1920s used a variety of proprietary engines, from Aza, Climax and Villiers, but were all single-cylinder machines of between 150cc and 293cc. They also cost considerably less than their prewar counterparts, the 1926 range comprising six models costing between £25 and £40. Haden hit difficulties in 1927, and for 1928 to 1930 offered just one model — the Super Sports — which used a 172cc Villiers single engine and sold for £38. Variants on this formed the basis of 1931's two New Comets, but the year also saw a temporary suspension of their manufacture, which was never lifted. Haden's returned to the supply and production of motorcycle components.

New Gerrard

New Gerrard Motors Ltd
Gayfield Square, Edinburgh
Liverpool St, Nottingham
25 Greenside Place, Edinburgh

One of the few Scottish makes, the New Gerrard was produced from 1922 onwards by Jock Porter, a successful TT rider, and his company (New Gerrard Motors). Using proprietary parts in a frame of his own design and construction, power was mostly provided by Burney & Blackburne 350cc or 549cc single-cylinder engines. Production was transferred to the Campion works in Nottingham between 1924 and 1927, but had returned to a new site in Edinburgh by 1928. The largest range of New Gerrards — five machines — was offered in 1926, whilst production was at Nottingham, but this had been reduced to just a single model by 1930. Named, appropriately enough, the Standard, it used a J.A.P. 346cc single-cylinder engien and cost, in 1934, £59 10s 'complete with Magdyno Lighting', as the catalogue boasted. This remained in production until 1936, but stocks were left at dealers as late as 1940.

New Henley — see Henley

New Hudson

New Hudson Cycle Co Ltd
Parade Mills, 29-35 Summer Hill St, Birmingham 1
New Hudson Ltd
St George's Works, Icknield St, Birmingham 18
Waverley Works, Birmingham 10

The New Hudson was one of Birmingham's more enduring marques. Founded in 1903 to make bicycles, the firm added motorcycles to its production in 1909, using both its own make and proprietary engines. Of the pre-World War 1 models, the longest produced was a 499cc single with a three-speed gearbox, selling for £55 in 1911 and £65 by 1916. There was also a 771cc twin, introduced in 1913, which sold for £92 7s 6d in 1916.

As with many other manufacturers, New Hudson production was interrupted by the war, but resumed by 1919 in new premises called St George's Works, in Icknield Street, Hockley, Birmingham. By the mid-1920s the company's motorcycle range was impressive. That for 1926 comprised 12 models, all of which were named: Popular Sports; De Luxe Semi Sports; De Luxe Tourist; Super Sports; Super Vitesse, etc. Power was

Left:
Rider H. Berwick sits astride a Birmingham-registered, pre-World War 1, New Hudson, probably a 499cc single modified for racing. Formerly bicycle manufacturers, New Hudson made their first motorcycle in 1909 and remained in the business continually until 1933. *Jim Boulton Collection*

provided by the company's own make of single-cylinder engines — of either 346cc, 499cc, or 600cc capacity — and prices ranged from £44 10s, for the 'Popular Sports', to £72 10s, for the 'Super Vitesse'.

This set the scene for New Hudson motorcycle production on into the 1930s. The model range was slightly slimmed, down to nine or 10, but use of the firm's own single-cylinder engines continued — in 249cc, 346cc, 493cc, 496cc, 500cc, and 550cc capacities. A new range was introduced for 1931, with 10 variants on the 'Standard', 'De Luxe' or 'Special' name. These had inclined engines, the lower part of which, together with the gearbox, was enclosed. A 493cc 'Sports' was added for 1932, but there were signs of trouble in 1933, when just two models were announced: a 346cc for £45 and a 493cc for £50. The following year production was suspended, but the firm continued by making brakes and suspension units for Girling.

A brief return to motorcycle production came in 1940, with the introduction of a New Hudson autocycle, but manufacture of this was discontinued until after the war. By that time the rights to the name and the autocycle had been acquired by BSA, who revived both in 1946. With revisions, production of the autocycle continued until 1957.

New Imperial

New Imperial Cycles Ltd
Lower Loveday St, Birmingham 19
Princip St, Birmingham 4
New Imperial Motors (1927) Ltd
Princip St, Birmingham 4
New Imperial Motors (1927) Ltd
Spring Rd, Hall Green, Birmingham 11

Established in the late 19th century, New Imperial built up a strong reputation for its bicycles. Experimentation from 1903 by N.T. Downs led to the introduction of the first New Imperial motorcycle in 1911. Their three pre-World War 1 models were all based around the company's own 292cc single-cylinder engine, and had two-speed gearboxes; selling for between £36 15s and £45 2s 6d. New Imperial also dabbled in cyclecar manufacture in 1914, but this was not continued. Motorcycle production was suspended in 1916, but had resumed by 1919.

The range of machines produced in the 1920s was widened by the company's development of its own engines. These were available in 246cc, 300cc, and 346cc single-cylinder form, and as 674cc and 980cc twins. In 1927 alone this stable of engines was used to offer no fewer than 15 different models of New Imperial motorcycles and combinations, ranging in price from £38 15s to £85. Particular emphasis was placed upon the sidecars available for the majority of the motorcycle range; the catalogues telling of 'Model "F" Sports Sidecar for Motor Cycle 6 (Aluminium) with screen luggage grid and back £15 15s.'

In December 1927, the motorcycle production side of the company was reformed as New Imperial Motors (1927) Ltd. At that time New Imperial motorcycles were being made in three works in Princip Street, Birmingham, and in one at Hall Green. In January 1929, work began on a large new factory in Spring Road, Hall Green, covering six acres. Completed that August, the new factory opened on 1 September 1929.

New Imperial's output was revolutionised by the 1932 model range, announced in August 1931. The company moved to a form of unit construction for its motorcycles, which provided a common base for the engine and gearbox, and refined suspension. This was introduced on the models 16 and 23 of 1932, but went further into the range from 1933 onwards. Even the names of the cycles reflected this change: 'Unit Minor', 'Unit Super', etc, and for 1934 there was also the 'Unit Major' and the 'Unit Plus', as well as the more exotically-named 'Blue Prince de Luxe', 'Semi Sport' and 'Grand Prix (Speed Model)', which were of conventional build.

None of New Imperial's motorcycles cost more than £60, which made them competitive on price. Production continued through the 1930s, with the range being gradually reduced as the decade progressed. Financial problems arose in 1939 and the motorcycle company was sold to Jack Sangster, of Triumph Motor Cycles in Coventry. Sangster intended to move New Imperial production there, but with the war this was not to be. The last New Imperials were produced in the early months of 1940.

New Ryder

New Ryder Motor Cycle Co Ltd
76 Belmont Row, Birmingham 4
41 Cape Hill, Smethwick, Birmingham 40
7-8 Broad St, Birmingham 1

Birmingham loved its 'New' motorcycle and bicycle companies. This, the New Ryder Motor Cycle Co Ltd, produced J.A.P.-engined machines for three years from 1914 to 1916. Originally based in Belmont Row, an area of Birmingham dominated by the goods facilities of the mainline railways, the firm moved to Cape Hill, Smethwick, where Mitchells & Butlers had a huge

brewery. New Ryder produced just two machines: a fixed gear 269cc single, for £28 7s 6d, and a 292cc two-speed single, for £34 12s 6d. Production continued, like so many, until 1916, and was then suspended for the war effort, resuming briefly, from premises in Broad Street, until 1922.

Newmount

Newmount Trading Co Ltd
5 Warwick Row, Coventry
Victoria Garage, All Saints Lane, Coventry

The word 'Trading' in the Newmount company name is the give-away here, for this was a 'badge-engineered' Zundapp, from Nuremberg in Germany, using a 198cc or 298cc single-cylinder engine. Transfers were applied in Coventry from 1930, but in the following year locally-made Rudge Python engines of 349cc and 499cc were used to power a three model range that cost from £60 up to £88 for the 'Special'. Newmounts were not listed after 1931.

Norman

Norman Cycles Ltd
Beaver Rd, Ashford, Kent
Raleigh Industries Ltd
177 Lenton Boulevard, Nottingham

Bicycle manufacturers, in the unlikely setting of Ashford in Kent, now the site of a major Channel Tunnel station, Norman ventured into motorcycle production in 1939 with two models: an autocycle called the Motobyke and a lightweight. These were

Above:
The 249cc B3 Sports (left) and Roadster (right) models from the 1959 Norman catalogue, the last full year of the company's independence before being swallowed by Raleigh Industries; ending 20 years production of stylish lightweights and autocycles. *Jim Boulton Collection*

developed for 1940, but then production was suspended for the duration of the war. Resuming in 1946, Norman revived both cycles until 1948, when they were replaced by more up-to-date models, all of which used Villiers engines. Throughout the 1950s, Norman produced a range of autocycles, mopeds and lightweight motorcycles using a mixture of Villiers and imported engines. By 1959 a total of eight models was being produced, but in 1960 the company was taken over by Raleigh and production quickly ended.

Norton

The Norton Mfg Co Ltd (to 1913)
Bradford St/Floodgate St/Bracebridge St, Birmingham
(from 1913): Norton Motors Ltd/Norton
Motors (1926) Ltd
Bracebridge St, Birmingham/44-45 Plumstead Rd,
London SE18
(from 1966): Norton Villiers Ltd
(from 1973): Norton Villiers Triumph Ltd
NVT Ltd
Lynn Lane, Shenstone, Staffordshire

One of Britain's most famous motorcycle marques, the 'Norton' developed out of a bicycle component manufacturing business — The Norton Manufacturing Co — established by James Lansdowne Norton in Bradford Street, Birmingham, in 1896. Mechanically-minded from an early age, Norton was soon experimenting with 'motorised bicycles' and produced his first machine, powered by a 1.5hp engine by Birmingham makers Clément-Garrard, in 1901.

Production continued, these early Nortons using a variety of continental engines by Clément, Moto-Reve and Peugeot, all with belt drive. By 1907 a V-twin-cylinder Peugeot-engined model was in production, a development that was to shape the company's destiny. With rider H. Rem Fowler, Norton entered the first ever Isle of Man TT, held in 1907. The Norton twin won its class and made the firm's reputation.

Expansion of the business required moves, first to Floodgate Street and then to Sampson Road North, in Birmingham, before they settled into what was to become their home in the city: a works in Bracebridge Street, due north of the city centre. Times of rapid growth are always difficult ones for any company, including the Norton Manufacturing Co, which went into voluntary liquidation in 1913. Saved by amenable receivers, the company was re-formed as Norton Motors Ltd and placed under the management of William 'Bill' Mansell.

One of the company's more famous products at this time was the 'Big Four', a long-stroke 4hp single-cylinder machine introduced in 1907. This found considerable favour with military buyers, a contract to supply the Russian Army with the machines buoying Norton through World War 1. The rest of their prewar models were based around two engines, both singles, of 633cc and 490cc, fitted to a range of machines costing between £50 and £68 17s 6d.

Production for the domestic market resumed in 1919 and saw the introduction of chain drive for the first time. At about this time too the company acquired its now famous advertising slogan, via an unsolicited testimonial. A delighted Norton owner wrote in to say that no other machine on the road could match his own, from which the company fashioned the slogan: 'The Unapproachable Norton'.

During the 1920s Norton consolidated their already enviable reputation for reliability and build-quality, something tested daily by owners of the machines, annually during the racing season, and on special occasions. In the early 1920s a standards award for production quality — the Maudes Trophy — was instituted. Awarded annually by the Auto Cycle Union, officials from this organisation visited the Norton factory in 1923. A motorcycle was assembled from components they chose at random, and then run for over 12hr, during which time 18 world records were set. Norton won the Maudes Trophy again in 1924, 1925 and 1926.

The company founder, J. L. Norton, died in 1925, but by this time its management was in the hands of skilled engineers and technicians. They produced a comprehensive range of models to cater for those seeking 'speed, ordinary touring, solo riding or the companionableness of the sidecar', as the 1930 catalogue put it. Ten models were featured — all singles — using engines of 348cc, 490cc, 588cc or 633cc, ranging in price from £49 15s for the No 16H to £73 15s for the No 22 'Two-Port'.

Norton's racing success was phenomenal, with victory topping victory both at home and in Europe. The 1930s brought even greater successes, and a remarkable achievement in the Isle of Man TT races: a victory in every Senior and Junior race, with two exceptions, between 1931 and 1938. On the technical side, the 1930s was a period of innovation for Norton. They introduced a sleek, lower frame and shorter wheelbase for 1938, together with new front forks, first incorporating rebound springs, and, in 1939, telescopic ones. The most major revision of the models came with the 1938 range. No less than 10 mechanical and styling changes were listed in the accompanying brochure, including completely enclosed valve gear; a smoother crankcase, easier rocker and tappet adjustment, a new silencer, improved foot-change gear pedal and an optional sprung frame (on some models).

During World War 2, Norton were once again busy making motorcycles and sidecar combinations for the Armed Forces. When peace returned, domestic production resumed once more, but the company's racing

Model No. C.J
3.48 H.P. O.H.C.   Code Word : DERBY

Price - £71 . 10 : 0   or Deposit £17 : 17 : 6,
balance by gradual payments

Model No. C.S.1
4.90 H.P. O.H.C.   Code Word : CLENT

Price - £79 : 0 : 0   or Deposit £19 : 15 : 0,
balance by gradual payments

Model No. 40 International
3·48 H.P. O.H.C.   Code Word : TENBY

Price - £86 : 10 : 0   or Deposit £21 : 12 : 6,
balance by gradual payments

Above:
Norton motorcycle production resumed in 1975, from a factory in Shenstone, Staffordshire, produced by a small company employing 20 people and styling itself 'NVT'. Produced that first year, this 850cc Norton Commando made much of its electric start. *Jim Davies*

Left:
In 1988 the Shenstone-built Nortons returned to racing. Here Trevor Nation awaits the start of that year's Isle of Man Senior TT race on his 500cc rotary model. *Jim Davies*

Right:
Although famed for the excellence of its V-twin machines, when NUT production resumed after World War 1, the company also produced single-cylinder models with its own engines, such as here. The leg and chain guards were by no means standard for the time. *VMCC*

ambitions focused upon the USA. They had entered 100- and 200-mile events at Daytona in 1941, and won, continuing this success with six more victories in the years up to 1953. Innovations continued also, 1949 seeing the first Norton twin, and 1950 the introduction of a duplex-framed machine with ride so comfortable that it was soon nicknamed the 'Featherbed'. A cradle-style frame was also introduced for 1953.

Always makers of large machines, Norton were late responding to the public's demand for lightweight machines. The first Baby Norton — a 250cc model — did not appear until 1958, the firm's Diamond Jubilee year. This move was a direct result of the firm's take-over by Associated Motor Cycles Ltd in 1956. As with the other AMC take-overs, appearances were deceptive. Things carried on as before at Bracebridge Street, and the 1957 and 1958 model ranges were still basically Norton-designed machines. The latter was smaller than some of previous years — just six models — and ranged from the Model 50 348cc single (£189 10s) to the Manx 30/40M, a 499cc or 348cc single (£398).

Caught up in the shambles that AMC became in the early 1960s, Norton production at Bracebridge Street, Birmingham, ceased in 1962, when everything was transferred to AMC's works at Woolwich. Following their collapse in August 1966 AMC's assets were bought by Manganese Bronze Holdings; with these came the rights to the Norton name. Already owners of Villiers, a new motorcycle division was created: Norton-Villiers. On the sale of the BSA Group to Norton-Villiers on 17 July 1973 another 'new' company was formed: Norton-Villiers-Triumph Ltd.

Norton motorcycle production resumed in 1975, from a factory in Shenstone, Staffordshire, produced by a small company employing 20 people and styling itself 'NVT'. Together with a thriving parts manufacturing business, and selling the Meriden-built Triumphs on behalf of the workers' Co-operative, these Nortons

continued to be built until 1993. In 1998 an attempt was made to produce 'Norton' motorcycles in Germany, and, possibly, from a factory in the UK; but any remaining connection between this and the founders of the original Norton firm was nominal in every sense of the word.

NUT

The N.U.T. Engine & Cycle Co Ltd
N.U.T. Works, Station Rd, Walker, Newcastle upon Tyne

The unfortunately-named NUT was actually christened thus after the place in which it was made: Newcastle upon Tyne. Founded in 1911, the company moved three times, beginning in Newcastle itself, moving to Derwenthaugh, before settling in Walker. The company launched a range of J.A.P.-engined twin-cylinder machines. By 1915 this comprised eight models, ranging from a 348cc fixed-gear machine for £56 5s to a 976cc three-speed model with chain-cum-belt drive for £82 15s.

No models were listed for 1916, but production resumed after World War 1, by which time the company was producing its own range of one- and two-cylinder engines, supplemented by some Villiers 172cc singles for 1928 only. The NUT single-cylinder engines came in 248cc, 346cc and 350cc sizes, their twins being 500cc, 692cc, 700cc, 746cc and 750cc. Model names were used for the 1927 and 1928 seasons, for the Standard, Dynamo, Sports, Super-Sports, Pillion and Overseas cycles. Sidecars were offered with all models, at between £18 and £22 extra.

An ambitious range of seven cycles was announced for 1933, but only four of these were actually produced and, after 22 years, NUT motorcycle manufacture ceased altogether.

OEC; OEC Atlanta; OEC Blackburne; OEC Temple

Osborn Engineering Co Ltd
Atlanta Works, Lees Lane, Gosport, Hampshire
OEC Ltd
Atlanta Works, 5-7 Highbury St, Portsmouth,
Hampshire
Atlanta Works, Stamshaw Rd, Portsmouth, Hampshire

John Osborn and Fred Wood established the Osborn Engineering Co Ltd just after World War 1, in Atlanta Works, Lees Lane, Gosport in Hampshire. They produced their first motor cycles around 1921, using Blackburne or J.A.P. engines. These early machines were conventional enough, but it would be the sometimes innovatory technology that OEC used, after they moved to a new Atlanta Works in Portsmouth, that would be the hallmark of their cycles.

First up was a duplex frame, ie one with two front down tubes, introduced in 1924. This was followed by optional rear suspension in 1926, and by duplex steering in 1927, a system employing a pair of linked tubes, to one of which the front wheel was attached, through the other of which the steering acted, via a system of linkages. Complex as it may sound, the duplex steering worked very efficiently and was very stable and good at self-centring, largely due to the separation of the functions of supporting the wheel and turning it that this system afforded.

OEC's 1927 range comprised 12 models: seven singles and five twins, powered by Aza, Blackburne or J.A.P. engines. Bottom of the range was a 350cc J.A.P.-engined single for £54, top being a 1,000cc J.A.P.-engined twin, for £140, but rear suspension was still an option, the catalogues noting 'Rear-sprung Frame any model, £4 10s. extra'. In the late 1920s/early 1930s, much space was occupied in the motorcycle retail guides attempting to detail the options and complex technology of the diverse OEC range. A variety of engines was being used, including units by Blackburne, J.A.P., Sturmey Archer and Villiers, with, from 1928 onwards, the occasional use of OEC's own 500cc single and 998cc twin.

Perhaps OEC's strangest product was the Whitwood Monocar, a kind of fully-enclosed motorcycle, with two in-line seats, and a pair of stabiliser wheels that popped down whenever it was stationary. This was made between 1934 and 1936, at new premises OEC occupied in Portsmouth. Production broke for the war in 1940, but did not resume until 1949. This was from a second factory in Portsmouth, in Stamshaw Road, from where OEC concentrated upon competition and trials bikes, using Villiers engines and a J.A.P.-engined speedway machine. There was also a lightweight road machine. Sadly, despite some old flashes of technical innovation, such as a dual chain rear drive, OEC found it hard to repeat their prewar commercial or competition success. They tried diversifying into the production of tubular steel furniture, but this only staved off an inevitable collapse, which came late in 1954.

In the 1920s, OEC also produced motorcycles under the names of the OEC Atlanta, OEC Blackburne and OEC Temple. The first two of these ceased production after 1926, the Blackburne being a brief continuation of designs acquired from Burney & Blackburne when they had stopped production earlier that year. Slightly longer-lasting was the OEC Temple, which remained in production until 1928. The range included a 1,000cc twin, selling for £119. This formed the basis of the motorcycles with which OEC first captured then held the world motorcycle speed record — a staggering 150.7mph in 1930.

OK; OK Junior; OK Supreme

Humphries & Dawes Ltd
Hall Green Works, Birmingham 28
O.K. Supreme Motors Ltd
Bromley St, Bordesley, Birmingham 9
Warwick Rd, Greet, Birmingham 11

Humphries & Dawes were one of Birmingham's pioneering motorcycle makers, producing their first machines in 1899. At first the company adopted the 'OK' brand for its products, but by the 1910s they were being sold under the 'OK Junior' name. As such, by 1914 a range of three single-cylinder machines was being produced, using Humphries & Dawes' own engines: a 269cc fixed-gear model for £27 5s, a 190cc two-speed chain-cum-belt drive one for £36 15s, and a similar cycle, but with a 292cc engine, for £38. These were made up to 1916, when war work took over.

The OK re-emerged around 1919, and shortly afterwards the company changed its name to O.K. Supreme Motors Ltd, renaming its motorcycles the same. There was also a move, to new premises in Bromley Street, Bordesley in Birmingham. The postwar OK Supremes used the company's own engines, plus those by Blackburne and J.A.P., although the latter were used exclusively from 1927 onwards. Between six and 10 different models were produced each year, and from 1934 onwards they all had names: 'Britannia', 'Flying Cloud', 'Hood' and 'Phantom'. Production continued at new premises in Warwick Road, Greet, in Birmingham, until the outbreak of war. Although a 1940 range was announced, it is unlikely that it was actually produced. The company went over to war work once more and became accessory manufacturers afterwards.

Olympic

Frank H. Parkyn/Olympic Cycle & Motor Co Ltd
Granville St, Wolverhampton

Frank Parkyn was one of Wolverhampton's more established cycle makers, having been producing his 'Olympic' bicycles in Green Lane, Wolverhampton, since the early 1880s. By 1896 Parkyn had moved to larger premises in Granville Street, from where, in the early 1900s, he began first to experiment with, and second to produce, his own Olympic motorcycles.

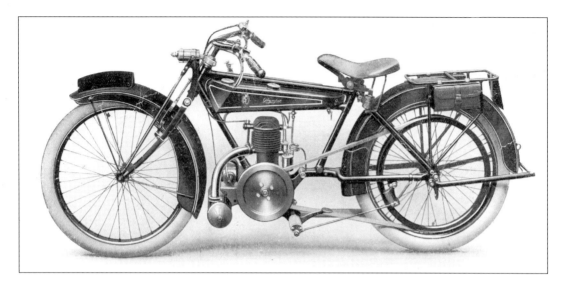

Above:
When Frank Parkyn revived his Olympic marque after World War 1 he produced machines with Blackburne, J.A.P. or Villiers engines. This 261.5cc 2.75hp machine was launched in November 1920, for 1921. The details of the frame, for which the Olympics were noted, are especially clear. Despite their engineering excellence, the last Olympic motorcycle was built in 1923.
Jim Boulton Collection

Right:
This shot of the Omega Motor Cycle Co's stand at the 1909 Stanley Show illustrates the revolutionary nature of the company's design. The 1.5hp engine was positioned in such a way as to allow the pedals to pass through the crankshaft, and the rider to retain a familiar riding position. Standing proudly beside their creation are R.S. Roberts and S. Dorsett. Unfortunately, only a few of these well-designed machines were produced between 1909 and 1910.
Jim Boulton Collection

These used MMC motors from Coventry, but few were made. The marque was revived in 1919 when a two-speed 268cc Verus-engined machine was produced, and continued until 1923, using Blackburne, J.A.P. and Villiers engines.

OMC – see SOS

Omega (1)

Omega Motor Cycle Co
St James's Square, Wolverhampton

The first Omega might have changed the way that motorcycles in general developed, had it caught on. Aimed at cyclists who were wary of motorcycles, the Omega was a motorised bicycle, with its 1.5hp engine at the bottom of the frame, positioned in such a way as to allow the pedals to pass through the crankshaft and the rider to retain a familiar riding position. The idea of Messrs Dorsett and Roberts, only a few of these well-designed machines were produced between 1909 and 1910. Dorsett was the 'D' of DF&M, makers of the Diamond motorcycle. He later went on to produce the Orbit in 1913 and in the 1920s.

Omega (2)

W.J. Green Ltd
Hill Street, Coventry 1
Croft Road, Coventry 1
Omega Works, Swan Lane, Coventry 2

Omega was also the name chosen by W.J. Green for his

motorcycles. Green was an engine maker who turned to cycle production around 1914. Just two models were offered: a two-speed chain-cum-belt drive one powered by Green's own 336cc 3hp engine, and a similar machine using a 2.5hp J.A.P. engine, both costing £39 17s 6d. Then the war intervened, and Green undertook military contracts until able to resume motorcycle production around 1920.

For the postwar models a combination of Green and J.A.P. engines were used, ranging from 170cc to 490cc. In 1926 Green also began to produce a three-wheeled car, using a 980cc J.A.P. engine. But this put a severe strain upon what was both a small company and a small works and the business collapsed in 1927. That had been the year when the first twin-cylinder Green — the Model 7 — had been introduced using a 680cc J.A.P. engine and selling for £60. All of the available spares were bought up and sold by Holland's of Hearsall Lane Corner in Coventry.

Orbit

S. Dorsett
Sedgley St, Wolverhampton

The third venture of Diamond's S. Dorsett was the Orbit, powered by the maker's own 250cc two-stroke engine. This was sold for £50 and first appeared in 1913, but was not produced in any quantity until 1919. By 1923 the engine had become a Bradshaw 350cc and the cost had risen to £60, and very few of a new model announced for 1924 were made before all production had ceased.

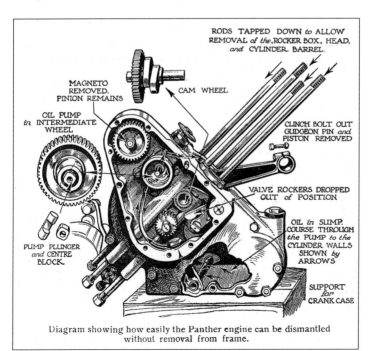

RODS TAPPED DOWN to ALLOW REMOVAL of the ROCKER BOX, HEAD, and CYLINDER BARREL.

MAGNETO REMOVED. PINION REMAINS

CAM WHEEL

OIL PUMP in INTERMEDIATE WHEEL

CLINCH BOLT OUT GUDGEON PIN and PISTON REMOVED

VALVE ROCKERS DROPPED OUT of POSITION

OIL in SUMP. COURSE THROUGH the PUMP to the CYLINDER WALLS SHOWN by ARROWS

PUMP PLUNGER and CENTRE BLOCK

SUPPORT for CRANK CASE

Diagram showing how easily the Panther engine can be dismantled without removal from frame.

Left:
A feature of the redesigned Panther motorcycles of the late 1920s was an engine that could be dismantled without removing it from the frame — this diagram shows how it could be done. *Jim Boulton Collection*

Above right:
The 1929 Panther, showing the company's distinctive feature: the use of the engine in place of the front down tube in the frame. A choice of 500cc or 600cc engine was offered, through which passed four steel rods to give structural support. *Jim Boulton Collection*

P & M; Panther

J.C. Phelon/Phelon & Moore Ltd
Horncastle Street Works, Cleckheaton, Yorkshire
Albany House, 324 Regent St, London W1

Jonah Carver Phelon was a motorcycle pioneer. Experimenting from the late 1890s, he produced his first machine in 1900. Like so many others, Phelon's starting point was a bicycle frame, but rather than squashing the engine into this he took the bold decision to redesign the frame. Working with Harry Rayner, out came the front down tube and in went the engine in its place. The machine had another far-sighted innovation — chain-drive — at a time when most motorcycles were belt-driven.

Resources were very stretched and few machines were made. Convinced of the soundness of his design, Phelon offered it to Humber who paid him 7s 6d for each one made. Humber continued to make the motorcycles under licence through 1902 and 1903, but in the latter year Jonah Phelon was joined by Richard Moore, who recognised the value of the former's design. The manufacturing rights were retrieved and in May 1904 Phelon & Moore formed a partnership to produce the machines themselves.

Known as P&Ms, the motorcycles added a two-speed gearbox to Phelon and Rayner's original design. Built to an exceptionally high standard, these machines enjoyed great success in reliability trials. The basic model was a 3.5hp 499cc single which by 1914 cost £65. For 1915 this was joined by a 6hp 771cc V-twin, with four-speed gearbox, for £81 17s 6d.

Production was maintained during World War 1 through P&M machines being used by the then infant Royal Flying Corps as Official Dispatch Rider motorcycles. Sales to the domestic market resumed in 1919, with the same models as had been offered before the war. These continued, with minor revisions, until 1926,

when the entire range was brought up to date. Saddle fuel tanks were introduced, as was a new model name — the Panther. One innovation was in the frame and engine design that allowed the latter to be dismantled without being removed from the machine.

The following year a new 246cc V-twin-engined machine, with an engine and four-speed gearbox designed by Granville Bradshaw, was introduced. This had a drop-forged steel main frame member that ran from the handlebars to the saddle, the engine being in a duplex steel cradle, bolted to the frame. Christened the 'Panthette', the machine boasted a maximum speed of 60mph and petrol consumption of over 100mpg — all for £37 10s! A machine with a 600cc unit was introduced in 1928 for use in sidecar combinations, but this engine was not a success, and in 1929 a Villiers unit was used instead. That year's range comprised six models and introduced the 147cc Panther, with a Villiers engine, which sold for just £24 18s 6d.

Like many British motorcycle manufacturers, P&M had a hard time of things in the early 1930s. They were saved by a deal struck with London dealers Pride & Clarke. In 1932, the company's engineer, Frank Leach, designed a light 249cc machine which Pride & Clarke sold as the 'Red Panther'. This was painted red and sold for £29 17s 6d; a low price made possible by the use of a basic specification and the cheapest components, production processes and assembly methods possible. Around 3,000 Red Panthers were produced each year almost three times the regular output of the Cleckheaton factory.

During World War 2 P&M made aircraft components, and they found the return to motorcycle production far from easy after 1945. Richard Moore retired in 1947 and there were other boardroom and management changes. One result of these was a programme to modernise the works. Old, worn machinery was refurbished and modern handling systems introduced with some success. Less successful was the replacement of belt-driven machines by electrically-powered ones. Old though the other ones may have been, many at the works believed that their modern replacements were not as accurate, and they could not get on with them.

This was perhaps then not the time to be introducing new models, but P&M were planning to enter the ranks of British scooter makers. The latter would join a range of 10 or so Villiers single- and two-cylinder two-strokes, ranging in price from £150 19s to £258 17s 2d. Launched in 1959, the Panther 'Princess' had a 175cc Villiers engine and three-speed gearbox, but came too late into a saturated market. Although parts for around 1,000 were made, only about 250 were assembled and sold.

The 'Princess' did not give P&M an ideal start to the 1960s, and worse was to come. Sales nosedived in 1961 and, despite a partial recovery, receivers were appointed in October 1962. Rather than close the firm

Belqw:
No-one could fault the accuracy of naming this 1954 machine a motorised bicycle. Phillips, then part of the Raleigh Group, were long-established bicycle manufacturers, and this was one of the company's staple designs — motorised. Power came from a 49cc two-stroke engine, with pedals and motor having separate chain drives. *Jim Boulton Collection*

down, they chose to assemble as many machines as possible from the stock in hand, a declining business that drifted on into 1967. Attempts were made to launch a new model, but component supplies, especially Villiers engines, were proving hard to obtain. Spares were sold from the original factory until 1977.

P&P

Packmann & Poppe Ltd
Moor St, Coventry 5
37 Ford St, Coventry 1
P&P Motorcycle Co Ltd
Orleans Rd, Twickenham, London
Wooler & Gittins/P&P Motorcycle Co Ltd/Almack
Engineering Co Ltd
Chatsworth Avenue, Wembley, London

One of Coventry's lesser-known marques was the P&P. The initials stood for Packmann & Poppe but the machines were built at the Montgomery Motors works on Walsgrave Road from 1922. The disastrous fire there in 1925 forced P&P to find another manufacturer, and the operation was moved first to Twickenham, and then to Chatsworth Avenue, Wembley. Here a range of five P&Ps was produced using proprietary parts and

Blackburne, J.A.P. and M.A.G. single-cylinder engines of between 340cc and 499cc. Twin-cylinder models, using J.A.P. 680cc and 976cc engines, were added to the range in 1928, selling for £78 15s and £115 10s, respectively. Two more seasons followed, 1930's range of four single-cylinder machines being the last P&Ps ever produced.

Phillips

Phillips Cycles Ltd
Smethwick, Birmingham

Part of the Raleigh Group, and famous for their pedal cycles, Phillips launched a motorised bicycle 'for maximum pleasure at minimum cost', at the 1954 Motorcycle Show. Costing £49 15s this was essentially a permanent bicycle and clip-on arrangement which used a 49cc two-stroke engine, driving the machine through the cycle chain. Other more moped-like models followed, including the 49cc 'Panda' of 1959 for £55 2s 6d. Variations appeared each season up to and including 1964, whereupon Raleigh pulled the plug on the venture.

Phoenix (1)

Phoenix Motors Ltd
Blundell St, Caledonian Rd, Islington, London N7

Phoenix Motors was established in May 1903 by Joseph Van Hooydonk to manufacture engines. Van Hooydonk had connections with the Belgian firm Minerva of Antwerp, and so it is possible that their engines may have formed some part of those purport-edly made by Phoenix. The company occupied premises in Blundell Street, just off the Caledonian Road in Islington, London. Quite quickly they also turned to the production of motorcycles and three-wheelers — the Phoenix Trimo.

In 1905, the 'Phoenix' motorcycle was available in nine models, with a range of engines from 2hp to 3.5hp and a choice of either belt or chain drive, fixed- or two-speed gears. Contemporary advertisements commented that the company was 'selling them in large quantities', and noted that 'Nothing that ought to be in a perfect motor bicycle is omitted from the Phoenix.' Car production was flirted with from time to time during the 1900s, but when it was decided to make cars in quantity in 1910, Phoenix moved to a new works in Letchworth, Hertfordshire, and that was the end of their motorcycle days.

Phoenix (2)

H.B. Engineering Co
34 Commerce Rd, London N22

The Phoenix was another British scooter. Introduced in 1956, the 'Nifty and Thrifty' Phoenix 150 used a Villiers 147cc two-stroke single-cylinder engine and three-speed gearbox, selling for £147 4s. This was joined by the De Luxe 150, with its 'Eyeability — with Reliability' which had the same technical specification, but a higher standard of trim, for £157 10s. Both models ran on, and were joined by machines using 198cc single and 247cc twin engines. The last Phoenix scooters appeared in 1964.

Pouncy

A. J. Pouncy
Owermoigne, Dorchester, Dorset
St John's Hill, Wareham, Dorset

A. J. Pouncy made motorcycles with names about as far removed from the norm as possible. Based in the small Dorchester parish of Owermoigne, Pouncy announced his first motorcycle early in 1931. This, and all of his machines, used a Villiers single-cylinder engine, coupled to a three-speed gearbox. Production was under way sufficiently towards the end of 1931 for a 1932 range of machines to be announced. These were the 'Kid', 'Sports Cub' and 'Triple S', using Villiers 147cc and 346cc engines and costing £26, £39 18s and £45 respectively.

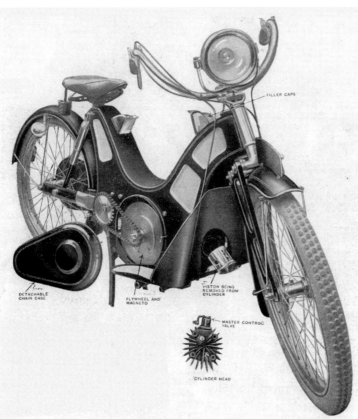

Pouncy moved his motorcycle production to St John's Hill, Wareham in Dorset, and for 1933 a new three model range was introduced, the: 'Pup', 'Pal' and the 'Mate', using Villiers 148cc, 249cc and 346cc engines. These models were continued into 1934, but production difficulties were then encountered. When these had been overcome production resumed, with a revised 'Pal', but it was short-lived, the last machines being made in 1936.

Premier — see Coventry-Premier

Pride & Clarke

Pride & Clarke Ltd
158 Stockwell Rd, London SW9

One of A.J. Pouncy's model names lived on briefly in a motorcycle produced for just one season by the London motorcycle dealers, Pride & Clarke Ltd. Long-established agents for such makes as P&M, Panther, Pride & Clarke produced their own lightweight motorcycle — the Cub — from proprietary parts and a Villiers 122cc engine. Unfortunately, the season they chose to launch this bike was that for 1939, the war putting paid to any further hopes they may have had of making as well as selling motorcycles.

Priory

Priory Engine Co
82 Priory Rd, Kenilworth, Warwickshire

Another of the Coventry area's post-World War 1 marques, the Priory lasted just eight seasons. Founded in 1919, three or four models of Priory motorcycle appeared each year up to and including 1926. In addition to the company's own-make 'Arden' engines, Villiers 147cc or 269cc single-cylinder engines were used, the only named model being the Ladies, at £25. All the 147cc models sold for between £23 and £27 10s, the 269cc one costing £38. When production ceased, the spares were to be found in the glory-hole that was Holland's, on Hearsall Lane Corner in Coventry.

Pullin; Pullin-Groom

Cyril Pullin/The Pullin-Groom Motor Co Ltd
24 Buckingham Gate, London SW1

Some names keep recurring through the history of British motorcycles, one such being that of Cyril Pullin. To racing aficionados, he was the winner of the Senior TT on the Isle of Man in 1914, but it is as a designer and sometime manufacturer that Pullin is of interest here. In 1920 he designed and launched the Pullin motorcycle; the model was sometimes known as the Pullin-Groom. In the autocycle/moped mould, the frame was made from pressed-steel sheets, as were the front forks. Pullin also designed the engine, which was a 348cc single-cylinder two-stroke, set horizontally, forward in the machine.

Years ahead of its time, the Pullin sold for just £51 9s, but not well enough, production lasting until only 1925. Cyril Pullin next appeared in 1928 as one half of the Ascot-Pullin, described earlier and later, in 1951, as the designer of a clip-on device called the Powerwheel, which was produced and sold by Tube Investments Ltd, a group of companies established in 1919, and describing itself as: 'The world's largest producer of bicycles and cycle components'. Finally, in 1955, Pullin designed a scooter, which he tried to find a manufacturer for, but in which no-one showed much interest.

PV

Ellison & Fell/P.V. Motor Cycles Ltd
PV Motor Works, Perry Vale, Forest Hill, London SE23

Messrs Ellison & Fell appear to have embarked upon motorcycle making in the unfortunate year of 1914. As a result, their PV machines — named after the initials of the road they were built in — are listed only for that one year. Six models were made, with three different J.A.P. engines being used. Bottom of the range models were belt-driven and used a 248cc single, available either with a fixed gear, for £48 10s, or with a three-speed gearbox, for £59. Middle range models used a 654cc twin, with the same options on transmissions, for £57 and £67 10s respectively, and the top of the range models used a 771cc twin, again with a choice of gears, for £61 10s or £72.

Quadrant

Quadrant Cycle Co Ltd
Sheepcote St, Birmingham 15
March, Newark & Co Ltd
Quadrant Works, 45 Lawley St, Birmingham 4
Quadrant Motors Ltd
Quadrant Works, 97 Woodcock St, Birmingham 4

The Quadrant Cycle Co was established in the 1890s, occupying premises in Sheepcote Street, which linked Broad Street with the Monument Lane area of Birmingham. They produced bicycles, motor cycles, from 1899, and a tricar, called the 'Carette'. By 1905 two models of Quadrant motorcycle were being offered: a 2hp or a 3hp, at £29 8s and £42 each, respectively. Both machines were very bicycle-like, belt-driven, with the engine and fuel tank fitted into the central diamond of the frame. A number of extras were offered, including: a Spring fork, extra £2 10s; a B100 Suspension Saddle, extra £0 7s 6d, and a Combination Luggage Rack and Stand, extra £0 15s 0d. Prospective purchasers were also exhorted to acquire the booklet: *Special Hints on Quadrant Motor Cycles*.

By the 1910s the company had experimented with car production, between 1906 and 1907, and moved to a new works at 45 Lawley Street, Birmingham, in the heart of the city's railway goods depots. Here they produced two models, both based around a 565cc single-cylinder engine, with three-speed gearboxes, but differing with regard to their final drives: by chain-cum-belt — £55, by chain — £57. When production resumed after World War 1, it was in another location: Quadrant Works, at 97 Woodcock Street, just two streets away from Lawley Street. Here they used two versions of their own make of single-cylinder engine, in either 490cc or 624cc forms, to produce three different models each year up to 1930. This would be Quadrant's last year of production and would see their only use of a J.A.P. engine, in a 490cc single costing £56.

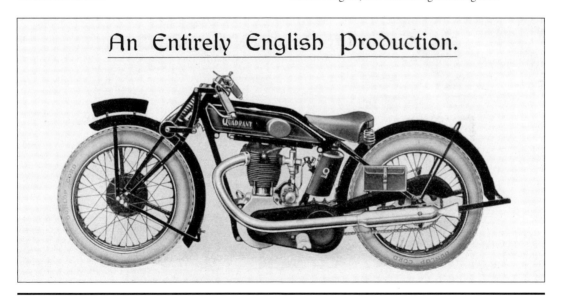

An Entirely English Production.

Radco

E. A. Radnall & Co Ltd
Vauxhall Works, Dartmouth St, Birmingham 7

Founded in 1895 to manufacture cycle components, E. A. Radnall & Co Ltd also produced motorcycles under their 'Radco' brand-name. One model was listed before production was halted in 1916: a two-speed, belt-driven machine, powered by a 211cc single-cylinder engine. After the war Radco motorcycles reappeared, with a much wider range of machines, powered by either the company's own or J.A.P. singles. The models offered in 1928 were typical. There were seven machines, two powered by Radnall's own 247cc engine, and five by J.A.P. 250cc 300cc and 500cc units. The economy model was the 'A', with the Radnall 247cc engine, for £32 10s, the top of the range being the 'K', with a J.A.P. 500cc engine, for £58; there was also the 'H', or the Radco Ace, which had the same engine, for just £45 10s.

For their motorcycles from 1930 onwards, Radco moved to an increasing use of Villiers singles instead of J.A.P. units, the entire 1931 range, for instance, relying entirely upon the Wolverhampton engines. The 1930s Radcos were also promoted as being 'All Electric', but they didn't have long to prove this. For 1932, eight models were offered, but the following year this was reduced to just three, two using Villiers 147cc and 196cc engines, the other having Radnall's trusty 247cc unit, and all priced between £21 and £28 7s. Then, motorcycle production was suspended, the trade catalogues showing a bald 'No New Models' against the marque.

For the next 25 years or so Radnall's produced bicycle components (listing cycle hubs, head fittings, handlebars, brakes, caliper brakes, footrests and spanners amongst their product range), but they also began to harbour thoughts of a return to motorcycle production, particularly in the face of the rise in interest in ridership created by the scooter and moped boom of the early 1950s. A new lightweight machine was planned, and prototypes tested, but the company had cold feet and the project was shelved. Another attempt was made in 1966, when Radnall's announced the Radcomuter — from Radco and commuter — a foldaway machine designed to be stowed in the average car boot, but this too was quietly forgotten.

Raleigh

Raleigh Cycle Co Ltd
Faraday Rd, Renton, Nottingham
177 Lenton Boulevard, Nottingham

Raleigh are probably the most famous name in British cycling. The company also had an early involvement in motorcycle production, making its first machines in 1899. Derived from one of the company's bicycles, two basic types were produced: a 3hp motorcycle and a 3.5hp forecar-style three-wheeler, the 'Raleighette'.

The motorcycle was belt-driven and was sold for £25.

Bicycle production at Raleigh was continuous, but that of motorcycles and cars, in which the company also dabbled in 1905 and 1916, was more fitful. War-related work occupied the firm from 1916, but motorcycle production had resumed by the 1920s. Raleigh produced their own engines, but also bought in units from Sturmey Archer, with whom they already traded for bicycle components. A modest range of five machines was offered each year, and up to 1928 these included one two-cylinder cycle, powered by Raleigh's own 798cc twin. But from 1928 onwards, it was singles all the way.

Model designations were unusually complex; perhaps they made sense to the company accountants, but 'Model MT-30', apart from having a year code, is not a very sexy way of selling motorcycles! Production continued until 1933. That year the five models ranged from a 298cc single, for £33, to a 496cc single, for £44, and included a 598cc machine for £42 10s. By this time Raleigh had decided to drop motorcycles in order to scale up production of a three-wheeled car and van — the Super Seven — designed by Tom Williams. This began in 1933, and so there were no Raleigh motorcycles for 1934.

Three-wheeler production continued until 1936, when the company abruptly dropped it. Convinced of his design, and that a market existed for it, Tom Williams bought the manufacturing rights back from Raleigh and set up his own company in Tamworth — Reliant (any similarities and puns to be found in this choice of name were probably intended).

Thus Raleigh approached World War 2 as just a bicycle manufacturer, and remained in this vein until the lure of the scooter/moped market in the late 1950s proved too great. In 1958 they announced a very bicycle-like moped — the RM1 — powered by a 49cc Sturmey Archer engine. Other models followed, until the RM series peaked at the RM12. The 1960s brought a major change of tack. At the end of 1960, Raleigh began two associations with European motorcycle manufacturers. The first was with the French company Motobécane, to produce a version of their Mobylette under licence; the second was with the Italian Bianchi firm, to sell their Orsetto scooter as the 'Roma' in Britain.

These arrangements set the style of Raleigh's production for the 1960s, the only unusual departure being in 1967 with the introduction of the RM7 'Wisp', based around a Raleigh small-wheeled bicycle — then the latest trend. The company continued to produce these forms of motorcycle until 1969.

Ray

W. H. Raven & Co Ltd
223 Castle Boulevard, Nottingham
later in Leicester

Raven's 'Ray' motorcycles were small single-cylinder machines, using either their own-make or Villiers engines of 172cc or 198cc. Four models were produced, all priced between £35 14s and £39 18s. The company had moved to Leicester by 1924, but their manufacture was discontinued after 1927.

Raynal

Raynal Manufacturing Co Ltd
41-43 Fleet St, Birmingham 3
Woodbarn Rd, Handsworth, Birmingham 21

The Raynal Manufacturing Co had produced a small number of motorcycles using Precision and Villiers engines before World War 1, and continued this, using Villiers 269cc units, into the 1920s. In 1935/6, from new premises, they took up a prototype design of an autocycle which G. H. Jones had produced in conjunction with Villiers. This used a 98cc Villiers engine, fitted into a conventional bicycle frame. Raynal's production version of Jones' design — the 'Auto' — appeared in 1937. This had retained the 98cc Villiers engine, but omitted some of Jones' refinements under the pressure to produce the machines in quantity and to cost. A De Luxe version of the Auto appeared in 1939, but all this boasted was a set of sprung forks.

Below:
In 1959 successful trails and scramble riders Derek and Don Rickman entered motorcycle production. Despite ever-present component supply problems, the brothers managed fitful production runs until the early 1970s, including this stylish 700cc Interceptor model. *Jim Davies*

Production continued until 1940, and resumed in 1947, continuing until 1953.

Regina

S. Barnett
Pelham St, Derby

The patriotic Regina came in three versions, all of which were powered by proprietary 292cc and 349cc single-cylinder engines. Listed from 1914, the cheapest Regina was belt-driven, with a fixed-speed gear, and sold for £26 10s. Next came a two-speed model, with chain-cum-belt drive, for £33 5s, and completing the range was a three-speed belt-driven machine with a 349cc engine, selling for £55. These machines were produced in 1915 and 1916, but production was discontinued thereafter, never to resume.

Revere

W. H. Whitehouse & Co Ltd
Friars Rd, Coventry

Whitehouse's were cycle makers in works in Friars Road in Coventry, an area now dominated by that city's inner ring road. They produced motorcycles for a few years around the time of World War 1. Two models are listed for 1915 and 1916, both using a 269cc single-cylinder engine. One is a fixed-gear machine selling for £28 7s 6d in 1915; the other a two-speed one at £35 15s. Revere's are not listed beyond 1916.

Rex; Rex-Acme — see Acme

Reynolds' Special Scott; AER

Albert E. Reynolds
9 Berry St, Liverpool

Some motorcycle dealers produced accessories and parts for the machines they sold, others even going so far as to produce their own modified versions of certain makes. One such was Albert Reynolds, a Scott dealer in Berry Street, Liverpool. Following approaches by Reynolds, Scott agreed to produce motorcycles to a specification he had drawn up. Known as Reynolds' Special Scotts, these were luxury machines. In 1933, two Reynolds' models were offered: the Special and the De Luxe. Both had a 596cc 5.95hp Scott two-cylinder engine and were available either as a cycle or sidecar combination. The Special cycle sold at £105 (combination £130) and the De Luxe at £115 (combination £140).

Reynolds offered the same models in 1934, adding an unnamed Villiers 249cc 2.5hp single-cylinder machine, which sold at £44 2s, to the range. Sadly, the venture was thwarted, partly by the high cost of the machines. Undaunted, Reynolds had a second stab as a motorcycle maker three years later. Called the AER, after Reynolds' initials, these two-cylinder machines were made in a workshop above his shop in Berry Street. Full production began in 1938 and continued into 1939, but came to an end with the outbreak of war.

Rickman

Rickman Bros (Engineering) Ltd
Queensway, Stem Lane, New Milton, Hampshire

Derek and Don Rickman were two highly successful trials and scrambles riders who progressed to motorcycle production, with greater success than many who had preceded them. Born out of a desire to make something better for their own use, the brothers designed a 'Tribsa' — so named because it combined a Triumph engine in a BSA frame — in 1959 which they christened the Metisse. The brothers enjoyed continued success on their own machines, but were faced with an ever-mounting demand to build them for others. Component supply problems precluded production of the machines, but once these had been overcome by 1963 the Metisse was offered in kit form.

Some production became possible in 1964, through an arrangement with the Spanish firm Bultaco, but when this lapsed it left the Rickmans to scour Europe for component and engine suppliers. Various alliances were formed, but none endured, and so in the early 1970s the brothers turned to producing motorcycle body accessories such as panniers.

Rockson

J. S. Rock & Sons
Beecher Rd, Cradley Heath, West Midlands

J. S. Rock & Sons were a long-established iron and steel firm with a factory in Beecher Road, Cradley Heath, in the Black Country. The Rockson motorcycle was introduced as a sideline in 1920, born out of an enthusiasm for motorcycling shared by the younger Rock brothers. Three models were made, all using a Villiers engine. The 'A' had a fixed gear and sold for £56 14s, the 'B' had a two-speed gearbox and sold for £65 2s, whilst the 'C' had a two-speed gearbox, plus a kick start, and sold for £73 10s. A healthy export trade was developed with India, which sustained motorcycle production in Cradley Heath until 1923, by which time over 400 machines had been produced.

Rolfe

Rolfe Manufacturing Co Ltd
Bridge St, Smethwick, West Midlands

The Rolfe took its name from Rolfe Street, where the London & North Western Railway had a station, which crossed Bridge Street where the machines were made. Production, which was always low-key, began in 1911. Both single and V-twin machines were produced using proprietary engines, the rest of the parts being made by the company. The only unusual feature of the Rolfes was the use of a band brake on the front wheel. A Rolfe cyclecar was proposed too, but all production ceased in 1914, never to resume.

Roper

J. Roper
Curzon St, Wolverhampton

A cycle component and fittings maker, J. Roper also produced a few motorcycles at his Curzon Street premises, between Dudley Road and Green Lane (later Birmingham Road) in Wolverhampton. There are no details of the machines, but it is thought that production, which began in 1901, was discontinued around 1905.

Rover

J. K. Starley & Co Ltd/The Rover Cycle Co/The Rover Motor Co Ltd
Meteor Works, West Orchard, Coventry

John Kemp Starley was the nephew of James Starley — the Father of the Cycle Industry. In partnership with William Sutton, Starley established the Meteor Works, in West Orchard, Coventry, in 1879, for the production of bicycles. In 1884 Starley produced the first of a series of designs for a bicycle with equal, or near equal, sized wheels. He gave these designs the name 'Rover', and they proved so successful that he renamed his firm The Rover Cycle Co in 1896.

In 1899 Starley began to experiment with designs for a motorcycle, a task which was left uncompleted when he died in 1901. The first Rover motorcycles were introduced in 1902 and production continued until around 1915 when the Meteor Works was given over to the production of Maudslay trucks and the chassis for Sunbeam staff cars.

The motorcycles used Rover's own make of 499cc single-cylinder engine, and three basic model variants were produced: a free engine version, selling for £55, and produced up to 1914, a fixed-gear version, for £48, produced from 1912, and a three-speed machine — the top of the range — which sold for £66 10s in 1916, the last year of production.

After World War 1, the Rover company decided to concentrate upon the production of light cars, particularly after the acquisition of their new plant at Tyseley, Birmingham, in 1921. Motorcycles were gradually phased out, the range offered in 1924 being the last.

Royal Enfield; Enfield

Enfield Cycle Co Ltd
Hunt End Works, Redditch, Worcestershire
Enfield Precision Engineers Ltd
Upper Westwood, Bradford-on-Avon, Wiltshire
Enfield (Bavanar Products Ltd)
Unit 3, Therapia Trading Estate, Therapia Lane, Croydon

Royal Enfield is another marque to emerge from a bicycle manufacturing business. The firm of George Townsend & Co entered into needle manufacture in Redditch in 1855. In 1885 they branched out into the production of cycle components and in 1888 they began to produce complete cycles under the 'Townsend' name. The firm became a limited liability concern in November 1890. Twelve months later they were seeking additional backers and secured support from a number of Birmingham businessmen, including one Albert Eadie. Around 1892/3 the needle-making side of the business was discontinued and the Townsend family withdrew from the company, leaving Albert Eadie in control.

Eadie brought in the former Assistant Manager of the cycle makers Dan Rudge & Co, Robert Walker Smith, as Works Manager. Still trading as George Townsend & Co, the firm continued to specialise in the production of cycle components (being renamed the Enfield Manufacturing Co Ltd). They produced their first cycle with the name 'Enfield' on it in October 1892.

Having rapidly outgrown their premises at Hunt End, work began on a new factory in 1896, built in Lodge Road and Union Street, Redditch. The business was also reorganised at this time, George Townsend & Co being renamed The New Eadie Manufacturing Co Ltd

Left:
The 'Royal Enfield Works from the Air', a vignette from the cover of the company's 1929 catalogue showing its factory at Redditch. *Jim Boulton Collection*

on 25 June 1896, and a new company, the New Enfield Cycle Co Ltd, was formed on 1 July 1896 to manufacture complete cycles. The New Eadie Manufacturing Co built complete cycles, which were sold to agents and small assemblers who put their own trade names on them, as well as producing cycle components. They occupied their new premises in 1896/7, their old ones being taken over by the New Enfield Cycle Co. Shortly after this move the original company, renamed as the Enfield Manufacturing Co Ltd, was wound up on 8 January 1897.

The New Enfield Cycle Co made ladies', gentlemen's, roadsters and tradesmen's carrier bicycles, diversifying into the production of motorcycles in 1900. Their first machines were powered by Minerva engines and followed a series of de Dion Bouton-engined tri- and quadricycles produced from 1898. The motorcycles were in fact motorised bicycles using a form of 'clip-on' attachment mounted in front of the steering column tube, which drove the rear wheel by means of a long, crossed belt.

Albert Eadie expanded his interests to include car manufacture, forming the Enfield Autocar Co in 1904. This put further strain upon the two factories and so the original Hunt End site was extensively redeveloped in 1906/7 to provide a vastly expanded works complex with its own water and electricity supplies, all of the machinery being electrically driven.

Early in 1907 the BSA Group made an offer for the assets of the Eadie Manufacturing Co, excluding the Enfield Autocar Co and the Enfield Cycle Co (the 'New' having been dropped). This was accepted and in June 1907 the Eadie Manufacturing Co went into liquidation. BSA took over Eadie's Lodge Road works, Albert Eadie becoming a member of the BSA main board and within two years Chairman of the company.

Volume motorcycle production did not begin until 1910, by which time the company were using V-twin engines based upon a design by the Swiss Motosacoche firm, the completed machines also having other close similarities with comparable Motosacoche models. For 1915 a range of four chain-driven models was offered:

a 225cc two-speed single (£39 17s 6d), two versions of a 424cc two-speed twin (£52 10s) and a 771cc J.A.P.-engined, two-speed twin combination (£84).

Motorcycle production continued into World War 1 and picked up again in 1919. By the mid-1920s Enfield were using their own make of engines in their motorcycles exclusively, but whilst these were in development they used Vickers and Wolseley units. For 1929 the Royal Enfield range comprised eight models, including the '201', a 225cc two-speed, single two-stroke, available in Standard or Open-frame form (£28 17s 6d or £30), the '202 Standard' and '203 Sports', using the 201's engine but with a three-speed gearbox (£32 10s), the '501 Standard', '502 De Luxe' and '505 Two-port', three-speed 488cc singles (£45 10s; £53 15s, or £52 10s) and the '182', a 976cc V-twin three-speed (£62 10s).

In 1931 the company introduced the 'Cycar', a 148cc two-stroke motorcycle with a completely enclosed frame and engine, selling for just £22 1s. They also launched a range of models aimed at sporting riders — the 'Bullets'. First seen in the 1933 model range, they were available with 248cc, 346cc and 488cc engines, for £42 17s 6d, £46 17s 6d and £53 17s 6d respectively. For 1937 a 1,140cc side valve engine was introduced for the model 'K' which had previously had a 976cc unit. This four-speed machine could be had for £72 10s or, for an extra £5, it could be adorned with 'detachable and interchangeable wheels, tank chromium plated with frosted silver panels'.

During World War 2 Enfield made around 55,000 dispatch rider machines and a paratrooper's collapsible motorcycle — the 'Flying Flea' — designed along the lines of the Corgi, built by Excelsior, but strikingly similar to a German model by DKW. When peace returned, the company bought back many of the motorcycles it had made for the war effort, painted them black, and then sold them to the public. No new models were launched until 1948, when two were announced for the 1949 model range. One was a revival of the Bullet name, but in a new 346cc machine that was offered in road, trials and scramble form. The other

TRADE DELIVERY OUTFITS

Fitted with coach-built box carrier, the 9.76 h.p. Royal Enfield Motor Cycle is the ideal outfit for small tradesman or large store. The specifications of these motor cycles are similar to Model 182, but have a different type of frame and tank.

MODEL 185

9.76 h.p. Delivery Outfit

Coach-built box carrier with hinged lid, painted green to match the motor cycle. As supplied to bakers, butchers, billposters, boot repairers, drapers, fishmongers, grocers, and others.

Inside dimensions of the Box Carrier : Length, 4 ft. 5 in. Depth, 1 ft. 8 in. Width, 1 ft. 7 in. Capacity, approximately 13 cubic feet.

OVERALL LENGTH of Outfit, 7 ft. 2 in. ; **WIDTH**, 5 ft. 3 in.

MODEL 165

9.76 h.p.
Dairyman's Outfit

We have sold large quantities of this type of outfit to dairymen, farmers, and greengrocers. It has a wide and exceptionally strong chassis. Milk float attached is capable of carrying three milk churns, besides cans, tools, spares, etc. Inside dimensions of body : Length, 4 ft. 6 in. Width, 2 ft. 7 in. Depth, 1 ft. 6 in.

OVERALL LENGTH of Outfit, 7 ft. 2 in. ; **WIDTH**, 6 ft.

MODEL 175

is a similar outfit, but on the standard chassis, the length and width being the same as the box carrier of Model 185. This is designed to carry two milk churns instead of three, and is invaluable to the man with a smaller business.

MODEL 155

9.76 h.p.
G.P.O. Type Outfit

As supplied to the G.P.O. Authorities. Capable of carrying loads up to 4 cwt. The large box has a lid in front and double doors at the rear. This model has, of course, the wide chassis mentioned above.

Dimensions of Box : Length, 4 ft. 9 in. Depth, 3 ft. 3 in. Width, 2 ft. 9½ in. Capacity approximately 31 cubic feet.

Overall measurements as Model 165.

Prices:

MODEL 185 Delivery Combination complete as above	...	...	**£77 10 0**
MODEL 165 Dairyman's Combination, complete as above	...	...	**£79 10 0**
MODEL 175 Dairyman's Combination (not illustrated)...	...	...	**£77 10 0**
MODEL 155 G.P.O. type Combination, complete as above	...	...	**£85 0 0**

Insurance rates for Trade Delivery Vehicles vary according to actual trade and district in which used. Gradual payment prices for these Outfits, therefore, can be supplied on receipt of this information.

We issue a separate list for Trade Delivery Outfits and shall be pleased to send a copy, post free, on request.

new model was a Twin, with an upright 496cc engine.

By 1952 a range of eight models had been developed, from the 143cc 'Ensign' to the 692cc 'Meteor' twin, and including a 346cc and 499cc Bullet, and the 496cc Twin. A less conventional model was launched in 1956. The 248cc 'Crusader' used unit construction, and was aimed at the lightweight market, adding some additional fairings around the mudguards, a dual seat and an enclosed chain. Unfortunately, at a touch under £200 prospective buyers found they could get more for their money from other manufacturers.

In 1958 the Crusader was offered in an 'Airflow' form, with additional glass fibre fairings fitted. These weighed 18lb, but offered improvements in the machines: Looks — beautifully smooth lines and flowing curves; Performance — a 20% improvement in fuel consumption and an 8% improvement in fuel consumption and Protection — you're out of the weather riding the Airflow. No need to dress like a diver! This wonder package sold for £257 1s 6s and became a factory-fitted option on other models the following year.

Enfield entered the 1960s in confident mood. Their model range catered for most tastes, from the 148cc two-stroke Prince to the large twins. A number of new models were introduced, most notably the 736cc vertical-twin-engined Interceptor, which was launched in 1963 and was produced for the home market until 1965, export production continuing at another Enfield works in Bradford-on-Avon. Sadly, by this time, things were far from well with the company, and events were set in train that would eventually lead in March 1967 to a take-over of the motorcycle manufacturing business by Norton-Villiers. Divorced from this was the spares side of the firm, which was sold to Velocette in April 1967.

Export production of the 750 Interceptor continued at Bradford-on-Avon, and in October 1968 the Series II Interceptor was launched from there. It had a revamped version of the 736cc vertical-twin engine — simplified and lightened, but with even more power, as the brochure proclaimed — the last one being produced in June 1970. Some years earlier, tools and dies for the 350 model had been sent to India, where production continued at the Tiruvot-Tiyur factory near Madras. From there 'Enfield India 350s' are still being made, and have been imported into Britain, for a price, since 1977.

Ruby; Royal Ruby

Ruby Cycle Co Ltd/Royal Ruby Cycle Co Ltd
Cannel St, Ancoats, Manchester
(from 1919): Moss Lane, Altrincham, Cheshire
Horrockses Ltd
Bradshawgate, Bolton, Lancashire

The Ruby/Royal Ruby motorcycle has a complex, and often misunderstood, history. It all began with the Ruby Cycle Co, a bicycle manufacturer in Ancoats, Manchester. In 1909 it introduced a motorcycle which,

in later versions, would become the Royal Ruby. This was so successful that the company changed its name to the Royal Ruby Cycle Co and branded all its bicycles and motorcycles thus.

By the time that production was suspended in 1916 for World War 1, the company was producing a range of seven models, each using a different J.A.P. engine. There were three singles, of 269cc, 292cc and 482cc plus four twins, of 496cc, 654cc, 771cc and 964cc, all using chain-cum-belt drive. From 1919 the company was based in premises in Moss Lane, Altrincham, Cheshire, where production was continued until around 1927. The name of, and rights to produce, the Royal Ruby were acquired by the Bolton-based firm of Horrockses Ltd, and production resumed in their Bradshawgate factory in 1927. As stocks of J.A.P. engines dried-up, Horrockses switched to using Villiers single units the following year.

Production continued, with varying numbers of models available each year. These were designated as the Standard, Sports and Super Sports. Only one model was produced in 1931, but 1932 saw both the Club and the Standard, and 1933 no fewer than five models of the Sports. These used Villiers 248cc or 348cc engines and sold for between £30 and £40. Unfortunately, this was to prove the last year that any Royal Rubys would be made.

Rudge; Rudge-Whitworth

Rudge-Whitworth Ltd
34 Spon St, Coventry 1
(from 1938): Dawley Works, Hayes, Middlesex

Dan Rudge kept The Tiger's Head Inn, Church Street, Wolverhampton, and was a keen cyclist, building his own machines. In 1870 Rudge built his first machines for sale, and continued in this way until his death in 1880. So successful was Rudge's venture that his widow kept it on, selling out to George Woodcock, who moved the business to premises in Spon Street, Coventry, once the heart of that city's watchmaking trade, in 1888. The Rudge Cycle Co was reorganised in 1896, becoming Rudge-Whitworth Ltd.

Motorcycle production began in 1910. Like the company's bicycles, they were branded Rudges, and used the firm's own make of single-cylinder and twin engines. Only singles were produced until 1915, using either a 499cc or huge 749cc engine, the latter having a massive 132mm stroke. The models using these engines sold for £58 15s and £63 15s respectively in 1914. In 1915 they were joined by a pair of motorcycles — the Multwin and Twin — using Rudge's own 998cc two-cylinder engine, and having four-speed gearboxes and chain-cum-belt drives. These sold for £75 a piece.

Rudge-Whitworth also dabbled in car production in 1912 and 1913, but this was dropped in favour of motorcycles which were manufactured until 1916 when they were displaced by war work. Production resumed in 1919 when the bikes were sold under the company's full title — Rudge-Whitworth. All the machines were

Right:
Rudge made their mark early through racing and trials successes. Sitting astride this London-registered machine is none other than the famous Cyril Pullin, later to become a motorcycle designer and manufacturer, seen on the Isle of Man, probably in 1914, where he won the Senior TT on this machine that year. *Jim Boulton Collection*

Above:
A Rudge model that was very successful in trials was the Multi. This referred to its variable gearing arrangement, which offered a range of ratios from 3.5 to 1 to 7 to 1, and everything in between. The gear ratio was raised by pushing the lever forwards and lowered by pulling it back, this acting to vary the diameter of the engine and back wheel pulleys. *Jim Boulton Collection*

Right:
Rudge-Whitworth was taken over by EMI, of Hayes, Middlesex, and reformed on 6 April 1934. Motorcycle production continued, but the problems associated with working a factory to under capacity from another part of the country were faced in 1938 when EMI moved Rudge production to Hayes. This 499cc Special model was made in 1938, and is seen at a rally in 1972. *Jim Boulton Collection*

singles, using the firm's own or J.A.P. engines. There were three basic model variants: Standard, Special and Sports, all of which used a 499cc engine, and cost £64, £74 and £76 respectively; four volt electric lighting was available on all models at £4 extra.

The success of a 499cc Rudge-Whitworth in the 1928 Ulster Grand Prix led to the introduction of a £69 'Ulster' model in the range for 1929 which continued for 1930. That year also saw the addition of a 'Dirt Track' model, using the trusty 499cc engine, which was presumably introduced to cash in on the craze for Speedway, introduced into Britain from 1928. Another racing success, this time in the 1930 Isle of Man TT, was followed by two 'TT Replica' models, using a new Rudge-Whitworth 349cc engine, for £82 or £85, in 1931. That year the company also began to produce proprietary engine and gearbox units, which they sold under the 'Rudge Python' name.

Yet, despite this diversification, and continued racing success, Rudge-Whitworth hit financial difficulties in 1934, with receivers being appointed. The company was taken over by EMI (the former Gramophone Co, of Hayes, Middlesex), and re-formed on 6 April 1934. Motorcycle production resumed with the reduced range of just four models introduced for that year, using own-make engines, namely the Standard, Sports, Special and Ulster, the first two having 249cc units, the others a 499cc one, and costing from £52 10s to £73 10s.

The problems associated with working a factory to undercapacity from another part of the country were faced in 1938 when EMI moved Rudge production to Hayes. There it continued until the start of the war, when space was needed to build radar equipment, and so motorcycle manufacture ended. EMI sold its Rudge-Whitworth interests on to Sturmey Archer and Norman Motor Cycles in 1940, and in turn they passed to Raleigh in 1943.

Rudge Wedge

Rudge, Wedge & Co
Mander St, Wolverhampton

Dan Rudge's eldest son, Harry, remained in Wolverhampton after his father's death. There he worked for Humber, and in 1891 he went into partnership with a local businessman, Mr C. Wedge, and established a cycle works in Pelham Street (later the home of Clyno). By 1902 the firm had moved to Mander Street, and it is from there that they also produced motorcycles. A choice of two engines, 1.75hp or 2.5hp, was available, the respective machines costing £40 and £42. It is not believed that many of these motorcycles were made, and the partners continued to concentrate upon the production of their bicycles.

RW Scout

R. Weatherell
Motorcycle Works, South Green, Billericay, Essex

A short-lived venture by a motorcycle builder who went on to form his own equally brief eponymous marque. The RW Scouts used a 318cc Dalm two-stroke engine and were introduced in 1920, surviving until the following year.

Saxel

Saxelbys Ltd
Sax Works, Much Park St, Coventry 1

Saxelbys Ltd were a Coventry-based firm of cycle and motorcycle accessory manufacturers, who branded their products 'Saxessories'. In 1923 they embarked upon motorcycle production, using proprietary parts and

Right:
The R.W. Scout was a short-lived venture by motorcycle builder R. Weatherell. Introduced in 1920, the RW Scouts used a 318cc Dalm two-stroke engine, surviving until the following year. In this advertisement, Mr Weatherell himself is seen lapping at speed.
Jim Boulton Collection

Right:
In addition to its road machines, Scott also made specials, one of the most legendary being this, the Sprint Special, introduced for 1931. Available with either a 498cc engine (£85) or a 650cc unit (£95), each machine was bespoke-built in the firm's Competition Department.
Jim Boulton Collection

engines from Barr & Stroud, Burney & Blackburne, J.A.P. and Villiers. At first the cycles were also called Saxessories, but by 1925 they had adopted a contracted version of their company name — 'Saxel' — for them. An amazing range of single-cylinder machines is listed for 1926 and 1927, no fewer than 24! This suggests that the firm was working to a bespoke-style production, building more-or-less to order, and that the catalogues merely list the possible variants. The cheapest Saxel had a Villiers 150cc engine and cost £26; the dearest had a Barr & Stroud 500cc unit and cost £64 10s. None was listed after 1927, and Saxelbys returned to making their Saxessories.

Scott

Scott Engineering Co
Mornington Works, Bradford, Yorkshire
Scott Engineering Co Ltd/Scott Motorcycle Co Ltd
Saltaire Road, Shipley, Yorkshire
Scott Motorcycle Co Ltd/Scott-Aerco Jig & Tools Ltd
(from 1950): 2 St Mary's Row, Birmingham 4
Scott-Aerco Jig & Tools Ltd
(from 1965): Carver St, Birmingham 1
(from 1969): 558 Bromford Lane, Birmingham 8

The Scott marque took its name from a Saltaire dyer's technician — Alfred Angus Scott — who built his first motorcycle at home in 1902. Further experimentation, allied to participation in hill climbs and other trials events, led Scott to produce an advanced two-stroke machine on which he swept the board at the Daventry Hill Climb in 1908. This success gave Scott the fillip he needed to embark upon motorcycle production, and with his cousin, Frank Phillipp, and a fellow enthusiast, Eric Myers, he established the Scott Engineering Co in premises in Bradford. There, Alfred Scott made a number of design and production advances, including the use of all-chain drive; the enclosed, sprung, front fork; the foot-change gear pedal; and the kick starter.

By 1912 the company had outgrown its Mornington Works in Bradford and moved to premises on the Saltaire Road in Shipley. That year a Scott won the Senior TT on the Isle of Man, a success repeated in 1913. The pre-World War 1 Scott was basically just one model — a chain-driven, two-speed machine using a water-cooled 322cc two-cylinder two-stroke engine. Over the years from 1911 its price rose from £57 15s to £71 10s in 1916.

During World War 1 Alfred Scott developed a shaft-driven sidecar combination for use as a mobile gun emplacement. When motorcycle production resumed in 1919, Scott sold his interest in the company and concentrated upon the production of the Scott Sociable, a permanent sidecar combination, driven from inside the sidecar. This venture was short-lived and outlasted Scott's death in 1923 by only two years.

Under new management, Scott motorcycles were developed, and in 1922 the first of a long-running series of models bearing the 'Squirrel' name was launched. The first was a 486cc dropped-handlebar sports. By the mid-1920s the company had developed a range of 10 to 12 models, all using either their own 486cc, 498cc or 596cc engines. Each was named, usually with a variant on the Squirrel theme: 'Super Squirrel', 'Flying Squirrel', 'Touring Flying Squirrel', 'De Luxe Flying Squirrel', 'Replica Flying Squirrel', etc. From 1929 Scott also made some singles, using their own design of 298cc engine. Prices ranged from around £60 to just under £100.

By 1931 the company had hit financial difficulties and receivers were appointed. They had the foresight to allow the company to continue trading. Somehow it survived — just — and they even managed to work on a machine with an advanced three-cylinder water-cooled engine, but this did not enter production and the company's continuing financial problems cast a pall over the operation at Shipley. For 1935 the model range was reduced to just one — a Flying Squirrel was available, with either a 497cc or 598cc engine. Although other more powerful models were announced, this was all the company produced in any volume until the outbreak of war.

No Scott motorcycles were manufactured during World War 2, whilst the company turned to making 'intricate mechanisms for the Services' — as their postwar literature proudly boasted when announcing that 'the thoroughbred returns' in 1946. But, at £194 10s, plus £52 10s 3d purchase tax, and an extra £5 1s 8d for a speedometer, cheap it was not, especially for a prewar design in a competitive market. As a result sales were low, and the company just managed to tickover a lot less smoothly than its product. This situation could not continue, and in 1950 the company went into voluntary liquidation.

The rights to manufacture Scotts were purchased by Matthew Holder, the owner of a jig and tool company based in Birmingham. Trading as the Scott Motorcycle Co, it took almost six years before the first of these 'new' Scotts appeared in June 1956. Thus returned the Flying Squirrel, but only on a bespoke basis. Some of the machines were also built at the company's two official service depots: Geoff Milnes at 74 Dewsbury Road, Leeds, and Murphy Motors at 54 Sutton Common Road, Sutton, Surrey. In this way the famous marque was kept alive, with the Flying Squirrel as its mainstay. Other machines were developed, especially in the early 1960s, but none of these entered production. In 1965 the base of operations was moved to Carver Street in Birmingham, and in 1969 on to Bromford Lane in the northeast of that city. Here it

finally petered out in 1978, although spares were made into the early 1980s.

Seal 'Sociable'

Haynes & Bradshaw/Seal Motors Ltd
348 Stretford Rd, Hulme, Manchester

The Seal is one vehicle that will be found in both motorcycle and motor car histories. It was a three-wheeler of the 'Sociable' type, ie a permanent motorcycle and sidecar combination, where the driver sat in the sidecar and steered with a tiller. Devised by Haynes & Bradshaw of Hulme in Manchester, the first Seals appeared in 1912. A 770cc J.A.P. twin engine was used and the ensemble sold for £78 15s. From 1914 a more powerful 964cc J.A.P. twin was used and other revisions were made, including the use of three-speed gears and a wheel rather than a tiller for the steering, all of which put the price up to £84.

When Seal production resumed after World War 1, in 1920, the company had become Seal Motors Ltd, but the Sociables were little changed. The 1920s saw three- and four-seater bodies being produced, the latter being called the 'Family', plus a delivery vehicle version — the 'Progress' which perched the driver above the motorcycle portion so as to leave the sidecar free for goods. Seals were listed throughout the 1920s, the last models being produced in 1931.

Sharratt

J. Sharratt & Sons
Carters Green, West Bromwich

Gilbert and Gordon Sharratt shared their father John's interest in motorcycles, and when they returned from the Army in 1919 they began to build their own

Below:
Gilbert and Gordon Sharratt turned their interest in motorcycles into a business when they returned from the Army in 1919. By 1923 they were offering lightweight machines using a J.A.P.-made 149cc AZA engine. *Jim Boulton Collection*

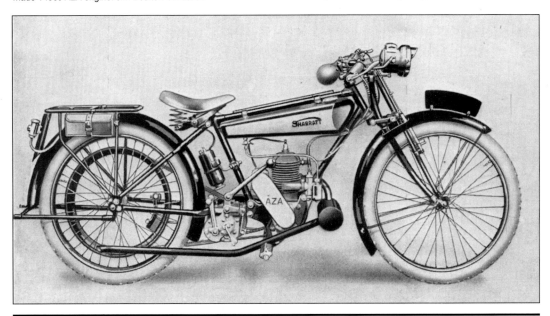

machines. A hobby had turned into a business by 1923 and was operating from their father's bicycle business in Carters Green, West Bromwich. The Sharratts were lightweight machines using either Aza or J.A.P. engines.

By 1928 the range comprised four models, the V, F, FS and FSS, and used either a Villiers 172cc engine (in the V), or a J.A.P. 346cc unit, and cost between £35 and £57. The machines were much in demand and were used in the then popular sport of motorcycle football. Only the FS and FSS were offered for 1931, but before the previous year's end the last of the Sharratts had been built, the company going into car dealership.

Silk

Silk Engineering (Derby) Ltd
Boar's Head Mill, Darley Abbey, Derby

After many years of research and development, Scott enthusiast and motor engineer George Silk embarked upon the production of his own marque. In the late 1960s, in partnership with Maurice Patey, George had formed Silk Engineering, a company that overhauled Scotts and made special motorcycle parts. The company moved into Boar's Head Mill, an old water-mill on the River Derwent at Darley Abbey, near Derby, in 1972 and from there, using a network of outworkers, they produced a score or so of Silk Scott Specials. A completely new design, the Silk 700S, entered production in 1975, but this was dogged by a few technical, and many component supply, problems.

Silk Engineering was taken over towards the end of 1976, a move that offered a sounder financial backing to the enterprise. But the production difficulties

endured and the price of the 700S soared from a launch figure of £1,355 to almost £2,500 by early 1979. Production ended that year, another example showing that technical excellence does not necessarily translate into commercial success.

Singer

Singer & Co Ltd/Singer & Co (1909) Ltd/Singer & Co Ltd
Canterbury St, Coventry 1

George Singer founded his cycle-making company in 1874. He moved to a new, purpose-built works in Canterbury Street in 1891, and from there, towards the end of the century, began to experiment with motorcycles and motor tricycles. In 1899 the company acquired the rights to a motor wheel device, patented by Messrs Perks & Birch of Coventry. This was a cycle wheel, complete with engine, fuel tank, etc, that could be used to replace the rear wheel of any bicycle or the front wheel of a tricycle. Singer manufactured and marketed this device from 1900 onwards, and it proved a great success, incorporating the company's own make of 2hp engine.

The first Singer motorcycle proper appeared in 1904, and for the next 11 years the company produced a variety of machines with both two- and four-stroke engines. Possibly the most successful model incorporated the company's 500cc single, four-stroke engine. Singer had been experimenting with cars since 1905, and when the company's motorcycle department was closed down in 1915 owing to the war, it was destined not to reopen.

Sirrah; Verus

Alfred T. Wiseman Ltd
Glover St, Birmingham 9

Wiseman's built engines, and in the early to mid-1920s combined these with proprietary parts to produce motorcycles under the brand-names Sirrah and Verus. The Sirrah used a Wiseman 292cc single-cylinder engine and was available in two versions costing £23 10s and £40. Verus models were more expensive, using Burney & Blackburne or J.A.P. 350cc singles, and selling for between £55 and £95. Neither marque was listed for 1927 or for any year thereafter.

SOS; OMC

SOS Motor Cycles Ltd
Hallow, nr Worcester
SOS Motor Cycles (1932) Ltd
S.O.S. Works, Camp Hill, Birmingham 12

Although the name SOS might inspire images of disaster, the initials stood for 'Super Onslow Special', and the preferred imagery was genteel. The brainchild of Leonard Vale-Onslow, the SOS was made in the very rural setting of Hallow, a small village just outside Worcester. First listed for 1928, that year just two SOS models were produced: the 'C', using a 247cc Villiers single and costing £43, and the 'E', which had a 343cc Villiers single and sold for £45. The following year the range had grown to five, with two Villiers-powered machines — the 'M' and 'Super K' — and three J.A.P.-powered ones — the GS1-GS3, the latter being top of the range with its 490cc engine and £58 10s price tag.

Production quickly outgrew its rural setting, and in 1932 the company was re-formed and moved to a factory in the Camp Hill area of Birmingham. No models are listed for that year, but a limited range of three was produced for 1933. Later in that year the company was taken over by the Redhill (Surrey) motor-cycle dealer Tommy Meeten, who stamped his mark upon the following year's production. All the models were given names: Speed A, Club B, Magnetic C, Club D, Superb E, Magnetic F and Superb G, and had Villiers engines from 172cc up to 346cc. Prices ranged from £39 18s up to £51 9s. SOS motorcycles remained in production until 1939.

A footnote to the SOS story is the OMC, which stood for 'Onslow Motor Cycle'. This was the brainchild of C.G. Vale-Onslow — Leonard's brother — and made at the SOS factory in Hallow in 1930. It was a lightweight machine and used a Villiers 172cc engine, selling for £35. Very few seem to have been made, and the OMC was listed only for 1930.

Sparkbrook

Sparkbrook Manufacturing Co Ltd
Paynes Lane, Coventry 1

For a firm with such a Birmingham name it is surprising to find that the Sparkbrook Manufacturing Co were actually based in Coventry. They were also one of that city's longer-established bicycle makers, beginning first in Much Park Street in 1883, quickly moving to a works on Paynes Lane. It was from there

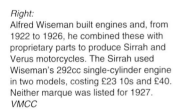

Right:
Alfred Wiseman built engines and, from 1922 to 1926, he combined these with proprietary parts to produce Sirrah and Verus motorcycles. The Sirrah used Wiseman's 292cc single-cylinder engine in two models, costing £23 10s and £40. Neither marque was listed for 1927.
VMCC

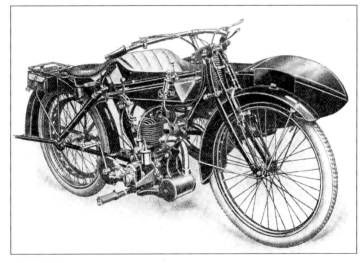

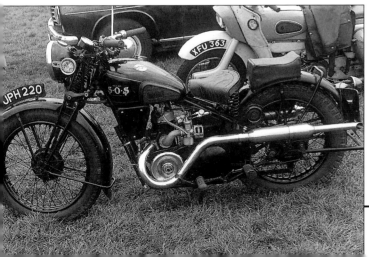

Left:
This 'So-Obviously-Superior' Super Onslow Special, or SOS, is reputedly the last to leave the company's Hallow works before the operation was moved to Birmingham. Photographed in 1970, it has a water-cooled 343cc Villiers engine and would have cost £42 when new.
Andrew Marfell/Jim Boulton Collection

Above:
In 1964, trials and scrambles rider Frank Hipkin went into
motorcycle production with business partner Fred Evans in
Oldbury. Christened the 'Sprite', their bike was Villiers-powered
until the supply of these engines was cut-off in 1968, from
when imported Sachs units were used, as in this 1971 175cc
model. Production ended in 1974. *Jim Davies*

that the company began to make motorcycles in 1912.
By 1915 their range was only two models, both using a
269cc two-stroke single-cylinder engine and with
chain-cum-belt drive. For £31 10s a fixed gear machine
could be bought, and for £37 15s a 2-speed one. Both
of these models were listed for 1916, but not thereafter.
The company had an abbreviated (sic) attempt at motor
cycle manufacture from 1921 to 1923, producing the
'Spark', which used a 247cc Villiers engine.

Sprite

Hipkin & Evans
Eel St, Oldbury

Another successful trials and scrambles rider who went
into motorcycle production was Frank Hipkin. In the
usual way, Hipkin made machines for his own use, and
was then asked to make them for others. As a result, in
1964, with business partner Fred Evans, the bikes were
put into production.

Premises were taken in Eel Street, Oldbury. The bike
was christened the 'Sprite' and was powered by a
Villiers engine. It was sold either as a complete
machine or in kit form, the latter proving very popular
with people wishing to avoid purchase tax, and as an
export item. Problems were encountered with the
supply of Villiers engines in 1968, so Hipkin and Evans
imported what they needed. The cancellation of a large
export order in 1974 forced the end of motorcycle
production, but the company survived and diversified
into other areas.

Star-Griffon

Star Cycle Co Ltd
Pountney St, Wolverhampton

Edward Lisle, a Wolverhampton tinsmith, built a
velocipede at his house in Franchise Street in the late
1860s. He also competed successfully in cycle races,
and fellow competitors ordered machines from him. By
1869 Lisle was listed as a cycle maker, but this venture
founded. Lisle's son, also Edward, later built a cycle in
the family cellar and, in partnership with a Mr Sharratt,
entered manufacture from 1876 at the Star Works in
Pountney Street. When Lisle later took the company
over, he renamed it 'Star' after the works and cycles.
Registered on 16 December 1896, the Star Cycle Co
made motor cars from 1898, but quickly hived their
production off to a subsidiary — the Star Motor Co —
and in 1899 introduced motorised tricycles and forecars.

With the declining cycle trade, a range of Star and
Star-Griffon motorcycles was introduced in 1903.
Griffon was a French marque, upon which this £42 2hp
machine have been based. The introduction of a low
priced car — the Starling — halted motorcycle production in 1905, but this resumed in 1911, when two

models were made using 4.5hp and 6hp engines. The latter, a three-speed twin, was expensive at £68 5s, and both machines were offered for only a season. Motorcycle production finally ended in 1915 and Star, taken over by Guy Motors in 1929, went into receivership in March 1932, when the marque died.

Stevens

Stevens & Bowden Ltd
Retreat St, Wolverhampton

Following the sale of AJS to AMC in 1931, the Stevens brothers remained interested in producing motor vehicles. The terms of the sale had left their former factory in Retreat Street in their possession, together with some machine tools, jigs and patterns. For their first venture under their family name the Stevens chose a three-wheeled delivery van, with a single front wheel, that incorporated much motorcycle technology including an over-square 588cc own-make engine. The vans could carry a 5cwt payload and cost £79 5s.

Stevens motorcycles proper appeared in March 1934. They were produced with either a 250cc, 350cc or 500cc Stevens engine, and all had four-speed gearboxes, with a choice of foot or hand control for the gear change and prices from £50. New models were introduced for 1935, 1936 and 1937, including a competition machine, and many thought the company's proud boast that a Stevens motorcycle was: 'The Most Refined Sports Machine in The World' to be well justified.

Stevens & Bowden were also general engineers, and production levels of both the delivery vans and motorcycles were modest, as befitted the size of the company and its works. The firm also had other work, which was escalating with the run-up to the war, and so to make room for this, vehicle production came to an end in 1938.

Sun

The Sun Cycle & Fittings Co Ltd
Phoenix Works, Aston Brook St, Birmingham 6
Raleigh Industries Ltd
177 Lenton Boulevard, Nottingham

Sun's entry into motorcycle production followed a familiar course. Established in 1885 by the Parkes family as a producer of bicycles and cycle fittings, the company made its first motorcycle in 1912. Like all of their pre-World War 1 models, this was based around a 269cc single-cylinder two-stroke engine. Production continued until 1916, when war-related work took over. These last models comprised a fixed-gear, belt-driven machine for £28, and a two-speed, chain-driven one for £34.

When production resumed after World War 1, it was with proprietary engines supplied by Aza, Burney & Blackburne, J.A.P. and Villiers. The 1929 product range, for example, comprised nine models, three of which were powered by Villiers 172cc engines, another using a Villiers 247cc unit, all priced between £25 4s and £34 10s. All five of the remaining machines were J.A.P.-powered, three having 350cc engines and two a 500cc one, being priced between £36 5s and £56 10s.

The company changed tack with its 1931 models, moving towards smaller engines, in the 98cc to 350cc

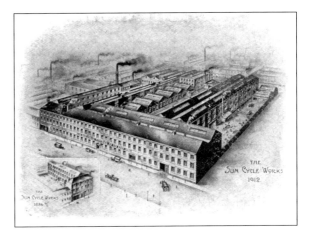

1½-h.p. SUN-VILLIERS
Model De Luxe.
Very Strong Carrier for occasional passenger.

range, in less expensive machines, costing from £25 to £49. This was a prudent reading of the market and the times, something that many other motorcycle manufacturers failed to do. From 1933 onwards the product range was reduced further by dropping the 350cc machine, leaving just four models powered by Villiers 98cc, 147cc, 148cc and 196cc engines, costing between £16 16s and £25 10s.

Production of Sun motorcycles was suspended from 1935 to 1940, the company continuing to produce components and fittings. The return was with an autocycle, powered by a Villiers 98cc engine, but the manufacture of this was soon suspended due to the war. It returned to production in 1946 and was joined by a more conventional motorcycle in 1948. The autocycle was dropped for 1951, and the motorcycle range was developed and refined throughout the decade.

Sun always responded to the market, and so they too made a scooter — the Geni — introduced in 1957. Unlike many other 'British' scooters, this does not seem to have been produced in conjunction with a foreign firm. A 99cc Villiers engine was used and the design was a curious motorcycle hybrid that retained spoked wheels and lacked the flat floorpan so characteristic of Italian derived machines. Moderately successful, production of the Geni continued past the end of Sun motorcycle production in 1959 and on until

1961. That year marked the retirement of Fred Parkes, who had run the firm for almost 50 years. Raleigh bought the rights to the Sun bicycle, but the company's motorcycle marque retired with Mr Parkes.

Sunbeam

John Marston Ltd/Sunbeam Cycles Ltd
'Sunbeamland', Paul St, Wolverhampton
Associated Motor Cycles Ltd
44-45 Plumstead Rd, Woolwich, London SE18
Sunbeam Motorcycle Division of BSA Motorcycles Ltd
48 Armoury Rd, Small Heath, Birmingham 11

Wolverhampton tin plate and Japanware maker John Marston was short in the leg, and he began to make bicycles only after an employee built one especially adapted for him in 1886. Upon seeing the finished bicycle, Marston's wife remarked upon how well the black and gold finish on the machine reflected the sun, which led to the name 'Sunbeam' being registered as a trade mark. Bicycle production began in 1887.

Many bicycle producers tried their hand at making motorcycles, and Marston was no exception. Launched in 1912, the Sunbeam motorcycle was a 350cc 2.75hp two-speed machine, with a dark green fuel tank bearing a silver panel. Carried over from the company's bicycles was their patent 'Little Oil Bath' chain and gear case, introduced in 1892. Flagged as 'The Gentleman's Motor Bicycle', the 'Sunbeam' sold for £63.

For 1913 the machine's finish was changed to black lined in gold leaf, and a twin, powered during its production life by Abingdon (AKD), J.A.P. and Swiss M.A.G. engines, was introduced. The quality and finish of the machines was extraordinarily high — as was their price. In 1915 a 550cc Sunbeam three-speed single cost £73 10s, and a 992cc twin £94 10s!

Quickly into racing, the Sunbeam team enjoyed great successes; their riders included Howard Davies, who, after World War 1, would make the HRD motorcycle. Domestic motorcycle production ceased in 1916 and the company turned to war work, which included making motorcycles for the Armed Forces, including the Russian Army, as did James and Norton.

Before the war ended, the Marston family suffered the triple blow in 1918 of the death, in February, of Roland Marston, John's third son, of John Marston himself in March, followed almost immediately by his widow, who had christened the company's products 32 years earlier. Charles Marston, the founder's eldest son, became Chairman, but was heavily involved with Villiers Ltd and sold his shares to Explosive Trades Ltd who would soon become Nobel Industries, and, in 1928, ICI.

Very much behind the scenes, these changes did not affect the production of Sunbeam motorcycles directly, at least not immediately. Two new models were launched in 1919 — a 3.5hp single and an 8hp twin — at £99 15s and £120 15s respectively. The company also launched itself back into racing, winning the 1920 and 1922 Isle of Man Senior TT races.

From the mid-1920s through to the early 1930s Sunbeam made a succession of sturdy singles, using engines from 246cc to 600cc, with prices from £72 9s to £110. Sunbeam's prices had begun to fall, but had started so high, and thus continued to fall into the

1930s. Under ICI control from 1928, new models were introduced, the first being 1931's 'Lion', a 492cc single, selling for £65 — it was also the first named model. More Lions appeared in 1932, followed by a 'Little 90', on a 246cc machine costing £56 10s.

Isolated manufacturers within the portfolio of large companies are always vulnerable to corporate whims, and in 1937 ICI sold Sunbeam motorcycles to Associated Motor Cycles Ltd, who already owned the ex-Wolverhampton marque AJS. Production was transferred to the giant AMC plant at Woolwich, where it continued until just after the war began. In 1943, AMC sold the concern on to BSA, where it became the Sunbeam Motorcycle Division of BSA Motorcycles Ltd. Under this brand-name BSA produced two remarkable machines: the S7 and S8. Both powered by 500cc overhead cam in-line twin-cylinder engines, the S7 boasted a 'liquid-smooth' engine and transmission, selling for £264, whilst the S8 was 'quicker' and 'more eager', aimed at the rider who 'desires an appreciable gain in performance but in return is ready to sacrifice a fractional degree of comfort' — it was a bit lighter — and sold for £240.

At the heart of both machines was sound engineering, including a chain-driven overhead camshaft, shaft drive, a worm reduction gear 'of robust proportions' and a four-speed gearbox, with single plate dry clutch, housed in a single unit with the engine. Despite having produced 'The Immaculate Motorcycle' under the Sunbeam name, BSA had its own models to make, and so the former Wolverhampton marque, an almost perpetual 'bridesmaid' since 1919, was dropped in 1957. Sad as this loss was, it should have been the end, but late in 1959 BSA launched two scooters bearing the Sunbeam name. Powered by either a 172cc two-stroke single or a 249cc four-stroke twin, the machines were produced until 1964, marking the end of the Sunbeam motorcycle.

Above left:
The Sun-Villiers Model De Luxe lightweight of 1929 had a Villiers 147cc two-stroke engine and a two-speed gearbox. It included a full toolbox, with 'Tecalemit' grease gun, all for £23.
Jim Boulton Collection

Right:
Sunbeam began to make motorcycles in 1912, and the following year introduced a new black finish, lined in gold leaf. In this photograph, an immaculately kited-out Baruch Beckley, a Brierley Hill Sunbeam Agent, shows obvious pride in his pre-World War 1 Sunbeam sidecar combination.
Graham Beckley/Jim Boulton Collection

Left:
Sunbeam motorcycles enjoyed great success in races all over the world. Here, works rider Arthur 'Digger' Simcock is pictured after winning the 1929 Austrian Six Hours Grand Prix.
IMI Marston/Jim Boulton Collection

Right:
Whilst Sunbeam participated less-and-less in road racing from 1934, the company maintained an active trials team. One member of this was Frank Williams, seen here on a modified machine with a raised exhaust.
IMI Marston/Jim Boulton Collection

Left:
One of the first AMC Sunbeams was the 598cc B28 of 1939, seen here in modified form on a 1969 tour of Birmingham.
Andrew Marfell/Jim Boulton Collection

Above right:
Under BSA ownership from 1943, a number of striking machines were produced by the Sunbeam Motor Cycle Division of BSA Motor Cycles Ltd. This £240 500cc Model S8 twin of 1955 was 'planned for the motorcyclist who desires an appreciable gain in performance but in return is ready to sacrifice a fractional degree of comfort'. Two years later BSA dropped the former Wolverhampton marque on motorcycles.
Jim Boulton Collection

Swallow

Swallow Coachbuilding Co (1935) Ltd
Walsall Aerodrome, Aldridge Road, Walsall

Swallow Coachbuilding was formed in Blackpool in 1922 by William Lyons and William Walmsley to produce motorcycle sidecars. The firm expanded into producing specialist motor car bodies, a move that would eventually lead to them becoming full-blown car manufacturers following a move to Coventry in 1928. By 1934 the balance of the firm's production had swung in favour of cars, and so the original company was split into two: cars being the province of S.S. Cars Ltd (an abbreviation of Swallow Sidecars), the original business continuing under the style of the Swallow Coachbuilding Co (1935) Ltd.

When car production resumed after World War 2, William Lyons made two important decisions. The first was that, in the light of recent events, any car called the S.S. was unlikely to be very popular, and so the company's name was changed to Jaguar Cars Ltd. Lyons's second decision was that, despite his obvious affection for the sidecar business, it was no longer a major part of his commercial operation, and so it was put up for sale. The buyer was Helliwells Ltd, a motor components firm (founded in Dudley in 1899 as a producer of fenders and fire-irons) which had factories on the Treforest Industrial Estate, near Caerphilly in South Wales, and at Walsall Aerodrome.

Seeking products for their new acquisition, Helliwells pre-empted the British scooter craze of the 1950s by introducing its 'Swallow Gadabout' in 1946. First produced in the company's Treforest works, the Gadabout was of conventional scooter design, powered by a 122cc Villiers two-stroke engine, with a three-speed gearbox, operated by a foot change, and a top speed of a little over 30mph — all for £99. Production was soon transferred to Walsall, where the line was developed. First came a £115 light delivery version, with — naturally enough — a sidecar that could carry up to 2cwt, followed, in 1951, by a Mark II version of the Gadabout — the Major — with a more powerful 197cc Villiers engine and a £126 15s 3d price tag.

Promoted by the company under the slogan: 'The Daily Round … The Common Task … Is Made Easier With The Famous Swallow Gadabout', sales began to suffer in the face of the more stylish imported Italian Lambretta and Vespa scooters, and so production of the Gadabout ended late in 1951.

Swift

The Swift Cycle Co
15 Cheylesmore & Quinton Works, Coventry 1

The Swift brand-name first appeared in 1865 when the Coventry Sewing Machine Co launched into bicycle manufacture through the initiative of Joseph Turner. Arguably Britain's oldest cycle manufacturer — their first machines appearing almost a year before the first Humbers — Swifts introduced a motor tricycle in 1898 and a voiturette the following year. They also produced their first motorcycle in 1898, and these would feature as part of their production until World War 1.

By 1902 the car-making side of Swift's business had grown to such an extent that the manufacture of the two products was made the province of two separate companies: The Swift Cycle Co (bicycles, motorcycles, motor tricycles) and The Swift Motor Co (motor cars), although later this clarity would become foggy when the Cycle Co also produced a cyclecar. Motorcycles were never a principal product for Swift, and their production had ceased well before World War 1.

Above:
The Cornish-made Teagle clip-on device was introduced in 1952. It used a 50cc two-stroke engine, crankcase and fuel tank assembly, that was mounted directly over a bicycle's rear wheel, as shown. Transmission was by a friction roller directly on the rear tyre. The device cost £18 12s 11d and production began in 1954, continuing until 1956. *Jim Boulton Collection*

Tandon

Tandon Motors Ltd/Indian Commerce & Industries Ltd
29 Ludgate Hill, London EC4
Tandon Motors Ltd
Colne Way, By-Pass Rd, Watford, Hertfordshire

The postwar demand for virtually any form of motorised transport spawned a number of marques formed especially to exploit it. One such was the Tandon, the brainchild of Devadutt Tandon, who was born in India and had formed the chain of photographic shops that still carries his name to this day.

The Tandon Special wasn't particularly special, rather utilitarian in fact, and used a Villiers 122cc engine mounted in a rather angular tubular frame. It had been designed with export sales in mind, to be shipped to India in CKD (Completely-Knocked-Down) kit form ready for assembly using unskilled labour with simple tools. These were produced at premises in Bushey Hall Road, Watford. Sales were poor, and motorcycle testers and reviewers had a field day trying to top each other with adjectives and phrases to sum up the sheer awfulness of its build, quality and performance.

The export orders had failed to materialise either, but, undaunted, Tandon moved his operation to Colne Way, on the Watford By-Pass, and began the development of improved models with a more conventional motorcycle appearance. New models, and refinements thereof, continued until 1955 when the company, which had always led a somewhat precarious financial existence, narrowly escaped receivership. Tandon battled on and sold the company to another of his interests — the Indian Commerce & Industries Ltd — and somehow managed to remain in motorcycle production until 1959.

Teagle

W. T. Teagle (Machinery) Ltd
Blackwater, Truro, Cornwall

In the early 1950s, the cheapest way for cyclists to become motorcyclists was to buy a clip-on device for their current bicycle. One such was the Teagle, produced by a company of machinery makers in Blackwater, near Truro in Cornwall. Introduced in 1952, the Teagle used a 50cc two-stroke engine, crankcase and fuel tank assembly that was mounted directly over a bicycle's rear wheel. Production began in 1954 and continued until 1956, by which time a range of reliable mopeds was available to lure cyclists away from pedal power.

Three Spires

Coventry Bicycles Ltd
Osborne Rd Works, Osborne Rd, Coventry

Coventry Bicycles Ltd were comparative latecomers to that city's cycle roster of manufacturers. Established in 1921, the company led a peripatetic existence during that decade, having works in Priory Street, at 85-6 Gosford Street, and in Wellington Street, before settling in Osborne Road. The company branded itself after Coventry's famous landmark, the three spires of its city centre churches that were so visible from quite a distance.

Three Spires motorcycles were introduced in 1932. They were lightweight machines powered by a single-cylinder 147cc Villiers engine. Two models were produced: the Three Spires Standard, selling for £18 18s, and the Three Spires, with lighting set and leg shields, available for £21. For whatever reason, these bikes did not sell well, and their production was discontinued.

Toreador

Toreador Engineering Co
Ribble Bank Mills, Preston, Lancashire
Bow Lane, Preston, Lancashire

An obscure marque, the Toreador was the product of the appropriately-named Toreador Engineering Co, who were based in Ribble Bank Mills in Preston. Listed for only the 1927 and 1928 seasons, the first Toreadors were powered by a Burney & Blackburne 349cc single-cylinder engine and available as either a standard or Super Sports model, for £57 or £66. For 1928 the range was revised and expanded to feature five models, all using J.A.P. engines of between 344cc and 498cc. This produced a range varying in price from £58 to £97, which should have pleased most pockets, but didn't, and no more was heard of the Toreador.

Triumph

Triumph Cycle Co/Triumph Cycle Co Ltd
Gloria Works, Earl's Court, Much Park St/Priory St, Coventry
Triumph Engineering Co Ltd
Meriden Works, Allesley, Coventry
Triumph Motorcycles (Meriden) Ltd
Meriden Works, Allesley, Coventry
Triumph Motorcycles Ltd
Jacknell Rd, Dodwells Gridge
Industrial Estate, Hinckley, Leicestershire

The marque that is now the standard-bearer of the British motorcycle industry began life as a company founded by two Germans. Siegfried Bettmann came to

Britain in 1884, when he was just 21. Based in London, Bettmann became the agent for a number of companies, and in 1885 he began to export bicycles. These were made in Birmingham and sold under the 'Triumph' name. Wanting complete control of this operation, Bettmann and his new business partner, the engineer Mauritz Schulte, set up their own factory — Gloria Works — in 1887, occupying a court, shared with a ribbon factory, off Much Park Street in Coventry. A private company was also established to produce bicycles, using the name Bettmann had coined for his machines: The Triumph Cycle Co.

Business went well, especially after a massive cash injection by financier and industrialist Harvey DuCros. In May 1896 the partners invested in a redundant, seven-storey silk-spinning mill in Coventry's Priory Street, close by the cathedral. Expansion began immediately, and a timber yard run by Messrs Booth & Earle was bought and flattened to double the size of the works. Later in 1896, more land adjoining the factory was acquired and further extensions were built, until the complex also included most of Dale Street too.

Formed into a public company in 1897, the New Triumph Cycle Co Ltd made Mauritz Schulte its chief engineer. He had imported a German Hildebrand & Wolfmüller-powered bicycle in 1895 and began to experiment with producing motorcycles by 1898. A cautious and painstaking person, Schulte searched for a suitable engine. In 1901, after much research, he lighted upon a 2hp unit produced by the newly formed Minerva company of Anvers in Belgium. Fitted to the front down tube of a reinforced Triumph bicycle, the Minerva engine powered the company's first motorcycle — a single-speed, belt-driven model — produced in the Much Park Street works in 1902. More research followed, and both German Fafnir and British J.A.P. engines were tried until Schulte decided to produce his own.

Tests had shown that 3hp engines, mounted vertically in the middle of the frame, gave the best results. The first Triumph-built engines appeared in 1905, but

Right:
The vast expanse of the Triumph works in Coventry, from the company's 1922 catalogue. *Jim Boulton Collection*

Left:
An excellent study of a pre-World War 1 Triumph motorcycle, with its proud, pipe-smoking rider, who has such confidence in the reliability of the machine that he's still wearing his slippers!
R.M. Forder/Jim Boulton Collection

Schulte was still not satisfied, especially with the performance of the valves and piston rings. Higher quality materials were sought and tested until, in 1907, Schulte produced a 550cc 3.5hp engine that he was satisfied with. In the first ever Isle of Man TT, held that year, Triumph motorcycles using this engine came second and third in the single-cylinder class, and in 1908 they won it. Motorcycle production had been transferred to the Priory Street works in 1907, and a number of developments, including those with carburettors and magneto ignition, followed. These were all fitted to production machines — as was a three-speed gearbox — all of Schulte's design.

By 1914 Triumph were producing engines in three sizes, 225cc (2.25hp), 499cc (3.5hp) and 550cc (4hp), fitted to machines with fixed, single-speed, two- or three-speed gears, and belt or chain-cum-belt drive. The finish was grey and prices ranged from £42 for a 225cc machine to £63 for a three-speed 550cc one. Production was maintained during World War 1 as the company supplied a staggering 30,000 of the latter machines to the British Army for use by dispatch riders. Schulte kept up his research work during the war, and in 1920, a year after domestic production resumed, launched the first chain-driven Triumph. This was to be Schulte's swan-song for the company, upon his retirement.

The early postwar models are typified by the 1922 range, which still used the prewar engines. Four machines were offered: the 499cc/3.5hp Type R (£120), the 550cc/4hp Type SD (£115), the 550cc/4hp Type H (£105) and the 225cc/2.25hp Type LW (£65). That same year the company began racing again.

A move into car production was also planned in the early 1920s. The company took over the failed Dawson Car Co Ltd in 1921. They had used a works in Priory Street and it was from there that Triumph produced its

first motor car in 1923. This set the company upon a divided course with regard to its manufactures, one that would ultimately lead to its downfall. None of this was readily apparent in the 1920s, and the company's motorcycles continued to be developed and refined. Over the decade they began to loose their 'motorised bicycle' appearance and to take on a more low-slung, streamlined look. Their colour changed too, from the uniform and somewhat drab grey, to green and then black, with blue panels. New engines were developed, like the 'P' of 1925, a 494cc unit fitted to a motorcycle that sold for just £42 17s 6d.

Like most other motorcycle manufacturers, Triumph cut costs throughout the late 1920s/early 1930s. In 1926 the most expensive Triumph was the 499cc 'R' at £68; by 1932 it was the 493.2cc CD at £48 17s 6d. That year the company also introduced an economy model — the 'Gloria' — which used a 98cc Villiers engine, later available with a 147cc Villiers unit. But the company's main problems were internal. They were stretched three ways, trying to produce bicycles, motorcycles and cars and were heading for disaster. Bicycle production was the first to go, eventually being sold to Raleigh, which continued to make them in Coventry until 1954. Motorcycles were next, being bought by John Young 'Jack' Sangster, the son of the chairman of Ariel — Charles Sangster — for £28,000 in mid-1936. (The car-making side of the company passed to Standard in 1939.)

Re-formed as the Triumph Engineering Co Ltd, Jack Sangster appointed his chief designer at Ariel — Edward Turner — as General Manager and Chief Designer. Already at Triumph was another ex-Ariel designer, Val Page (formerly of J.A.P.), who had joined the Coventry firm in 1932, and Albert Camwell, who was one of the ablest of production engineers in the motorcycle industry. The runes were well cast. One of the first products of the new management was the 1936 'Tiger' range of single-cylinder models: the 250cc Tiger 70 (£46), the 350cc Tiger 80 (£56) and the 500cc Tiger 90 (£66), with their accompanying new appearance dominated by chromium plate on the tank and wheels. Augmenting these models in 1937 was the Speed Twin, which introduced a 500cc vertical twin-cylindered engine, still being used by the company in the 1970s.

The outbreak of World War 2 dealt a double blow to the newly re-formed company. They had given the Priory Street factory over to war production, making motorcycles for military use, only to lose it entirely in the devastating blitz that destroyed so much of the city on 14 November 1940. A temporary home was found at The Cape, in Warwick, an area later to find fame as the home of Donald Healey's sports cars. Given that the company had been engaged upon important war work, the Government looked favourably upon their plight and assisted with the erection of a new factory, five miles southwest of Coventry on a 22-acre site in Meriden. This was ready for occupation by July 1942.

After the war, Edward Turner embarked upon a policy of building only twin-cylinder motorcycles. This fostered an export trade, much to the delight of the Government, who had embarked upon their 'Export-or-Die' campaign. Racing resumed also, and the company enjoyed great successes, especially at Daytona in the USA. By this time Jack Sangster had become very wealthy, and in a move to defray death duties he sold the Triumph Engineering Co Ltd to BSA on 15 March

Left:
Triumph maintained its production during World War 1 when the company supplied a staggering 30,000 motorcycles to the British Army for use by despatch riders. Here are three members of the Signal Troop, 3rd South Midland Mounted Brigade, pictured on their Triumphs. *Jim Boulton Collection*

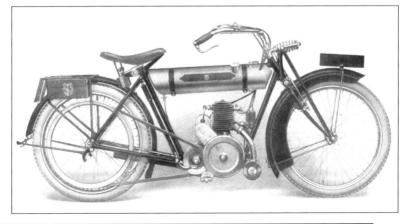

Right:
Bottom of Triumph's 1922 model range was this £65 Type LW, with a 225cc two-stroke single-cylinder engine. The finish was 'Black enamel on Coslettised frame; all bright parts heavily plated. Tank, enamelled grey, green panels, lined red'. *Jim Boulton Collection*

1951 for £2,448,000 — not bad for a £28,000 investment 15 years earlier! Despite these changes, the company carried on much as before. The range for 1952, announced on 1 November 1951, included some familiar models: the Speed Twin, Tiger 100 (introduced in 1939), the 650cc Thunderbird and the 498cc Trophy.

The company's production history is long and too complex to detail here. But two models are truly worthy of mention: the Bonneville and the Trident. Named after the Utah salt flats famous for being the scene of land speed trials, the Bonneville was launched at the 1958 Motorcycle Show. It used a 650cc vertical-cylinder engine. The Trident, or T150/T160, was announced in 1968 and produced from 1969 onwards. It had a 750cc three-cylinder engine, upon which development work had begun in 1964. In complete contrast was Triumph's March 1962 attempt to enter the already dying scooter market with the 'Tina', which had a 99.75cc two-stroke engine and fully automatic transmission. The Tina was plagued with transmission problems, ironed out in its replacement — the T10 of 1965 — which remained in production until 1969.

From the early 1970s onwards, Triumph motorcycles began to make more headlines on the business and political pages of most newspapers than in the sports section. The by then BSA Group sold the company to Norton-Villiers, to form Norton-Villiers-Triumph Ltd, on 17 July 1973, and within two months the Chairman, Dennis Poore, announced that Meriden would close and that production would be concentrated at the former BSA plant at Small Heath. Unfortunately for Poore, the workforce at Meriden would have none of this, and he set in train one of the longest and most bitter industrial disputes ever seen in Britain. This brought an ailing British industry first to its knees and then to near extinction.

For 10 years a workers' co-operative kept Triumph in production, consuming lots of Government subsidy and private capital; but bankruptcy came on 26 August 1983. Leicestershire businessman John Bloor bought the assets, selling spares to keep trading. Forming a new company in 1984, work on a new 10-acre factory site on a Hinckley industrial estate began in 1988. Pre-production started in 1990, and in February 1991 the four-cylinder 1200 Trophy model was produced. Further models were developed, and a worldwide distributor network formed; April 1996 saw the 40,000th Hinckley-made machine. A 12-model range has been developed, from the £6,449 Trident 750 Roadster, to the £9,999 Daytona T595.

Trobike
Trojan Ltd
Richmond Rd, Croydon, Surrey

Trojan was formed in 1913 to produce a distinctly unusual design of motor car by Leslie Hounsfield. World War 1 delayed production of the Trojan until 1922, when it was established in Kingston upon Thames; it moved to Croydon in 1928. Trojan cars were produced until 1935, by which time the company had been taken over by Leyland Motors, the Lancashire commercial vehicle firm.

The Trobike's only connections to this history are that it was made in the firm's Croydon factory and that, like its four-wheeled predecessor, it was very unusual. Classed as a mini-bike, the Trobike ran on 5in wheels, had an open tubular frame and used a 94cc two-stroke engine. Sold complete or in kit form, the Trobike had originally been intended for use at airports or in large industrial complexes where people needed to nip about from location to location quickly. Out on the road, with its top speed of 30mph, it was a bit lost. Produced from the late 1950s and on into the early 1960s, the Trobike shared one feature with Trojan cars — it had solid wheels. Alongside the Trobike, Trojan also assembled Lambretta scooters and, from 1961, made the Trojan 200, a British version of the German Heinkel 'bubblecar'.

Trump

Liphook Motor Engineering Works
Weybridge, Surrey
Trump Motors Ltd
Foxlake Works, Byfleet, Surrey
Trump Motors Ltd
36 John Bright St, Birmingham 1

Trump motorcycles were the creation of Angus Maitland and his cousin Frank McNab, both race enthusiasts. Their machines were designed mainly for racing and were all based around J.A.P. engines, including 250cc and 500cc singles and 1,000cc twins, mounted into lightweight frames. Trump machines enjoyed considerable road race success. Angus Maitland left the partnership in 1911 to form his own business. Production of Trumps was suspended during the latter part of World War 1 and when it resumed this was in Birmingham, where it continued until 1923.

Turner 'By-Van'

Light Delivery Vehicles Ltd
Lever St, Wolverhampton

Turners have been involved in engineering in Wolverhampton since the late 19th century, and in motor vehicle production since at least 1902. After World War 2 the company produced a farm tractor and then turned its attention to a curious design of two- and three-wheeled delivery vans. A subsidiary company — Light Delivery Vehicles Ltd — was set up to produce these machines, occupying part of Turner's Lever Street works in Wolverhampton.

The two-wheeled 'By-Van' had a large steel container that occupied the space usually taken up by the fuel tank and engine. This held 5.6cu ft, or 1.5cwt, and was accessed by means of a large lid, on top of which was the rider's seat. Power came from a Turner 'Tiger' 147cc single-cylinder two-stroke engine, mounted directly above the front wheel, the fuel tank being mounted on top of the handlebars. The By-Van came in a choice of four colours and sold for £120. Its larger brother was called the Tri-Van. The mechanics were the same, but behind these was a large 23cu ft, or 3cwt, steel box mounted between a pair of wheels; the vehicle selling for £150.

Launched at a motor show in Brussels in April 1946, no one was too sure what to make of the By- and Tri-Vans, and expressed their caution by not buying them, both vehicles quietly slipping into obscurity.

Tyler

Tyler Apparatus Co Ltd
11 Charing Cross Rd, London WC

The Tyler was a brief diversion by an established London firm of apparatus makers. Listed only for 1915 and 1916, just two models were produced, both using a 269cc single-cylinder engine. One was belt-driven, and had a fixed-speed gear, costing £27; the other had a two-speed gearbox and chain-cum-belt drive, selling for £33 15s.

Above:
In 1922 Vauxhall Motors developed the first four-cylinder shaft-driven motorcycle in Britain, but the project was quashed due to the high price such a technically advanced machine would have commanded. This lovingly-restored example shows what might have been. *Vauxhall Motors Ltd/Jim Boulton Collection*

Vauxhall

Vauxhall Motors Ltd
Kimpton Rd, Luton, Bedfordshire

Knowledge that Vauxhall Motors contemplated the production of a motorcycle came through the efforts of motorcycle enthusiast Robert Thomas, who, in the early 1950s, obtained substantive parts of the one surviving example, and over the next 20 years he painstakingly reconstructed it.

The story goes back to 1922, the year in which Vauxhall put into production their first small car, and these events are possibly not unrelated to the development of what was the first four-cylinder shaft-driven motorcycle in Britain. If Robert Thomas's machine is anything to go by, the Vauxhall would have been an excellent motorcycle. It seems probable that the project was quashed owing to the high price such a technically advanced machine would have commanded. Only two were completed, with additional frames and engines, both being sold off cheaply to Vauxhall employees.

Velocette; VMC; Veloce

Veloce Ltd
Fleet St, Summer Row, Birmingham 3
Victoria Rd, Aston, Birmingham 6
York Rd, Hall Green, Birmingham 28

The Velocette managed the rare distinction of being designed and manufactured by the same family-owned and run business throughout the 67 years of its existence. Founded in 1904 by Johann Goodman, Veloce Ltd had a works in Fleet Street, to the northwest of Birmingham city centre. Their early models were lightweight machines, marketed under the VMC name (for Veloce Motor Cycles) and later under the firm's name: Veloce — all using the company's own engines.

As production escalated they moved to a works in Victoria Road, Aston. From about 1912, all the company's machines were sold under the Velocette marque, one of the first to bear this name being a 221cc two-stroke with an automatic lubrication system, two-speed gearbox and all-chain drive.

Production continued until 1916 before the firm's productive capacity was put to war-related work. When motorcycle production resumed in 1919, Veloce produced a range of machines powered by two-stroke engines. They also embarked upon a very active racing programme, developing a series of sports two-strokes capable of speeds in excess of 70mph. Steady progress was made in the Isle of Man Junior TT races in the early 1920s, especially after Percy Goodman's development of the 350cc overhead camshaft 'K' series engine during 1924/5.

Exhibited at the 1924 Motor Cycle Show at Olympia, the motorcycle that this new engine went into caused quite a stir. In addition to the new engine, it also featured a positive foot-change gear pedal, developed by Harold Willis, which enabled riders to change gear without taking a hand off the handlebar. This would become a standard feature on most motorcycles. The first models went on sale in June 1925, and later that year, to cope with the demand for the machines, Veloce moved to a works in York Road, Hall Green, Birmingham, recently vacated by Humphries & Dawes, makers of the OK motorcycle, upon their move to Bramley Road, Acock's Green.

The 1920s also saw another first for Veloce. They were the first company to sell 'works' racing-style machines to the public, a move that came about following the success of the KTT model in winning the 1926 Isle of Man Junior TT. A road-going KTT was offered in 1928.

Each year saw a range of five or six models, using the company's own engines, of either 249cc or 348cc. In 1926 the range cost from £38 for the 'AC' to £75 for the 'KSS', but the above-mentioned KTT became top of the range upon its launch, costing £80. Established models continued on into the 1930s, to be joined by new ones. In June 1933 the £46 10s 'MOV' was introduced, a high-revving 248cc machine that proved popular with enthusiasts owing to its capacity for being tuned. This was followed by an enduring model — the 'MAC' — which used a 348cc engine modified from the MOV unit and sold for £49 10s.

A revised KTT was launched in 1935, featuring a modified engine mounted in a new cradle frame, and continued in production until 1937; it returned, further modified, in May 1938.

Veloce announced a model range for 1940, but these were not produced in quantity because the works was switched to war production. When domestic production resumed for 1946, the prewar range continued more or less unaltered for two years. Breaking the mould was the 'Little Engine' LE of 1948, whose introduction was marked by innovatory design. This featured a compact

engine and gearbox unit, the former being a 149cc water-cooled, horizontally opposed, four-stroke twin, set across a cradle frame. Complementing this was a hand start, a car-like gearbox and change lever, and a shaft final-drive, all of the mechanics being completely enclosed by pressed-steel shields. Quickly upgraded to a 192cc engine, the LE was adopted by many police forces in Britain and abroad.

Accompanying the LE through the 1950s and 1960s was a continuation of Veloce's more conventional designs. The MAC, a design of 1934, was revised, the 349cc engine receiving a new alloy cylinder head to give 'totally enclosed valve gear including valve stems', as the brochure stated. By 1956 Veloce had put together an impressive range of eight models: the 'Silent' LE, MAC, MSS, a 350 and a 500 Scrambler, a street version of the 500 Scrambler, called the 'Endurance', plus two new machines: the 349cc Viper and the 499cc Venom. In 1957 this range was expanded further to include the Valiant, which used a modified air-cooled version of the LE's engine, and in 1959 Veloce announced the Valiant Vee-Line which had a new: 'fibreglass streamlined fairing that puts it right in the forefront of modern motorcycle design (and) gives excellent weather protection to the rider'.

Right:
When Veloce motorcycle production resumed in 1919, the company produced a range of machines powered by two-stroke engines and also embarked upon an active racing programme, developing a series of sports two-strokes capable of speeds in excess of 70mph. This is Team Rider S. Jones, who came third in the 1922 Lightweight TT race.
Jim Boulton Collection

Below:
In 1925 Veloce Ltd moved into the recently vacated works of Humphries & Dawes, makers of the OK motorcycle, in York Road, Hall Green, Birmingham. This view shows Velocettes in production at the works. Note the table trestles and the small amount of line shafting, showing that motorcycle assembly was still largely a hand-powered business. *VMCC*

Feeling unable to ignore the scooter craze, Veloce decided to join it, late, in 1961. They produced the Viceroy, derived from LE mechanicals, but using a 247cc two-stroke twin-cylinder engine. This was enclosed in a rather heavy and bulky body which lacked most of the flair and style of a Lambretta or Vespa, and despite good build-quality and excellent handling and performance, it didn't sell, being dropped in 1964. The company's timing was poor to start in the scooter market. BMC had launched the Austin Seven/Morris Mini Minor 'Minis' in 1959, beginning a renewed attack on the small car market.

Despite such setbacks, the company pressed on and added a number of model variants to their range, such that by 1965 this comprised 17. But time and to some extent tradition was against Veloce, whose machines did not offer what the market wanted. 1970 would prove to be the company's last full year of trading. They opted for voluntary liquidation early in 1971.

Verus — see Sirrah

Victoria

Victoria Motor & Cycle Co Ltd
Victoria Works, Dennistoun, Glasgow

Not to be confused with the German Victoria motorcycles, these examples were one of the rare Scottish makes, produced in Glasgow in the 1920s. At their peak, in 1926, the Dennistoun-based Victoria Motor & Cycle Co were offering a range of 11 motorcycles, eight of which were Villiers-powered, the remainder having J.A.P. engines. Villiers 150cc, 172cc and 247cc engines were used for a range of low-priced cycles costing between £25 and £36; the J.A.P. engines being 293cc and 600cc, used in machines costing £40 to £60, the latter also being available as a combination for £75. This range was reduced to six Villiers and three J.A.P.-powered motorcycles for 1927, which was the last year of Victoria production.

Villiers

Villiers Cycle Components Co
Upper Villiers St/Marston Rd, Wolverhampton

Few entries in this book are free from a mention of the name Villiers, for this company was probably the largest supplier of proprietary motorcycle engines in Britain.

The company was established in 1898 by Charles Marston, the son of John Marston, founder of the Sunbeam Cycle Co. Established to produce pedals and

other components for Sunbeam cycles, Villiers produced their first engine, a four-stroke, in 1911, but this was somewhat ahead of its time and did not find favour with motorcycle manufacturers. Two years later Villiers produced their first two-stroke engine, of 269cc, which was more to the motorcycle makers' liking.

Munitions manufacture occupied the company during World War 1, engine production resuming thereafter. Engines of three basic capacities were produced: 150cc, 250cc and 350cc, with a 172cc unit being developed by the 1930s. Many other applications were found for these power units, including their use in generators, lawn mowers, etc. The company continued to produce engines of many kinds throughout World War 2, and on through the 1950s. A landmark was reached in 1956 when Villiers made their two millionth engine, the year also seeing the firm merge with J.A.P.

Villiers was taken over by Manganese Bronze Holdings in 1965, a company that would, in September 1966, take over AMC and effectively control motorcycle production in Britain. In July 1968, supplies of Villiers engines were denied to the surviving independent motorcycle makers, and within a year motorcycle engine production ceased, Villiers turning to the making of industrial engines.

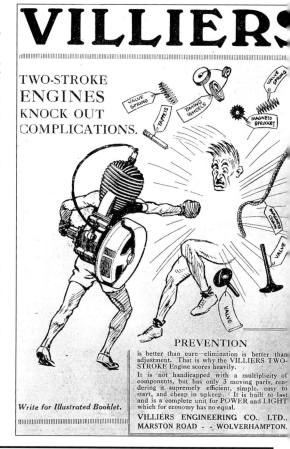

TWO-STROKE
ENGINES
KNOCK OUT
COMPLICATIONS.

PREVENTION

is better than cure—elimination is better than adjustment. That is why the VILLIERS TWO-STROKE Engine scores heavily.

It is not handicapped with a multiplicity of components, but has only 3 moving parts, rendering it supremely efficient, simple, easy to start, and cheap in upkeep. It is built to last and is a complete unit for POWER and LIGHT which for economy has no equal.

Write for Illustrated Booklet.

VILLIERS ENGINEERING CO., LTD.,
MARSTON ROAD - - WOLVERHAMPTON.

Right:
This 1924 advertisement didn't pull its punches when it came to promoting the virtues of Villiers two-stroke engines.
Jim Boulton Collection

Vincent-HRD; Vincent

Vincent 'HRD' Co Ltd/Vincent Engineers (Stevenage) Ltd
The Great North Rd, Stevenage, Hertfordshire

When production of Howard R. Davies' HRD motorcycles ceased in Wolverhampton in 1928, the rights were bought by an Australian enthusiast — Phil Vincent — who moved production of the machines to a factory on the Great North Road, Stevenage, in Hertfordshire. Vincent's interest was clear: HRDs had been billed as 'The World's Fastest Production Motorcycles', and this was one marque worth saving. In 1929 the first of the 'Vincent-HRD' machines, as they were now called, were manufactured. A range of five single-cylinder machines was offered, from a 346cc J.A.P.-engined model for £73 10s to one for £75 12s, with a 596cc J.A.P. engine.

Towards the end of 1931 another Phil — the designer and engineer Phil Irving — joined the firm. For the 1932 models a wider range of engines was used, including units from J.A.P., Rudge and Villiers. The following year saw the introduction of Irving's own design of spring-frame, and 1934 saw production of a lightweight machine powered by a 248cc Villiers two-stroke engine. But it would be for the company's larger machines that Vincent gained their reputation — using their own engines.

The Vincent team fared badly in the 1934 Isle of Man TT, let down by the J.A.P. engines they used. This set the spark for the company to design its own units, a desire fanned into flame by the onset of the difficulties that were to plague Rudge — its other main engine supplier — that led to the EMI buy-out in 1935. Design work and testing were completed in a few months during 1935, and the five models in the 1936 Vincent range all boasted own-make engines. Greatest of all the prewar Vincent-HRDs was the Rapide, announced for the 1937 model range. This had the company's own design of 998cc V-twin engine, and astonishing power and speed.

Production continued until late 1939, when production went over to war-related work. During the war 'the two Phils' continued to refine their motorcycle designs, paying particular attention to reducing the weight of the Rapide. A solution was to make the engine unit an integral part of the frame and to make extensive use of aluminium alloy for the engine castings. Difficulties were encountered in getting the new Rapide into production, and the first ones for sale were not made until September 1946. The effect of the Phils' efforts was immediately apparent: the machine weighed only 380lbs, but its engine developed 55bhp at 5,700rpm, giving these production motorcycles a top speed of 120mph!

With excellent build-quality, the postwar Vincent-HRDs assumed the niche vacated by Brough Superior. Around 1950 the company dropped the 'HRD' from its marque and was later renamed as Vincent Engineers (Stevenage) Ltd. In 1953 Vincents turned their attention to the other extreme of the motorcycling world — that

of the sub-50cc clip-on units then in vogue. So far as *aficionados* of 'The World's Fastest Production Motorcycles' were concerned, worse was to come with the announcement of the 1955 model range in November 1954. Vincent had linked up with the German NSU company and were offering a range of two 'NSU-Vincent' lightweights — the Fox 98cc and 123cc models — plus the 49cc NSU 'Quickly!' and the Firefly clip-on. Then, to top all this, the company had played around with the large Vincents — the Black Prince (late the 'Shadow'), Black Knight (late the 'Rapide') and Victor (late the 'Comet') — by enclosing the mechanical parts and the rear wheel in an overall mudguard, cowl, valance combination to produce 'The Twentieth Century "Knights of the Road"'.

Luckily, perhaps, the suppliers of the enclosure mouldings could not match Phil Vincent's demanding standards, and they were phased out. None the less, things were badly awry at the company, and a decision was made to discontinue motorcycle production. The last Vincents were made in December 1956, but the firm continued in existence, seeking new uses for its engines. A tenuous link with the motorcycle world remained until 1958 — Vincent continued to make the Firefly clip-on — an ignominious end for such a great marque.

Vindec

The South British Trading Co Ltd
13-15 Wilson St, Finsbury, London EC2
Brown Bros Ltd
22-34 Great Eastern St, London EC2

The 'Vindec' was a make of two-speed epicyclical hub gear that first appeared around 1905. Use of the name in association with these motorcycles may therefore have some connection with this device. Vindec cycles were made in the 1920s, first by the splendidly-named South British Trading Co, and, by the mid-1920s, by Brown Brothers, the large motor component factors who had previously made a motorcycle under their own name. Vindecs are listed up to 1930, used J.A.P. 170cc, 292cc, and 300cc singles and cost between £28 and £49. For 1931, 'Manufacture discontinued' was recorded against the marque in trade listings.

W&G

W&G Cycle Works
108 Windmill Rd, Brentford, Middlesex

Makers of their own engines, W&G production ended in 1928 with a single model. This was called the W&G Standard and used a 490cc two-cylinder engine, selling for £64.

Walco

W.A. Lloyd's Cycle Fittings Co Ltd
Clyde Works, 7 Freeman St, Birmingham 5

Walco is a well-known brand of cycle accessories and fittings — the name is a contraction of W.A. Lloyd Co. The company also produced motorcycles from 1903 and the following year experimented with car production. Neither product became a major feature of the company's output.

Wallis

Queens Mead Rd, Bromley, Kent

The Wallis is another obscure marque and the only models listed are those for 1927. These used Burney & Blackburne 348cc singles, and J.A.P. 346cc, 348cc and 490cc singles, in what were expensive machines. Bottom of the range was the Blackburne-powered model, at £65, whilst top of the range was the J.A.P. 490cc machine, for £110.

Wearwell; Wolf; Wulfruna

Wearwell Motor Carriage Co Ltd/Wearwell Cycle Co Ltd
Pountney & Gt Brickkiln streets, Wolverhampton
Wulfruna Engineering Co Ltd
Gt Brickkiln St, Wolverhampton
Wearwell Cycle Co (1928) Ltd
New Griffin Works, Colliery Rd, Wolverhampton

Wearwell were another of Wolverhampton's long-standing bicycle firms. The business had been founded in 1868 by Henry Clarke, who began making bone-shaker velocipedes in a workshop in Temple Street that year. Later, with his son, Clarke would make the 'Cogent' cycle. When Henry Clarke died in 1890 his four sons joined together and formed the Wearwell

Below:
Wearwell introduced their first motorcycle in 1901. Based upon their bicycle, a 2.5hp Stevens engine was inclined forwards up the front frame member. This 1903 model used a 3.25hp Stevens engine; that year Wearwell motorcycles also adopted the 'Wolf' name. Seen in 'as found' condition, DA 44 was discovered by a Mr Miller in a Wombourn barn in the early 1950s. *Jim Boulton Collection*

Wulfruna 3½-h.p. Motor Cycle.

Combined with Chain-driven 2-speed Gear.

Cash Price
Single speed
Belt drive,
43 Guineas

Cash Price
with 2-speed
53 Guineas

If anyone requires a powerful well-equipped and speedy machine for solo work, and ordinary Side Car work, this cannot be excelled.

The Gear Case Cover is now made to enclose the chain entirely on all 2-speed Models.

Above:
Wearwell's 'Wulfruna' range for 1914 included this 3.5hp 499cc single, which was available in fixed-speed or two-speed versions. The finish was black enamel, with optional lining, the tank being enamelled green and gold. *Jim Boulton Collection*

Right:
The pulling power of Wolf motorcycles was to the fore here on the cover of the marque's 1932 catalogue.
Jim Boulton Collection

Cycle Co, which operated out of their father's old works in Darlington Street. By 1896 the company had moved to Pountney Street and in 1901 it introduced its first motorcycle.

Based upon a Wearwell bicycle, the engine was a Stevens 2.5hp, inclined forwards up the main front member of the frame; the final drive was via a belt of twisted leather. This machine sold for £44 2s. A larger, 3.25hp Stevens engine was used for 1903, the same year that Wearwell adopted the 'Wolf' brand for its motorcycles. This kind of motorised bicycle was gradually improved and developed throughout the 1900s and early 1910s. By 1915, Wolf motorcycles were using a 269cc single-cylinder engine and were available with either a fixed gear and belt drive for £23 2s 6d or with a two-speed gearbox and chain-cum-belt drive for £29 7s 6d. The company also produced motorcycles under the 'Wulfruna' name.

Production was suspended from 1916, but resumed after World War 1. By the mid-1920s the range was impressive, comprising 17 models, each of which was given a letter code. All the cycles were single-cylinder,

Blackburne, J.A.P. and Villiers engines being used, ranging from 150cc to 550cc. Prices went from £28 to £61 10s.

No Wolf motorcycles are listed for the years 1928 through to 1931, reflecting major changes in the company. The Clarke family sold the concern in 1927, the new owners re-forming it as the Wearwell Cycle Co (1928) Ltd and relocating to the New Griffin Works in Colliery Road Wolverhampton. Motorcycle production was resumed from there in 1931, a new range of machines being offered for 1932, with appropriate names: Cub, Minor, Utility, Vixen and Silver Wolf. The latter had a 196cc Villiers engine, a lighting dynamo and a flywheel magneto, all for £29 10s. With value like this, sales were good and production was maintained until the outbreak of World War 2.

Once peace returned, only Wearwell bicycles followed suit, the last Wolf motorcycles having been made in 1939.

Whitwood Monocar — see OEC

Williamson

Williamson Motor Cycle Co Ltd
Cromwell Works, Cromwell St, Coventry 6

Williamson liked to have its motorcycles on three wheels. The company began to produce motorcycle combinations in 1912, and the following year it also made a three-wheeler — the Williamson Cycla — which remained in production until 1916. Both this and the company's motorcycles used Douglas engines. Just one model of combination is listed for 1912 to 1916. This used an 8hp Douglas 964cc two-cylinder water-cooled engine, with a three-speed gearbox and chain drive. From 1912 to 1914 this cost £98 10s, but the

price rose to £102 in 1915 and to £107 in 1916. Production was suspended that year, but resumed briefly in 1920, never to be heard of again.

Wooler

Wooler Engineering Co Ltd
Old Oak Common Lane, Willesden Junction, London NW10
Wembley, Middlesex

Wooler Engineering launched their motorcycle in 1911. It was of unusual design, having a two-stroke engine, placed horizontally, and a double-ended piston arrangement that was designed to remove the need for a crankcase. Unusually too for the period, front and rear suspension were fitted. Power came from a 345cc single-cylinder engine, the final drive being via a belt. In 1914 the machine cost £47 5s, and production continued until 1916, when the price had risen to £49 12s 6d.

When production resumed by 1920, Wooler were using flat-twin four-stroke engines. In 1925 they introduced a cycle with a 500cc engine, but this was to be the last year of the Woolers before World War 2, none being listed from 1926 onwards. The most noticeable feature of the prewar Woolers had been their fuel tanks, which extended forward, engulfing the head of the steering gear and standing proud of the front of the machines, incorporating the headlamp. This feature was retained in the postwar machines, an aspect of them that belied the technical innovations they included.

Both the engines and transmissions of the Wooler motorcycles announced in 1945 were revolutionary. The engine was a 500cc four-cylinder unit, laid on its side across the main frame, with two cylinders each side, one above the other, the engine's motion being transmitted to the crankshaft by a rocking beam. Final drive was by means of two drive shafts, one from each side of the engine, and the transmission was either four-speed or infinitely variable. It took two years to produce a prototype, and a further five before a revised specification was announced, signalling that production might be imminent. This was not to be.

Four more years passed before a further revised prototype appeared, but as tantalisingly close as production of the Wooler machines seemed, it never began, and no more was heard of them after 1956.

Wright

Wright Bros
Blackwell St, Kidderminster, Worcestershire

Above:
Stan and Reg Wright kept a general store in Kidderminster.
Keen motorcyclists, during the 1920s they built a number of
competition machines from proprietary parts. Here, Hillary
Greatwich, of Lickhill Manor, poses on a Wright, with one of the
Wright brothers in the sidecar. *Jim Boulton Collection*

Keepers of a general store in Kidderminster, Stan and
Reg Wright were the grandsons of the original owner
who established the business in 1862. Keen motorcyclists, they built a number of competition machines,
which they used in hill climbs and sprints in the 1920s
and early 1930s. Built up from proprietary parts, the
'Wright' machines provide ample evidence of just how
easy it was to enter the motorcycle business in those
times. Success in that business, alas, came a little
harder, as many, including the Wrights, found out.

Yale

T. Baxter
36 Great Eastern St, London EC2

Great Eastern Street was the home of many car and
motorcycle importers. T. Baxter's large twins may,
therefore, originally have been the product of the
Consolidated Manufacturing Co of Toledo, Ohio. They
had an over-square 982cc V-twin engine, two-speed
gearbox, chain-drive, and kick start, selling for £75, but
are not listed past 1916.

Zenith

Zenith Motor Engineering Co
101a Stroud Green Rd, Finsbury Park, London N4
Zenith Motors Ltd
Weybridge/Hampton Court, Surrey/Kennington Cross,
London SE11
Writers Ltd
Kennington Cross, London SE11

With only Birmingham's short-lived Zephyr (1922/3)
beneath them, briefly, on any dealer's list, the Zenith

was ever the last, but by no means the least, marque of
British motorcycle. They produced their first machines
in 1904, from a small works in Finsbury Park, North
London. The brains behind the company was its chief
designer F. W. 'Freddy' Barnes, to whom are credited
innovations in both frame and gear design.

Zenith first came to prominence in their early years
with the Barnes-designed 'Bi-Car', a 3hp Fafnir-
engined motorcycle that offered the luxury and ride of a
motor car. At its heart was a fully-sprung frame which
'ironed-out' the worst of the road's roughness. More
significant was Barnes' 'Gradua' gearing system, introduced in 1909. This used engine pulley flanges that
could be opened or closed by means of a rider-operated
handle, interlocked with a mechanism that moved the
rear wheel forwards or backwards to keep the drive belt
tension constant. The effect of this was to provide a
variable gear ratio in the range 5.5:1 to 3:1. In regular
road use this gear system conferred little advantage to
the Zenith-Gradua rider over someone on a more
conventional machine, but Zeniths came into their own
during speed hill climbs, where riders could vary the
gearing on the ascent. Protests abounded and Zenith-
Graduas were barred from entering speed hill climbs
from 1911 onwards.

As the company grew it moved, first to Weybridge in
Surrey and then to Hampton Court. They built an
impressive range of models, all using J.A.P. engines,
including 488cc and 493cc singles, and 496cc, 654cc,
976cc and 986cc twins. The Gradua gearing system
was used throughout the range, which began at £55 5s
and rose to £85 10s.

After World War 1 Zenith produced more conventional designs of motorcycle, assembled from proprietary parts, the firm's main contribution being the
Barnes-designed frames. Engines by Bradshaw, Fafnir,
J.A.P., Precision and Villiers were used, ranging from
just under 150cc to 1,100cc. Bottom of the range was
the 'Zenith 3', a 346cc single costing £48, the top being
the '8-45' 980cc twin at £149. For 1929, model names
were adopted. The Zenith 3 became the 'Zeni-three',
whilst others became the 'Club'. From 1932 the entire
range was offered in both Standard and De Luxe
versions, the difference generally adding around £14 to
the price. In 1934 Zenith offered their largest ever
range — 17 models — when all the De Luxes were
counted, and introducing the 'NP', a 1,096cc J.A.P.
twin-engined machine that sold for £72 15s and became
the 'CP' in subsequent years.

Zenith had hit financial difficulties in 1930 and the
company almost folded. They were taken over in 1931
by Writers Ltd, a large motorcycle dealership based in
Kennington Cross, London. For a time production was
maintained at Hampton Court, but was eventually
moved to Writers' site at Kennington. Halted for World
War 2, when motorcycle production resumed in 1945 it
was a very muted affair. The company found it hard to
obtain supplies of proprietary engines, and the few
Zeniths that were made used 750cc V-twin J.A.P.
engines held in stock from before the war. When these
ran out, production ceased in 1950.

Appendix: British Motorcycle Manufacturers

The following is a list of British motorcycle manufacturers who do not have an entry in the main part of this book. It was compiled from a variety of sources, including trade publications. Requirements of space have meant that certain abbreviations have been used and certain assumptions made, particularly in the addresses column. Many firms operated from a number of sites during their working history, but space here permits only one address to be included. Production dates can be assumed to be continuous, with pauses for World War 1 (generally 1916-1918/1919) and World War 2 (generally 1940-1945/1946). Companies whose production was not continuous for other reasons have this indicated by the use of the symbol '~' in place of the symbol '-'. The abbreviations following certain production dates refer to the type of motorcycle made by the company. Where no abbreviation is given it can be assumed that conventional motorcycles were the company's staple product. Elsewhere the following abbreviations have been used: co (clip-on attachment), kit (sold as a self-assembly kit), sc (scooter), sp (speedway model), tr (trials machine).

Marque	Maker	Place of Manufacture	Production Dates
Abbotsford	—	—	1919-1920 sc
ABC (ii)	A.B.C. Cycle Co	Aston, Birmingham	1922-1924
AEL	A.E. Lynes & Co Ltd	Coventry	1919-1924
Aeolus (i)	E.H. Owen	London W14	1903
Aeolus (ii)	Bowns Ltd	Birmingham B19	1914-1916
Airolite	Small Engines Co	Birmingham B10	1922-1923 co
Ajax	Ajax Motor Manufacturers Ltd	Birmingham B24	1923-1924
AJR	A.J. Robertson	65 Queen St, Edinburgh	1925-1926
AKD	Abingdon Works Ltd	Birmingham B25	1927-1933
Akkens	Thomas & Gilbert	Smethwick	1919-1922
Alecto	Cashmore Bros	Balham, London SW12	1919-1924
Alert	Smith & Molesworth	Freeth St, Coventry	1903-1906
ALP	Alperton Motor Co Ltd	Alperton, London NW10	1912-1917
Alta Suzuki	—	—	1969-1970 tr
AMC	Associated Motor Cycles Ltd	Plumstead Rd, London SE18	1931-1966
Anglian	Anglian Motor Co	Newgate St	1903-1912
Arab	Arab Cycles	Bellbarn Rd, Birmingham	1923-1924
Arden	Arden Motor Co Ltd	Balsall Common, Coventry	1912-1920
Armis	Armis Cycle Mfg Co Ltd	Heneage St, Birmingham	1920-1923
Armstrong (i)	Armstrong Cycle Works	Paddington, London	1902-1905
Armstrong (ii)	—	—	1913-1914
Arno	Arno Motor Co	Gosford St, Coventry	1906-1914
Arrow	Kirk & Marifield	Bradford St, Birmingham	1913-1917
Ascot	The Ascot Motor Co	Pentonville Rd, London N	1905-1906
Ashford		Ashford, Kent	1905
ASL	Associated Spring Ltd	Corporation St, Stafford	1907-1914
Aston	Aston Motoring & Eng Co	Witton Lane, Birmingham	1923-1924
Atlas (i)	Atlas Engineering Co	Coventry	1913-1914
Atlas (ii)	The Aston Motor & Eng Co Ltd	Witton Lane, Birmingham	1923-1925
Aurora (ii)	Aurora Motors	Douglas, Isle of Man	1919-1921
Austen; Austin	Austen Cycle Co	Lewisham, London	1903-1906
Autoglider	Autoglider Ltd/Townsend & Co	Gt Charles St, Birmingham	1919-1922 sc
Autoped	W T T Engineering Co Ltd	6 Dalling Rd Hammersmith	1920 sc
Autosco	Brown & Layfield	Sydenham, London SE	1920-1921 sc
Avon	Avon Motor Cycle Co	South End, Croydon, London	1919-1920
Ayres-Hayman	Viaduct Motor Co	Broadheath, Manchester	1920
Banshee	Banshee Mfg Co Ltd	Bromsgrove, Worcestershire	1921-1924
Bantamoto	Cyc-Auto Works Co	381 Uxbridge Rd, London	1951
Barnes	G.A. Barnes	Lewisham. London SE	1904
Baron	Baron Cycle Co	Summer Row, Birmingham	1920-1921
Barter	Humpage, Jacques & Pedersen	Luckwell Lane, Bristol	1902-1904
Bayliss-Thomas	Excelsior Motor Co Ltd	Kings Rd, Tyseley	1922-1929

Beardmore-Precision	F. E. Baker Ltd	Kings Norton Birmingham	1919-1924
Beaufort	Argson Engineering Co Ltd	South Twickenham	1923-1926
Beaumont	Beaumont Motors (Leeds) Ltd	Cleopatra Works, Harehills	1919-1923
Beeston	New Beeston Cycle Co Ltd	Parkside, Coventry	1898-1901
Berwick	Berwick Motor Co Ltd	Tweedmouth, Northumbria	1929-1930
Bikotor	—	—	1951 co
Binks	Charles Binks Ltd	Nottingham	1903-1906
Birch	J.N. Birch	Nuneaton, Warwickshire	1902-1910
Blackford	—	—	1902-1904
Blumfield	Blumfield Ltd	Lower Essex St, Birmingham	1906-1914
Booth	Booth Motor Co	Putney, London SW	1901-1903
Bord	Bord Motor Co	Finsbury Pavement, London	1902-1906
Bounds-J.A.P.	J. Bounds	Kilburn High Rd, London	1909-1915
Bowden	Bowden Patents Syndicate Ltd	Baldwin Gardens, London	1902-1905
British Radial	British Radial Engine Co	Kings Rd, Chelsea SW10	1921-1923
British Standard	British Standard Motors	145 Lichfield Rd, B'ham	1919-1923
Brown Bicar	J.F. Brown	40 Oxford St, Reading	1907-1910
Buck	The Buckman Eng (Parent) Co	Sherwood, Nottingham	1900
Bulldog	H.H. Timbrell	59 Slaney Rd, Birmingham	1920
Burford	Consolidated Alliance Ltd	1 Albemarle St, London W	1914-1915
Burney	Burney, Baldwin & Co Ltd	Oxford St, Reading	1923-1925
Butler	Chris Butler	Dalston, London E8	1963-1966 tr
Calvert	Stoke Newington Motor Co	Stoke Newington Rd, London	1899-1904
Camber	Bright & Hayles	Church Rd, Camberwell, Ldn	1920-1921
Carlton	Carlton Cycles Ltd	Clarence Rd, Worksop	1920 ~ 1940
Castell	Castell & Sons	Malden Rd, Kentish Town	1903
Caswell	Caswell Ltd	27 Great Eastern St, London	1904-1905
Cayenne	Hayes-Pankhurst Mfg Co	St Leonards on Sea, Sussex	1912-1913
CC	Charles Chamberlain	Bispham, Blackpool	1921-1924
Centaur	Centaur Cycle Co Ltd	West Orchard, Coventry	1901-1915
Century	—	—	1902-1905
Chase	F.W. & A.A. Chase	9 Station Rd, Anerly, London	1902-1910
Clarendon	Clarendon Mtr Car & Cycle Co	77 Moor St, Coventry	1901-1910
Cleveland	Cleveland Motor Cycle Co	Douglas St, Middlesborough	1911-1914
Clément	C.R. Garrard Mfg Co	Ryland St	1898-1910 co
CMC	The Cluelt Manufacturing Co	Tarporley, Cheshire	1900
CMM	Coventry Motor Mart	London Rd, Coventry	1920
Colonial	H.P. Carter	10-11 Bond Gate, Nottingham	1911-1913
Comery	Comery Motors	275 Vernon Rd, Nottingham	1923
Comet	Comet Motor Wks	New Cross, London	1902-1906
Commander	General Steels & Iron Co Ltd	Springfield Rd, Hayes, London	1952-1953
Condor	Condor Motor Co	182-184 Broad St, Coventry	1907-1914
Consul	Johnson, Burton & Theobald Ltd	4-6 Castle St, Norwich	1922-1924
Corah	The Corah Motor Mfg Co	Redditch Rd, Kings Norton	1905-1914
Corona	Corona Cycle Co	Maidenhead, Berkshire	1901-1904
Corona Junior	Meteor Manufacturing Co Ltd	98 Tollington Park, London	1919-1923
Coulson B	Coulson Eng Co	Albion St, Kings X, London	1919-1922
Coventry B&D	Coventry Bicycles Ltd	Wellington St, Coventry 1	1923-1925
Coventry-Challenge	Challenge Cycle Co Ltd	201 Foleshill Rd, Coventry	1903-1910
Coventry-Mascot	The Coventry Mascot Cycle Co	Camden St, Coventry 2	1922-1923
Crest	The Crest Motor Co	Leamington Spa, Warks	1923-1924
Croft Cameron	Croft Cameron	St Michael's Rd, Coventry	1923-1926
Crownfield	J. Perkins	299 High Rd, Leyton, London	1903-1904
Crypto	Crypto Works Co Ltd	29 Clerkenwell Rd, London	1902-1910
Cyc-Auto	Cyc-Auto Ltd	Bashley Rd, Park Royal, Ldn	1934-1956
Cykelaid	The Sheppee Motor Co Ltd	40 Thomas St, York	1919-1926 co
Dalesman	—	—	1968-1974 tr
Dalton	Dalton Motor Co Ltd	John Dalton St, Manchester	1920-1922
Dane	Dane Works	131a Uxbridge Rd, London	1919-1920
Dart (i)	F. Baker	Kingston-on-Thames, Surrey	1901-1906
Dart (ii)	Dart Engineering Co	Stoney Stanton Rd, Coventry	1923-1924
Davison	A.C. Davison	Viaduct Works, Coventry	1902-1908

DAW	Dalton & Wade	146 Spon St, Coventry 1	1902-1905
Day-Leeds	Job Day & Sons Ltd	Ellerby Lane, Leeds	1912-1914
Dayton (i)	Charles Day Mfg Co Ltd	221 High St, Shoreditch, Ldn	1913-1920
De Luxe (ii)	De Luxe Motors	174 Corporation St, B'ham	1920-1924
Defy-All	Defy-All Cycle & Mtr Cycle Co	Chapel St, Stalybridge	1921-1922
Dennell	Herbert Dennell Motor Cycles	Leeds	1903-1908
Derby	Ed. De Poorter Co Ltd	9-10 Great Tower St, London	1902-1910
Despatch Rider	Dreng Ltd	Fern Rd, Erdington, B'ham	1915-1917
Diamond (ii)	—	—	1965-1969 tr
Dreadnought	W.A. Lloyd's Cycles Ltd	Freeman St, Birmingham	1915-1924
Dreadnought, The	Harold Karslake	Brough Wks, Nottingham	1902-1903
Dunkley (i)	Dunkley's Ltd	Bromsgrove St, Birmingham	1913-1920
Dunstall	Paul Dunstall	—	1964-1969
Dursley-Pedersen	—	—	1905
Dux	Dux Motor Mfg Co	Coventry	1904-1906
Duzmo	JPortable Tool & Eng Co Ltd	Cedar Rd, Enfield Highway	1919-1923
Dyson-Motorette	—	—	1920-1921 co
Eadie	Albert Eadie	Redditch, Worcestershire	1898-1903
Eagle-Tandem	—	Altrincham	1903-1905
EBO	E. Boulter	Leicester	1910-1915
Economic	Economic Motors	Wells St, London W1	1921-1923
Edmonton	—	—	1903-1910
Elf-King	Bond & Cooper	Crown Wks, Birmingham	1907-1909
Elfson	Wilson & Elford	Manor Rd, Aston, B'ham	1923-1925
ELI	The E.L.I. Motor Mfg Co	Station Rd, Montpelier, Bristol	1911-1912
Elison	Wilson & Elison	Manor Rd, Aston, Birmingham	1923-1924
Elmdon	Joseph Bourne & Sons	Bath St, Birmingham 4	1915
Elstar	Alf Ellis	—	—
Elswick	Elswick Cycles & Mfg Co	Barton-on-Humber	1903-1920
Endrick	Endrick Engineering Co	Olton, Birmingham	1913-1915
Endurance	C.B. Harrison (1909) Ltd	Sheepcote St, Birmingham 15	1909-1924
Energette	J. L. Norton	Birmingham	1901-1906
ETA	G.E. Halliday	Mixenden, Halifax, Yorkshire	1921
Evart-Hall	Evart Hall Ltd	38 Long Acre, London WC	1903-1905
Fairfield	Alfred Foster Motor Cycles	Warrington, Cheshire	1914-1915
Farnell	—	—	1901-1905
FB	Fowler & Bingham Ltd	Coventry Rd, Hay Mills, B'ham	1913-1916
FEE	J. Barter/Light Motors Ltd	Orchard St, Bristol	1905-1908
Firefly (ii)	—	—	late 1960s
FLM	Frank Leach Mfg Co	Manor Wks, Headingley, Leeds	1951-1953
Frost	Romney Frost	Lichfield St, Wolverhampton	early 1920s
G&W	Guy & Wheeler	49 South John St, Liverpool	1902-1906
Gaby	Gaby Lightweight Motor Cycles	37 Corporation St, Birmingham	1914-1915
Gamage	A.W. Gamage Ltd	Holborn, London	1913 ~ 1923
Gaunt	Peter Gaunt	—	1969-1970 tr
GB	F. Glassen & Co/G.B. Motor Co	16 Water Lane, London EC	1905-1907
Gerrard	—	—	1914-1915
Glendale	—	—	1920-1921
Globe	Clarke, Cluley & Co	Globe Wks, Coventry	1901-1910
Gloria	—	—	1924-1925
Gough	—	—	1920-1922
Grandex	The Grandex Cycle Co	Gray's Inn Rd WC	1906-1917
Graves	J.G. Graves Ltd	Sheffield	1914-1915
Green	Green Motor Cycle Co	50 Jermyn St, London W1	1920-1923
Greyhound	Greyhound Motors	Ashford, Kent	1905-1907
GRI	Macrae & Dick	Inverness	1921-1922
Grigg	The Grigg Motor & Eng Co Ltd	Richmond, Surrey	1920-1924
Grose-Spur	George Grose/Carlton Co	Ludgate Circus, London EC4	1938-1940
GYS	—	Bournemouth	1949-1955 co
H&R; R&H	Hailstone & Ravenhall	132 Clay Ln, Coventry	1922-1925
Hack	Hack Engineering Co Ltd	44 Victoria Rd, Hendon, London	1920-1923
Haden-Precision	A. H. Haden	Princip St, Birmingham	1920-1924

Hampton	The Hampton Engineering Co	Lifford Mills, Kings Norton	1912-1914
Harewood	Harewood Motor Cycles	Long Lane, Bexley Heath	1920
Harper	Harper Aircraft Co Ltd	Exeter Airport, Exeter	1954 sc
Hawker	H G Hawker Engineering Co Ltd	Kingston-on-Thames, Surrey	1921-1923
Haxel-J.A.P.	—	—	1911-1913
Hazel	Cripps Cycle & Motor Co	Woodford Rd, London E	1906-1911
Hazlewood	Hazlewoods Ltd	West Orchard, Coventry	1905-1923
HEC (i)	—	—	1922-1923
HEC (ii)	Hepburn Engineering Co Ltd	Kings Cross, London	1938-1940
Hercules (i)	H. Butler	Derby	1902-1910
HJ	Howard & Johnson	179 Hockley St, Birmingham 18	1920-1921
HJH	H. J. Hulsman (Industries)	Canal Rd, Neath, Glamorgan	1954-1956
HMC	Hendon Motor Cycle Co	The Broadway, West Hendon	1913
Hobart	Hobart Cycle Co Ltd	Hobart Wks, Coventry	1913 ~ 1924
Hockley	Hockley Motor Mfg Co Ltd	126 Barr St, Hockley, B'ham 19	1914-1916
Holden	The Motor Traction Co Ltd	27 Walnut Tree Walk, Ldn SE	1898-1903
Holroyd	J.S. Holroyd	East St, Farnham, Surrey	1922
Hoskison	Hoskison Motors, Ltd	20 Digbeth, Birmingham 5	1919-1922
Howard	Howard & Co	Coalville, Leicestershire	1905-1907
HT	The Hagg Tandem Mtr Cycle Co	Park St, nr St Albans, Herts	1920-1922
Hulbert-Bramley	Hulbert-Bramley Motor Co	19 Grand Parade, Putney SW	1903-1906
Imperial	Imperial Motor Co	228 Brixton Hill, London SW	1901-1910
Iris	Iris Motor Co	58 Holland St, Brixton, London	1902-1906
Ivel	Dan Albone	Ivel Wks, Biggleswad, Beds	1902-1905
Jackson-Rotrax	—	—	1949 sp
JNU	J. Nickson	230 Station Rd, Bamber Bridge	1920-1922
Jones	G.H. Jones	—	1936
Joybike	H.V. Powell (cycles) Ltd	98 Birchfield Rd, Birmingham	1959-1960 sc
Juno	Juno Cycle Co	248 Bishopsgate, London EC2	1913-1915
Jupp	The Jupp Motor Co Ltd	86 Leadenhall St, London EC3	1921-1922
Kempton	A.B.C. Motors (1920) Ltd	Walton-on-Thames, Surrey	1921-1922
Kestrel	—	—	1903-1905
Kieft	Kieft Cars Ltd	Derry St, Wolverhampton	1955-1957
Kingsway	Kingsway Motor Cycle Co	Much Park St, Coventry 1	1921-1923
Kumfurt	Kumfurt Motorcycles & Accessories Co	Cookham Rise, Berkshire	1914-1916
Kynoch	Kynoch Ltd	Lion Wks, Witton Ln, B'ham	1903-1913
L&C	J. Leonard & Co	20 Long Acre WC	1904-1905
Ladies-Pacer	—	Guernsey	1914
Lancer	Lancer Cycle & Motor Co	Coventry	1904-1905
LDE	Frank Desborough	Commercial R, Wolverhampton	1951
Leonard	J. Leonard	Brockley Rd, Brockley, London	1903-1906
Letbridge	—	—	1922-1923
Lily	—	—	1914-1915
Lincoln-Elk	Kirby & Edwards/J. Kirby	Broadgate, Lincoln	1906-1924
Little Giant	—	—	1913-1915
London	Rex Patents Ltd	3 Exchange St, Clapham	1903-1905
M&M	Morgan & Maxwell	80 High St, Streatham, London	1914
M.C.C.	Motor Castings Co	London	1903-1910
Mabon	Mabob & Co	19 Clerkenwell Rd, London EC	1904-1910
Majestic	OK Supreme Motors Ltd	Warwick Rd, Greet, Birmingham	1931-1933
Marlow	Marlow Motorcycles	20a Emscote Rd, Warwick	1921-1922
Mars (i)	Mars Motor Co	Church End, Finchley, London	1905-1910
Mars (ii)	Mars Ltd	Whitefriars Lane, Coventry	1923-1926
Marseel	Marseel Eng Co	Victoria Park, Coventry	1920-1921
Martin-Comerford	Comerfords	Thames Ditton, Surrey	1930s tr
Martin-J.A.P.	—	London	1930s sp
Martinsyde	Martinsyde Ltd	Brooklands, Byfleet, Surrey	1920-1923
Matador	The Matador Eng Co Ltd	Deepdale, Preston	1922-1925
Maxim	—	—	1919-1921
May Bros.	—	—	1903-1906
McKechnie	McKechnie Motors	Kings Head Chambers, Coventry	1922
McKenzie	Geo. H. McKenzie	28 Warwick Row, Coventry	1921-1924

Mead (i)	Mead Cycle Co	11-13 Paradise St, Liverpool	1911-1916
Mead (ii)	—	Birmingham	1922-1924
Melen	F. & H. Melen Ltd	Cheapside, Birmingham 24	1923-1924
Metro-Tyler	Tyler Apparatus Co Ltd	Bannister Rd, London NW10	1920
Midget-Bicar	J.F. Brown	40 Oxford St, Reading	1908-1909
Millionmobile	Strettons Ltd	Cheltenham, Gloucestershire	1902-1905
Minerva	Minerva Motors Ltd	40 Holborn Viaduct, London EC	1905
Mini-Motor	Mini-Motor (Great Britain) Ltd	Trojan Way, Croydon	1949-1955 co
Mohawk	Mohawk Motor & Cycle Co Ltd	Chalk Farm Rd, London NW	1903 ~ 1925
Monarch	R. Walker & Son	Kings Rd, Tyseley, Birmingham	1919-1921
Morris (i)	William Morris	48 High St/16 George St, Oxford	1902-1905
Morris (ii)	John Morris/Morris Ltd	Bentley Heath, Knowle, B'ham	1913-1922
Morris-Warne	Morris Bros. & Warne	46 Churchfield Rd, London W3	1922
MPH	Peter Hay	67 Havelock R, Tyseley, B'ham	1920-1923
Neall	Neall Bros. Ltd	Daventry, Northamptonshire	1910-1914
Nestor	The 'Nestor' Motor Co	74 Church St, Blackpool	1913-1914
New Coulson	H.R. Backhouse & Co Ltd	Tyseley, Birmingham	1923-1924
New Era	Era Motor Co Ltd	Miller St, Dingle, Liverpool	1920-1922
New Knight	Holloway & Knight	84 Foster Hill Rd, Bedford	1923-1924
New Paragon/Paragon	Paragon Motor Mfg Co	Cressing Rd, Braintree, Essex	1921-1923
New Scale	New Scale Motor & Eng Co	Bank St, Droylsden, Manchester	1913 ~ 1925
Newton	Newton Bros.	Chapel St, Manchester	1921-1922
Nicholas	Nicholas Motor & Cycle Co	34 Stroud Green Rd, London N	1911-1915
Nickson	J. Nickson	250 Station Rd, Bamber Bridge	1920-1924
NLG	North London Garage	Corsica St, Highbury, London	1905-1912
Noble	Noble Motor Co	Blackfriars Rd, London SE	1901-1910
Norbreck	D.H. Valentine	24 Finedon Rd, Wellingborough	1921-1924
Ogston	The Wilkinson TMC Co Ltd	Southfield Rd, Acton, London W	1912-1913
Olivos	Olivos Motors	120 Bollo Bridge Rd, Acton W3	1920-1921
Onaway	Onaway Motor Eng Co	107 St Albans Rd, Watford	1904-1908
Ormonde	Ormonde Motor Co	Wells St; Oxford St, London W	1900-1910
Ortona	Ortona Motor Co	Egham, Surrey	1904-1906
Oscar	—	Blackburn, Lancashire	1953 sc
Osmond	Osmonds (1911) Ltd	Tomey Rd, Greet, Birmingham	1911-1924
Overdale	—	Scotland	1921-1922
Overseas	Overseas Motor Co Ltd	Johnstone St, Ladywood, B'ham	1913-1915
Pacer	Millards Cycles	Bosq Ln, Esplanade, Guernsey	1914
Pax	Pax Engineering Co	Station Rd, Acock's Grn, B'ham	1920-1922
PDC	Imperial Motor Co	228 Brixton Hill, London SW	1903-1906
Pearson	Pearson Bros.	Elm Grove, Southsea, Hants	1903-1904
Pearson & Cox	Pearson & Cox Ltd	Shortlands, Kent	1914-1917
Pearson & Sopwith	Pearson & Sopwith Ltd	60 Mortimer St, London W	1919-1921
Pebok	Pebok Motorcycle Co	98 Leadenhall St, London EC	1903-1910
Peco	Pearson & Cole Ltd	Duddeston Mill Rd, Saltley	1913-1915
Peerless (i)	Bradbury & Co	Wellington Works, Oldham	1902-1910
Peerless (ii)	International Mfg Co	76-77 High St, Birmingham	1913-1914
Pen Nib	H.W. 'Bill' Boulton	Penn Rd, Wolverhampton	1922-1925
Pennington	E.J. Pennington	Ford St, Coventry	1897
Perks & Birch; P&B	Perks & Birch	Coventry	1899-1901
Peters	Peters Motors Ltd/J.A. Peters	Ramsey, Isle of Man	1919-1925
Piatti	Cyclemaster Ltd	Byfleet, Surrey	1955-1958 sc
Pilot	Pilot Cycle & Motor Co	Soho Rd, Birmingham 21	1903-1915
Portland	Maudes Motor Mart	Gt Portland St, London W	1919-1911
Powell	Powell Bros. Ltd	Wrexham, Clwyd	1921-1926
Power Pak	—	162 Queensway, Bayswater	1950-1956 co
Powerful	H.W. Clarke & Co	Gosford St, Coventry 1	1903-1910
Precision (i)	Precision Motor Co	Derngate, Northampton	1902-1906
Precision (ii)	F E Baker Ltd	Kings Norton, Birmingham	1919
Premo	Premier Motor Co	Aston Rd, Birmingham 6	1906-1910
Prim	A. Money & Co	21 Eastern St, High Wycombe	1906
Princeps	Princeps Autocar Co	Northampton	1901-1910
Progress	—	Coventry	1902-1908

R&P	Robinson & Price Ltd	Chatham St, Liverpool	1902-1910
Radmill	Bradbury, Rinman & Co	230 Shaftesbury Ave, London E4	1912-1913
Raglan	Raglan Cycle Co/M Adler Ltd	Sampson Rd North, Birmingham	1903-1913
Ray (i)	Ray Motor Co	Brick St, Piccadilly, London W1	1919-1920
Reading	Stanley J Watson	Richmond	1920
Ready	D. Read & Co	Weston-Super-Mare, Somerset	1921-1922
Rebro	Read Bros.	Goods Stn St, Tunbridge Wells	1922-1923
Redrup	Boyle & Redrup/C. Redrup	St Stephens Rd, Leeds	1919-1921
Regal	Regal Motors	15 High St, Saltley, Birmingham	1909-1915
Regent	Regent Motors Ltd	116 Victoria St, London SW1	1920
Regina (i)	Ilford Motor Car & Cycle Co	High Rd, Ilford, London	1903-1915
Revolution	New Revolution Cycle Co Ltd	Birmingham	1904-1906
Rex-J.A.P.	Premier Motor Co Ltd	Aston Rd, Birmingham 6	1909-1916
Reynolds Runabout	Jackson Car Mfg Co	Pangbourne, Berkshire	1919-1922
Riley	Riley Cycle Co Ltd	City Works, Coventry	1901-1910
Rip	Rip Motor Mfg Co Ltd	Leytonstone Rd, Stratford, Ldn E	1905-1908
Roc	A.W. Wall Ltd	Hay Mills, Birmingham	1904-1915
Romp	—	Birmingham	1913-1914
Roulette	—	—	1918-1919
Royal-Ajax	British Cycle Mfg Co Ltd	1&3 Berry St, Liverpool	1901-1910
Royal-Eagle	Coventry-Eagle Cycle & Mtr Co	Stoney Stanton Rd, Coventry	1901-1910
Royal Scot	Donaldson & Kelso	Anniesland Glasgow	1922-1924
Royal Wellington	Shakespeare, Kirkland & Frost	Birmingham	1901-1905
Russell	—	—	1913
Saltley	Saltley Cycle Co	86 Snow Hill, Birmingham	1921-1924
Sapphire	Roger Kyffin	—	1963-1966
Saracen	Robin Goodfellow	Cirencester, Kent	1967-1973 kit
Sarco; Sarco Reliance	Sarco Eng & Trading Co Ltd	108 Fenchurch St, London EC3	1920-1923
Scorpion	Scorpion Motor Cycles Ltd	Ashburnham Rd, Northampton	1963-1965
Scout	Taylor & Hands	353a Coventry Rd, Birmingham	1912-1913
Service	Service & Colonial Ltd	292-293 High Holborn, Ldn WC2	1901-1912
SGS	Sid Gleave/Gleave Motors	Davenport St, Macclesfield	1926-1933
Shacklock	CH Shacklock	Manby St, Wolverhampton	1916
Shaw (i)	—	—	1904-1910
Shaw (ii)	—	—	1918-1922 co
Sheffield-Henderson	Henderson Motors Ltd	73 Fitzwilliam St, Sheffield	1919-1923
Silva	T & T Motor Co Ltd	52a Conduit St, London	1919-1920 sc
Silver Prince	New Tryus Cycle Co	Poplar Wks, Birchfields, B'ham	1919-1924
Simplex	Patrick Eng Co Ltd	Brearley St, Birmingham	1919-1922 co
Singer	Singer & Co Ltd	Canterbury St, Coventry 1	1900-1915
Skootamota	Gilbert Campling Ltd	1 Albermarle St, London W1	1919-1922
Spa-J.A.P.	Spa-Motor & Eng Co	Scarborough, Yorkshire	1921-1923
Spark (i)	Spark Motors	46 Upper Thames St, London EC	1903-1904
Spartan	Wallis & James	Nottingham	1920-1921
Speed King	—	—	—
J.A.P.	J.G. Graves Ltd	Sheffield	1913-1914
Stafford	Stafford Auto-Scooter	Holyhead Rd, Coventry	1920-1921 sc
Stag	Stag Co	Sherwood Forest, Nottingham	1912-1914
Stan	Stan Motor Co	Westwood Heath, Coventry	1919-1921
Stanger	Stanger Engineering Co	13 Steele Rd, Tottenham, Ldn	1921-1923
Stanley (i)	Stanley Bicycle & Mtr Co Ltd	Days Lane, Coventry	1902-1905
Stanley (ii)	Stanley Engineering Co Ltd	Egham, Surrey	1932
Stellar	Stuart Turner Ltd	Henley-on-Thames, Oxfordshire	1912-1914
Stuart	Stuart Turner Ltd	Henley-on-Thames, Oxfordshire	1911-1912
Sudbrook	Sudbrook Motor Works	Bristol Rd, Gloucester	1919-1920
Superb Four	Superb Four Motors	10 Genoa Rd, Anerly, London	1920-1921
Supremoco	Supreme Motor Co	Longsight, Manchester	1921-1923
Swan	Swan Motor Mfg Co	Frodsham, Warrington, Cheshire	1912-1913
Symplex	Symplex Motors	Alma St, Birmingham	1913-1922
Tailwind	Mr Latta	Berkhampstead, Surrey	1952 co
Tee-Bee	Templeton Bros.	535 Sauchiehall St, Glasgow	1908-1911
Temple	Osborn Eng Co	Lees Lane, Gosport, Hampshire	1924-1928

Thomas	J.L. Thomas	Barnet, London	1904
Thorough	G. Featherstone & Son	234 Bethnal Green Rd, London	1903
Tilston	—	—	1919
Torpedo	F. Hooper & Co Ltd	Barton-on-Humber, Humberside	1910-1920
Townend	New Townend Bros. Ltd	83 Far Gosford St, Coventry	1901-1903
Trafalgar	G. Lyons & Co Ltd	39 East St, Baker St, London W	1902-1905
Trent	Trent & Co	Shepherds Bush, London	1902-1910
Triple-H	Hobbis, Hobbis & Horrell	Alvechurch Rd, Birmingham	1921-1923
Triplette	—	—	1923-1925
Unibus	Gloucestershire Aircraft Co Ltd	Cheltenham, Gloucestershire	1920-1922
Val	Val Motor Co	314 Bradford St, Birmingham	1913-1914
Vanette	Yukon Engineering Co Ltd	West Mitcham, Surrey	1924
Vasco	Vasco Motors	Kingston-on-Thames, Surrey	1921-1923
Venus	Venus Motors	52 Plasket Lane, London E13	1922-1923
Victa	—	—	1912-1913
Vinco	—	—	1903-1905
Viper-J.A.P.	—	—	1919-1920
Viscount	—	—	1960
Vulcan	Vulcan Works Ltd	13 Stafford St, Birmingham	1922-1923
Waddington	—	—	1902-1906
Wakefield	Wakefield Motor & Cycle Wks	The Arches, Clapham, London	1902-1905
Ward	W. Ward & Sons	Wetherby, Yorkshire	1915-1916
Warrior	Warrior Motorcycle Co	Victoria St, London SW1	1921-1923
Watney	—	—	1922-1923
Watsonian	Watsonian Sidecars Ltd	44 Albion Rd, Greet, B'ham	1950
Waverley	Waverley Motors	137 Lichfield Rd, Birmingham	1921-1923
WD	Wartnaby & Draper	21 Caundon Rd, Coventry	1911-1913
Weatherell	R. Weatherell & Co Ltd	South Green, Billericay, Essex	1922-1923
Weaver	Alfred Wiseman Ltd	Glover St, Birmingham	1922-1925
Wee	—	—	—
MacGregor	Coventry Bicycles Ltd	Wellington St, Coventry	1922-1925
Weller	Weller Bros Ltd	West Norwood, London	1902-1905
Westfield	Rising Sun Motor & Eng Works	Brackley Rd, London SE	1903-1905
Westovian	R.V. Heath & Son	Catherine St, South Shields	1914-1916
Wheatcroft	New Era Eng Co	Moor St, Coventry	1924
Whippet (i)	Whippet Motor & Cycle Mfg Co	Falcon Terrace, Clapham Jn	1903-1910
Whippet (ii)	Brampton Eng Co	Cambridge Park, Twickenham	1919-1921 sc
Whippet (iii)	Dunkley Motors	Bath Rd, Hounslow, London	1957-1959
Whirlwind	Dorman Eng Co	Northampton	1901-1903
White & Poppe	White & Poppe Ltd	Lockhurst Lane, Coventry	1902-1922
Whitley	Whitley Motor Co Ltd	Cow Lane, Coventry	1902-1910
Wigan Barlow	Wigan Barlow Motors Ltd	Lowther St, Stoke, Coventry	1921
Wilbee	Wilbee Motor Co	Rickmandsworth, Hertfordshire	1902-1910
Wilkin	Wilkin Motors Ltd	91-93 Onslow Rd, Sheffield	1919-1923
Wilkinson-Antoine	Cadagan Garage & Mtr Co Ltd	102 Sydney St, Chelsea, London	1903-1906
Wilkinson-T.M.C.	Wilkinson T.M.C. Co	Southfield Rd, Acton, London W	1909-1913
Willow	Willow Auto Cycle Co	Willow St, London SW1	1920
Win-Precision	Wincycle Trading Co Ltd	106-107 Gt Saffron Hill, London	1910-1914
Winco	—	—	1920-1922
Witall	The Witall Garage	1a Lucas St, Deptford, London	1919-1923
Wizard	Wizard Motor Co	Rhondda, Cardiff, S Glamorgan	1920-1922
X.L.-All	Eclipse Motor & Cycle Co	John Bright St, Birmingham	1902-1910
XL	Norfolk Engineering Works	Chapel Rd, Worthing, Sussex	1921-1923
Xtra	Xtra Cars Ltd	41 London St, Chertsey, Surrey	1923-1924
Young (i)	Mohawk Cycle Co Ltd	Hornsey, London N	1919-1920
Young (ii)	Waltham Eng Co Ltd	Waltham Cross, London N	1921-1922
Zephyr	Small Engines Co	Birmingham	1922-1923